Wildflowers of the Southern Appalachians

John F. Blair, Publisher • Winston-Salem, North Carolina

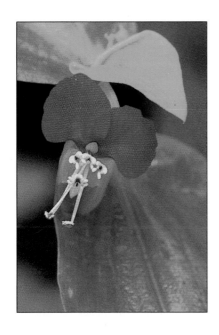

Wildflowers
of the
Southern Appalachians

How to Photograph and Identify Them

Kevin Adams and *Marty Casstevens*

The photographs in this book were scanned, placed on
Kodak Photo CD's, and color-corrected by Applied CD Technologies,
in Charlotte, North Carolina. The leaf drawings were converted
from slides by Keys Printing, in Greenville, South Carolina.

Photographs on front cover—
    Across the top from left to right: *Indian pink, Swamp pink,*
        and *Southern nodding trillium* by Kevin Adams
    Vertical middle row from the top: *Dayflower,* by Marty Casstevens;
        Wake robin, Bull thistle, and *Indian paint brush* by Kevin Adams

Photographs on back cover—
Eastern blue-eyed grass, and *Jewelweed* by Kevin Adams

Library of Congress Cataloging-in-Publication Data
Adams, Kevin, 1961–
    Wildflowers of the southern Appalachians : how to photograph and
identify them / Kevin Adams and Marty Casstevens.
        p.   cm.
    Includes bibliographical references (p.   ) and index.
    ISBN 0-89587-143-2 (alk. paper)
    1. Wild flowers—Appalachian Region, Southern—Identification.
2. Wild flowers—Appalachian Region, Southern—Pictorial works.
3. Photography of plants.   4. Photography of plants—Appalachian
Region, Southern.   I. Casstevens, Marty, 1954–   II. Title.
QK122.5.A435   1996
582.13'0975—dc20   95–51144

DESIGN BY DEBRA LONG HAMPTON
MAP BY LIZA LANGRALL
PRINTED AND BOUND BY R. R. DONNELLEY & SONS

To Jane,
for giving me my first camera, and for not taking it away
when it consumed our lives.

And to my little Brandie-girl.

Kevin

To Beth,
my friend in adventure.

Marty

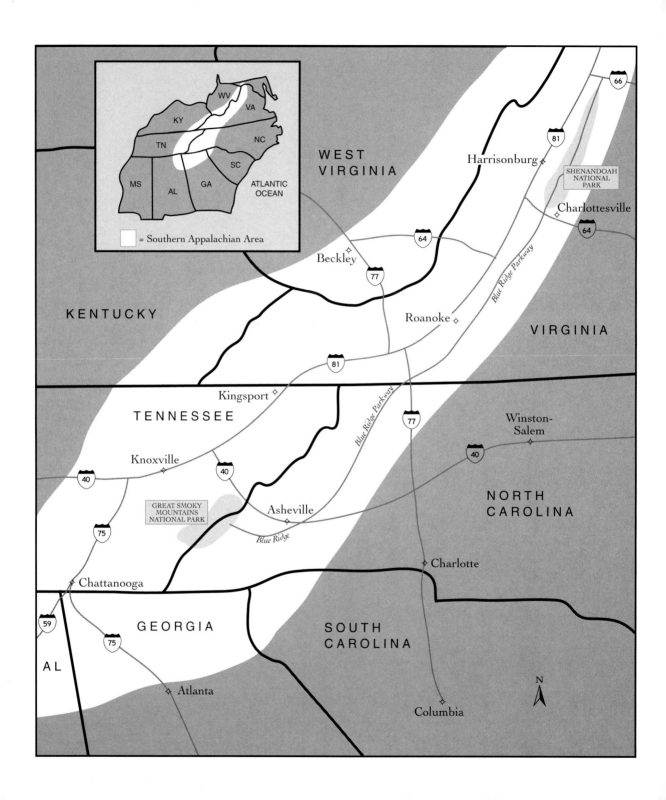

WEST VIRGINIA

KENTUCKY

Harrisonburg

SHENANDOAH
NATIONAL
PARK

Charlottesville

Beckley

Roanoke

VIRGINIA

Blue Ridge Parkway

Kingsport

TENNESSEE

Winston-
Salem

Knoxville

Blue Ridge Parkway

GREAT SMOKY
MOUNTAINS
NATIONAL PARK

Asheville

NORTH
CAROLINA

Blue Ridge

Charlotte

Chattanooga

GEORGIA

SOUTH
CAROLINA

AL

Atlanta

Columbia

N

WV
KY
VA
TN
NC
SC
MS
AL
GA
ATLANTIC
OCEAN

☐ = Southern Appalachian Area

Contents

Large whorled pogonia, page 168
75-300mm lens, 5T diopter, ¼ sec. at f/16   *Adams*

Pale touch-me-not, page 128
75-300mm lens, 5T diopter, ¼ sec. at f/16   *Casstevens*

Acknowledgments

From the beginning, we knew that for this book to become a reality we would depend on the efforts of many people. What we did not know was how unselfishly these people would give their time. We are indebted to everyone who participated in this project, and we regret that space does not permit us to name everyone. While working on this book, we had help from numerous respected authorities. However, we want to stress that any errors or misleading information is our responsibility. We are photographers first and naturalists second, and although we made every effort to be accurate, we realize that perfection is unattainable.

Thanks to Tony Ledford, Marc Parsons, and Al Spicer for providing technical computer assistance and advice, to David Duhl for helpful advice pertaining to photography, and to Johnny Moore for allowing his business partner to play in the woods for six months.

The digital aspect of producing this book was made possible by the technical wizards at Applied CD Technologies of Charlotte, North Carolina.

Numerous individuals provided location information, and some guided us to their favorite sites. Thanks go to Joe Christian, Jo Johnston, Opal Loflin, and Elizabeth Wheeler.

For allowing us to photograph on their property, we thank Glenn Bodenheimer, Buck Stafford, and Becky Studebaker. Also, Emily Allen of Winston-Salem, for making her fabulous garden available and for her spirited conversation. Thanks also to Ed and Lila Burney for sharing their retreat with us.

In addition to photographing in the wild and at private gardens, we depended heavily on the fabulous botanical gardens at the Highlands Nature Center. Several of the rare plants in this book were photographed there, allowing us to not disturb wild populations.

We relied heavily on botanical professionals for technical information as well as for help in locating species. Thanks to Moni Bates, a botanist from Greensboro; Roy Coomans, professor of biology at North Carolina A&T University; George Beatty from Pennsylvania, whose inspiring spring wildflower slide shows at Great Smoky Mountains National Park should not be missed; C. Ritchie Bell, former professor at the University of North Carolina and former director of the North Carolina Botanical Garden; Glenn Cardwell, Chief Ranger for Great Smoky Mountains National Park, who retired as this book went to press, and who will be missed; Doug Coleman, regional botanist and executive director of Wintergreen Nature Foundation; Bill Hooks, former naturalist with Great Smoky Mountains National Park; Karen Moore, with The Nature Conservancy in Virginia; and Gerry Roe, park ranger, and Randy Winstead, botanist, both with Shenandoah National Park.

A special thanks to J. Dan Pittillo, professor of biology at Western Carolina University, for reviewing the manuscript and offering advice and encouragement. This book is greatly improved by his involvement.

For putting Marty up in their "estate" while she photographed for five months in Shenandoah National Park, thanks go to Pat and Joe Novack, of Madison, Virginia. Also, special thanks to Mike Casstevens, for his patience, sacrifice, and support.

We are grateful to the entire staff at John F. Blair, Publisher. We would especially like to thank Liza Langrall, our computer specialist, Debbie Hampton, who designed the book, and Andrew Waters, our editor.

Finally, for providing location information, reviewing the manuscript, and being a partner in exploration, we thank our new friend and companion, Wayne Irvin.

Nodding wild onion, page 211
75-300mm lens, 5T diopter, ¼ sec. at f/16   *Casstevens*

Introduction

As a nature photographer and naturalist, I have spent countless days rambling the southern Appalachians in search of wildflowers and other photography subjects, and it seems I have read nearly every book published about the region. During the process, a seed was planted in the back of my mind about a detailed wildflower identification book that would include photography and conservation information. I believed the latter to be critical as more and more wildflower enthusiasts visited the region. The cumulative stress on the environment from these visitors is too much to be ignored. So after completing my first book, *North Carolina Waterfalls: Where To Find Them, How To Photograph Them*, I decided to make that idea a reality. My hope is that this book will encourage people to become better stewards of the environment by collecting photographs of wildflowers, rather than the wildflowers themselves.

Every author works with a deadline. I'm still not sure how I got myself into such a dilemma, but I had less than one year to write and photograph this entire book. Without forming a partnership with Marty Casstevens, the book would not have been published. We have worked together on all phases of the book, including the photography, and we share the same philosophy about its purpose.

Researching and writing the book was hard enough, but photographing 250 different wildflower species in one season was a tremendous challenge. Locating the flowers was not that difficult; anyone who learns their growth requirements and spends time outdoors can find them. The problem was making a good photograph in sometimes less-than-ideal conditions. We rarely had the luxury of enough time to return to a location over and over until the conditions were just right. A popular belief among beginning photographers is that professional photographers make great photos because they have more time to make them. That is only partly true. Once you become completely comfortable with the entire photographic process, you'll find yourself making good photos on a consistent basis regardless of how much time you have. We hope this book is a testament to that.

Of course, there were times when the shooting conditions or subject matter were too poor to make the ideal image. Unfortunately, deadlines must still be met, so in these cases we made the best image possible for inclusion in the book.

When I first came up with the idea for this book, I wanted to include *every* wildflower in the southern Appalachians, along with photographs, detailed descriptions, and all the other conservation and photography information. When I actually began work on the project, I immediately realized that a book of this nature would be roughly the size of a college-level encyclopedia and cost about the same. Obviously, a decision had to be made about which wildflowers to include. With over twenty-five hundred flowering plants in the southern Appalachians, and room for only a few hundred in the book, a great deal of thought had to be put into the selection process.

The first criterion was that the wildflowers in the book had to be herbaceous; that is, they could not have obvious woody stems, and they had to die back to the roots after fruiting. This seemed logical since most people consider the herbs as being the "true" wildflowers even though that is not botanically correct. As they are not herbaceous, you will not see any trees, shrubs, or vines included. (There are a few wildflowers included that are technically shrubs, for reasons given under each listing.)

Including only herbaceous wildflowers still leaves hundreds from which to choose. Obviously, we wanted to include the most popular and common native species, and the most popular and common of the showy introduced species. To choose beyond

Milkweed fruit, page 104
75-300mm lens,
5T diopter,
½ sec. at f/22
Adams

that, we used two additional criterion: those wild-flowers that the reader would likely have heard about and would want to find; and those which we felt the reader would most want to identify if discovered in the wild. As a result, you will find that several elusive wildflowers, such as some orchid species, have been included, while some very common plants, like the clovers and peas, have not.

Some readers may question the decision to include any rare wildflowers in a book that claims to be conservation oriented, believing it best to keep quiet about them. However, with so many people spend-ing time outdoors, it is naive to think that anything can be kept secret. We believe that education is the best environmental policy. Once you learn the name of a wildflower, you no longer pass it by as just an-other "weed," especially if you discovered and iden-tified it yourself. The flower then has an identity that is rooted not only in a guidebook, but in you as well. Some people may argue that by illustrating and describing certain plants, like ginseng, for instance, it encourages people to collect them. We disagree. We believe the vast majority of people will want to protect these plants once they learn about them, and the people who are poaching plants will do so with or without this book. At the same time, we are not encouraging people to search out rare flowers and tell everyone they know about them. A person is much more likely to develop a conservation mindset if they discover and identify wildflowers themselves. If you do discover a rare wildflower, you can report it to the state natural heritage program or a similar group.

Another issue that may create debate is our decision to produce this book using computer digital imaging. Anyone who has seen the motion pictures *Jurassic Park* or *Forrest Gump* knows what the computer can do with a photograph. However, the decision to go this route was based solely on finances. With the rising cost of paper, and the cost of traditional photography scanning, digital imaging was the only way to produce this book and keep the retail price reasonable. Now that we have used the process, we realize that cost is only one of the many advantages of digital technology. The computer enables us to restore color to a scene as we remembered it being when we made the photograph, in effect making the image even more "real" than the film recorded it. Also, the computer makes cropping images an easy task. Besides these two aspects, and removing pinholes and dust specs that were introduced during the scanning process, every photograph in this book appears exactly as it did through our viewfinders.

Although producing this book was extremely challenging, and at times quite difficult, we never considered it a chore. We looked forward to each and every day in the field, and we awaited each wildflower discovery with wide-eyed innocence. Being nature photographers first and naturalists second, we learned a tremendous amount about wildflowers during the process, and now have an even greater appreciation of the natural world. Anyone who spends time with a particular subject will learn it well and appreciate it more.

We wish for our readers the same satisfaction and fulfillment we experienced, though you may want to start out on a smaller scale. If you are a wildflower photographer or enthusiast, pick a particular region or group of plants and concentrate on that. Learn how to identify all the species of that group and collect photographs of each one. Then, move on to another region or group of plants. We promise you that your photographs will be better, and your satisfaction level higher, than if you simply head out the door to photograph and identify everything you happen to see.

Wildflowers are probably one of the most popular of southern Appalachian attractions, possibly exceeded only by scenic views. But too many people only view the flowers from their cars while tooling down the highway. We encourage you to get out of the car and take a close look. Visit a wildflower early in the morning when it is covered in dew. Return on a sunny afternoon to see how many insects it attracts. Learn about the natural history and the folklore.

Some people argue that attempting to explain and apply order to the natural world leads to a dulled appreciation of its beauty. We disagree and are reminded of the quote by the Dutch physicist M. Minnaert: "It is indeed wrong to think that the poetry of Nature's moods in all their infinite variety is lost on one who observes them scientifically, for the habit of observation refines our sense of beauty and adds a brighter hue to the richly colored background against which each separate fact is outlined."

We hope this book helps to refine your sense of beauty.

Kevin Adams

Bee balm, page 122
75-300mm lens, 5T diopter, 1 sec. at f/22

Adams

Photographing Wildflowers

It would be difficult to think of a subject we enjoy photographing more than wildflowers, and from the numbers of wildflower shooters encountered in the field, it's evident that other photographers share this enthusiasm. This thrills us because our hope is that people will become better stewards of the environment by photographing nature instead of harming it. We encourage people to collect photographs, not nature. But this new photographic emphasis raises concerns about the negative impact photographers are having on the environment. We should all feel obligated to protect nature, to leave the wildflowers for others to enjoy.

With all the workshops, seminars, books, and magazine articles pertaining to wildflower photography, you would think that photographing them would be easy. Yet many photographers have a difficult time interpreting what they see and translating it onto film. Beginning photographers, especially, seem to have trouble with the whole process of closeup photography. Part of the problem may be that there is too much information. Camera salesclerks and manufacturers bombard us with claims that their gear is ideally suited to the task at hand. Another problem may be that books and magazine articles often only list the various methods and types of gear available without fully explaining why the photographer should use one over the other. We think it's best to identify what works, explain how to use it, and forget everything else.

Please read this chapter all the way through *before* making any equipment purchases, or trying a new technique. Once you finish, you will realize that you can handle 99 percent of your closeup require-ments with proper technique and a few simple pieces of gear. In fact, you will learn that proper technique, not equipment, is the most important factor in good photography.

This chapter only deals with photography as it applies to wildflowers, and it assumes a basic knowledge of photography. A detailed treatment is beyond the scope of this book. For background reading on the subject we recommend *Closeups in Nature*, by John Shaw, published by Amphoto and available at your local camera store. This is the best book available on closeup photography. Another excellent book is *How to Photograph Insects and Spiders*, by Larry West. Though it is about photographing insects, the photography information applies equally to wildflowers, and West's insight into the natural world makes for great reading.

Cameras

Function, adaptability, convenience, portability, cost, and image quality are the factors to consider when purchasing a camera. For wildflowers, the 35mm Single Lens Reflex (SLR) wins hands down in all of the above categories except image quality. However, if you are only interested in photographing landscapes that include wildflowers, such as the spectacular sweeping scenics of the West, we recommend you look into a view camera system. This type of camera permits completely independent swings and tilts that provide precise control of depth of field. Also, the larger image size produces truly outstanding reproductions in books and calendars. But if you want to tackle all realms of closeup and wildflower photography, choose the 35mm system. This will prove the most practical for the varied approaches needed to photograph southern Appalachian wildflowers, and it is the system we discuss in this chapter.

People often ask what brand of 35mm camera we use. Well, it doesn't really matter because the answer has nothing to do with the quality of our photos. That has to do with technique. All the major brands of cameras work just fine, but if you are just starting out, we recommend either Canon or Nikon because of the excellent selection of lenses and accessories available for those brands. They aren't necessarily better, they just give you more options. Listed below are the important features to look for when purchasing a camera for photographing wildflowers:

AUTOMATIC EXPOSURE OVERRIDE

Having manual control over the exposure is often critical in any type of photography. Make sure the camera you purchase has a manual-exposure control, or at the very least, an exposure compensation dial.

DEPTH-OF-FIELD PREVIEW

The depth-of-field preview feature permits you to view the depth of field by manually closing the lens to the shooting aperture. This allows you to see what is in focus and how distracting the background may be. Many photographers complain that they cannot easily see what is in focus when pressing the preview button because the image is too dark. We also have this problem, but we use the preview mainly to determine what the background looks like. For photographing wildflowers, a depth-of-field preview is indispensable.

MIRROR LOCK

On most cameras, the instant you click the shutter the mirror that directs light to the viewfinder moves up out of the way, allowing light to reach the film. Because it must move very quickly, it slaps against the top of the camera, increasing the possibility of vibrations. These vibrations are most evident with shutter speeds ranging from $1/4$ to $1/30$ of a second, and they are especially noticeable when using high magnifications. A mirror lock allows you to manually move the mirror up before releasing the shutter, eliminating the possibility of a blurred picture from mirror slap. Some of the newer cameras have special dampening devices designed to lessen the vibration, but despite claims to the contrary, they have not totally eliminated the problem. Unfortunately, only the most expensive cameras offer mirror lock.

ISO OVERRIDE

Most cameras today feature DX Film Coding. An internal scanner reads the bar code on the film canister to determine the manufacturer's suggested ISO (film speed) setting. If, after making an exposure test, you discover your camera is overexposing or underexposing your pictures, you do not need to send the camera for repair. Simply use the ISO override feature to correct the problem. For example, if you are using ISO 50 film and your camera always overexposes by ½ stop, you would simply set the ISO dial to 80 when using that film. You will have fooled the camera into allowing ½ stop less light to reach the film. Using the ISO override to "push" or "pull" the film (expose it at an ISO value greater or less than its true value) will save you from making additional calculations.

We always use this feature when using Fujichrome Velvia film. Like many other professional photographers, we do not believe that Fujichrome Velvia is a true ISO 50 film as stated by Fuji and set the ISO dial to 40 when using this film. (Depending on how your particular camera is calibrated, you may need to set your ISO dial to a different setting than ISO 40 in order to achieve the same $1/3$-stop additional light.)

EXTERNAL SHUTTER RELEASE

When you use a tripod, as you should, tripping the shutter by hand can cause vibrations. Always use either a cable, an electronic, or a wireless remote shutter release unless you hand-hold the camera.

100-PERCENT VIEWING

Most cameras only allow you to view approximately 90 percent of what will actually be recorded on film. This can be quite annoying; you might get your film back only to discover some unwanted object jutting in on the edge of the scene. This is why cameras with 100-percent viewing are much better. Unfortunately, as with mirror lock, only the most expensive cameras have this feature.

TTL FLASH CAPABILITY

With TTL (Through The Lens) flash, the light meter in the camera reads the amount of light that is hitting the film and controls the flash output accordingly, thus taking much of the guesswork out of determining the exposure. We occasionally use flash for insects and wind-blown wildflowers, and would not consider using a manual, non-TTL unit.

These are the main features you will find useful in wildflower photography. There are others you may find helpful for general use. Examine the type of photography you want to do and carefully determine the features you need to accomplish this. For wildflowers, do not compromise on the above features unless necessary. You probably won't get the mirror lock and 100-percent viewing unless you buy one of the most expensive cameras on the market, and the TTL flash feature may be of little importance in your photography, but you should make sure the camera has the other features.

Tripods

A sturdy tripod is necessary for quality results in most photographic situations and is essential in closeup photography. Photographers often say they don't like tripods because they are heavy and bulky. If weight or extra baggage concerns you, then go ahead and leave the tripod behind, or carry a small, lightweight model. Just don't plan to come back with any good wildflower photos.

A tripod allows you to fine-tune the image by carefully examining the scene for composition. You can look at the edges of the frame to make sure there are no distracting elements jutting in. It encourages you to slow down and take a careful, studied approach—the only way to consistently make beautiful photographs. And, of course, it allows you to use slower shutter speeds. Another advantage is that on windy days you can get all your gear set up, and at the instant the wind calms, you're ready to fire the shutter. None of this is possible when hand-holding the camera.

Don't make the mistake of assuming that your pictures will be sharp just because you are using a tripod. A sturdy tripod used incorrectly is worse than a cheap model used properly. There is no substitute for good technique. Always extend the larger leg sections first, as they are more sturdy, and make sure to tighten the knobs securely. Firmly seat all three legs in the ground, and make sure they are not bouncing on top of spongy soil. A trick we use is to always leave the smallest leg section extended a couple of inches so it will more thoroughly seat itself in the ground. A good test is to firmly tap the tripod while looking through the viewfinder; if the scene dances wildly, the tripod is not stable enough.

These are our recommendations for tripods:

BOGEN 3021

Probably the best tripod buy on the market. Many, many photographers use this tripod because it is relatively inexpensive, fairly sturdy, and lightweight. It is the smallest tripod we recommend.

GITZO 320

For assured sturdiness, it is hard to beat the Gitzo line of tripods, though they are pricey. The Gitzo 320 is the pro's standard.

SLIK PROFESSIONAL

The Slik Professional tripod is the sturdiest and most

versatile tripod we have seen. This is truly a rock-solid tripod. However, it is not cheap and it is very heavy.

Regardless of which tripod you buy, look for the following features. First, make sure that it will extend to your viewing level while standing. You won't be shooting many wildflowers this way, but for other photography it will save your back a lot of pain. On the flip side, an extremely important consideration is how low to the ground the tripod will go. All else being equal, choose the model that sets up the lowest. This means you will not be buying one with braces extending from the centerpost. All the tripods listed above will go fairly low to the ground by themselves, and might be modified to go even farther. If you have a do-it-yourself mind-set, look at how the leg mechanism works. You should be able to figure out how to modify it. The Bogen 3021 requires unscrewing three nuts and filing the leg stops with a file or Dremel tool. The Slik Professional only needs a little filing at the leg's point of contact with the main assembly.

One problem you'll run into is that when you attempt to set up the tripod low to the ground (modified or not), the centerpost gets in the way. Saw it off; you don't need it anyway. Anything more than three inches is just extra weight. If you have to raise the centerpost to get the camera high enough, you need a different tripod. The only time you should raise the centerpost is when you need precise height adjustment while shooting closeups, and three inches is plenty for that. If anybody tells you that you should simply reverse the centerpost to shoot low to the ground, politely disregard the statement. That person obviously has little experience shooting closeups. Houdini could not contort his body to photograph that way on a regular basis.

Just as important as the tripod is the head to go with it. A cheap head, as with a cheap tripod, means poor results on film. Without question, our first choice in heads are the ball-and-socket design—as opposed to the pan-tilt type. The pan-tilt heads are just too bulky and cumbersome to work with, and they're ridiculously slow to use.

Here are our recommendations for tripod heads:

BOGEN 3055
This is a medium duty, inexpensive head, and about the smallest you should use.

BOGEN 3038
Rock solid and relatively inexpensive, but very heavy and bulky.

ARCA-SWISS B-1 MONOBALL
One of the smoothest and sturdiest on the market, but very expensive. There are several heads similar to the Arca-Swiss, with varying degrees of smoothness and sturdiness, and with different handle designs. All of them are acceptable.

You're also going to need some type of quick-release system that will allow you to quickly mount the camera on and off the tripod. Trust us, you need it. The Bogen heads come with a hex-plate system that is OK, but we much prefer the dovetail system that is standard with the Arca-Swiss-style heads. You can buy a dovetail clamp and mount it on a Bogen head if you like. Contact Really Right Stuff (see the appendix) and request their catalog and informational literature. It will tell you everything you need to know about tripod heads and quick-release systems. Kirk Enterprises has a similar line.

Other Methods of Support

When you need to set up the camera at ground level, you won't be using the tripod in the normal fashion because it won't set up that low. Even a modified tripod gives a minimum camera height of only 10 inches or so. As stated earlier, reversing a tripod's centerpost is not an option; the camera must remain in an upright position. Some of the devices photographers use for low-level work include bean bags, platform pods (a piece of ¾ inch plywood with a tripod head bolted to it), and a rolled up jacket. Each of these has drawbacks. We use a Bogen Super Clamp attached to one leg of the tripod for low-level work. The Super Clamp is a heavy-duty device that clamps onto just about anything up to 2 inches thick. It has various studs to which a ball head is attached.

To use the clamp, roughly determine the camera position needed and set up the tripod so that one leg extends into this area. Then clamp the Super Clamp onto this leg. Those of you who have tape or foam padding attached to all three legs will have to remove this from one of them. That is why our tripods only have foam padding attached to two legs. Now take the head off the tripod and attach it to the Super Clamp and begin the slow, careful process of composing the photograph.

This setup works beautifully in all low-level situations we have experienced. Furthermore, it permits photography in one other situation that defies conventional methods: when the camera needs to be positioned very close to a steep bank or rock wall. Just plant two tripod legs on the ground and extend the third horizontally against the bank. The Super Clamp is then attached to this horizontal leg at any point along its length. The Super Clamp/tripod combination works so well that it is the only method of support we use other than a tripod alone.

When we only need to set up a little lower than the tripod sets up, we simply flop the ball head into its vertical slot. Since we regularly use lenses that have tripod collars, we can shoot either verticals or horizontals from this position by simply loosening the knob on the collar and rotating the camera.

Filters

We only use filters to enhance a condition already present in the scene, never those that introduce strong colors or special effects. Consequently, the only filters we regularly use are the polarizer, warming filter, and graduated neutral-density filter. The graduated neutral-density filter is used mostly for scenics. The polarizer, although it does a great job of saturating foliage, cuts out roughly two stops of light, which is unacceptable for most close-up photography. Thus, the only filter regularly used for wildflowers is the warming filter. Scenes photographed in the shade, particularly under a blue sky, often have a cool, bluish cast (see the section on lighting for a detailed discussion of this effect). The bluish cast is greatly pronounced when photographing white-petaled species. Warming filters eliminate this coolness. They come in three strengths, designated 81A, 81B, and 81C; 81A has a faint amber tint, while 81C has a definite yellow cast. We use an 81A for most wildflower work because the stronger filters sometimes introduce a yellow cast to the scene.

We do not keep a skylight or UV filter on our lens for so-called protection. Any filter, regardless of quality, will degrade the image to some extent and increase the likelihood of flare. Protect your lenses by treating them properly and by keeping the lens cap on when you are not shooting.

Film

People often ask what kind of film to use, but this question is difficult to answer. What works for us may not work for you. However, if you plan to sell your photography for use in books, calendars, and magazines, you will need to shoot slide film because that is what the editors want. Also, with slides, the exposure you shoot is the exposure you get. The slides will be exactly as you shot them, good or bad. With negative film, you never know when the lab technician has altered the final print to match a preset standard.

For years our standard film has been Fujichrome Velvia. We love the fine grain and saturated colors, although its slow speed (rated at 50, but closer to 40) is a drawback for wildflowers. Most of this book was shot with Velvia, although we used some of the new crop of 100-speed films, such as Fuji's Provia and Kodak's Lumiere. The grain is as fine as, or finer than, Velvia, and there is a gain of $1^1/3$ stops of light.

We often hear that to photograph something like wildflowers or minerals you should use a truer film such as Kodachrome 64. Just what is true color anyway? A $^1/3$-stop difference in exposure will often alter the color in a wildflower more than using Velvia over Kodachrome 64, and some people see color a little differently anyway. Besides, wildflowers and other natural objects aren't always the same hue. They vary according to soil, moisture, time of season, and a host of other factors. So who's to say you're capturing the true color just because you use a certain film? Every time we have used one of these "true" films, we find ourselves wondering what happened to that beautiful red or green subject we remember seeing in the field. Those films just don't record the image as it is translated in our minds. Shoot the film you like and don't worry about it.

You may question the validity of some of the photographs in this book, but we can tell you that none of them represent wildly exaggerated color. We strive for great color not only by choice of film, but also by choice of lighting. If you photograph all your flowers in flat, midday, direct sunlight, then your photos will indeed be flat and boring. But if you photograph during the best lighting, then you will record great, saturated color with most films. Velvia just stacks the odds in our favor.

Magnification

Throughout this chapter, we mention image size and the implications of shooting at a given magnification. In photography, image size refers to the size of the subject on film relative to its size in reality. When this size is equal, the image is said to be "life

size," or 1X. Thirty-five-millimeter film is roughly 1 inch by $1^1/2$ inches. If you photograph a subject that is this size so that it fills the negative or slide from edge to edge, then you're shooting at 1X. If that subject only fills half the frame, then you're shooting at $^1/2$X, and if only half the subject fills the entire frame, you're shooting at 2X.

If this is confusing don't feel bad. You don't really need to know the exact magnification you're shooting at except for specialized applications. Even in an identification guidebook like this, it is usually less confusing to give the size of the plant instead of the illustration's image size. However, you should have a basic understanding of the principles. It's often useful to relate to real-life objects. If you photograph this book so that it fills the frame you are shooting at roughly $^1/7$X magnification. A credit card requires not quite $^1/2$X magnification and Washington's portrait on a dollar bill is about 1X.

So how does this apply to wildflowers? Well, unless you plan to record details of flower structure, you will almost never need to shoot at 1X or higher. Most images in this book were shot in the $^1/8$X to $^1/2$X range. By the way, there's a neat trick to determine the magnification you're shooting at if you ever want to know. Slip a millimeter ruler into the scene directly over your subject. Look through the viewfinder and count the number of millimeters across the long end of the frame. If you count 36 millimeters, the size of 35mm film, then you're at 1X. Eighteen millimeters means 2X, 72 millimeters means $^1/2$X, etc.

Using Accessories for Higher Magnification

Most newer lenses, such as the 75-300mm and 80-200mm zoom lenses will focus down to about $^1/8$X magnification all by themselves. Many have a built-in macro feature that takes them down to $^1/4$X or even $^1/3$X. This range will easily handle portrait photos of the larger wildflowers like Turk's-cap lilies and trillium; but when you photograph smaller species, or want to get closer to the larger ones, you need the accessories listed below.

EXTENSION TUBES

Any time you extend a lens's elements farther from the film plane, the lens will focus closer. Whether that extension comes from the lens's built-in focusing device or from a set of add-on extension tubes, the result is the same: closer focusing ability. Extension tubes are nothing more than a hollow, mechanical linkage added between the lens and camera to permit closer focusing. Two big drawbacks to extension tubes are that they add a wobbly linkage between the lens and camera, and they reduce the amount of light reaching the film. The more the extension, the more light it costs.

To determine the amount of magnification obtained with extension tubes, simply divide the amount of extension into the focal length of the lens while focused at infinity. For instance, if you add a 50mm extension tube to a 100mm lens, you are automatically at ½X when focused at infinity.

There are a few—not many—situations in which you'll need extension tubes. We'll discuss each in the lens section.

TELECONVERTERS

A teleconverter, or multiplier as it is sometimes called, is typically used to make long lenses longer (increase the focal length), but it can be used effectively for closeups as well. Consider this: a teleconverter has the unique ability to multiply whatever is placed in front of it. If you place a 1.4X teleconverter behind a 300mm lens focused at infinity, the result is an effective 420mm lens. However, if you first add an accessory to make that 300mm focus at say 1X, when you add the teleconverter you will be shooting at an effective 1.4X magnification. As with extension tubes, you do lose light. A 1.4X teleconverter costs one stop, while the 2X converter costs two stops. Two stops is often too much to lose, so you may want to stick with the 1.4X types. We use the now-discontinued Nikon 1.6X teleconverter for most work.

SUPPLEMENTARY LENSES

If your camera salesperson knows you enjoy photographing closeups, he or she has probably tried to sell you a set of cheap, single-element closeup lenses, or diopters. The +1, +2, and +3 closeup diopters usually come in a set of 3 and work just like a filter. If the sales pitch worked, and you bought any of these, immediately go to the nearest hardware store and buy a sledgehammer. Take this sledgehammer and smash these diopters into dust before you accidentally place one on your lens. Now go back to the camera store and purchase a quality, *two-element* closeup lens (also called a two-element closeup diopter) such as those made by Nikon. These lenses screw onto any brand lens, just like a filter, and give you instant magnification with almost no loss of light. Furthermore, the quality is superb, and the cost is not much more than the cheap diopters. Several manufacturers make two-element closeup lenses, but Nikon's are the easiest to find. Nikon calls them 3T, 4T, 5T, and 6T. The 3T and 4T are 52mm in filter size, and the 5T and 6T are 62mm in filter size. The 3T and 5T are the weaker of the two available strengths, while the 4T and 6T yield more magnification. Buy either the 5T or 6T, or both, and use step rings on lenses with different filter threads. We made most of the photographs in this book with these closeup lenses, usually the 5T. For more information about their use, see the section on telephoto lenses.

———

That's it. These three accessories are all you should need to make your lenses focus close enough to shoot wildflowers. So what about all that other stuff you hear or read about? What about bellows, reversing rings, and stacking lenses? What about macro converters, enlarging lenses, and short-mount lenses? Well, in certain circumstances—notably studio work with extreme magnifications—they may be OK, but for general field work they are just not practicable. Concentrate on what works and forget everything else.

Lenses and Making Them Focus Closer

The sharpness and clarity of a photograph is only as good as the lens that made it. Regardless of how expensive a camera you have or how good your technique is, if you have inferior optics, your images will suffer. This is why we usually recommend buying lenses from the manufacturer of your camera. If you shoot with Canon, use Canon lenses; if you shoot with Nikon, use Nikon lenses. There are a few good aftermarket brands such as Sigma, Tokina, and Tamron, but be careful, there are some lemons too. If you're on a budget, buy the best lens and tripod you can afford and skimp on something else.

WIDE-ANGLE LENSES

The classic lens choice for scenics is the wide-angle lens. It works well when you want to photograph an entire field or meadow of flowers because the great depth of field allows you to keep everything in focus. Although the southern Appalachians do not have the sweeping fields of wildflowers that are common in other parts of the country, there are a few instances when a wide-angle will be useful for wildflower photography. Often, trilliums grow in such abundance and over such a large area that a wide-angle lens is the only way to capture the scene. The same is often true with goldenrods, buttercups, and fringed phacelia, among others.

When we photograph such a scene, or any wide-angle scene for that matter, we rarely focus by looking through the camera. We use the depth-of-field scale on the lens barrel. If you are not familiar with this technique, ask your camera salesperson to demonstrate it for you. We always hedge our bet a bit by choosing the next smallest aperture than recommended by the scale. If you use a wide-angle zoom lens, it may not have a depth-of-field scale. That is one reason to use a fixed-focal-length wide-angle lens. Other reasons include the fact that the front element of a fixed-focal-length lens does not rotate (a decided advantage when using polarizing or gradu-

Goldenrod and
Mount Jefferson, page 134
28mm lens,
graduated neutral-density filter,
½ sec. at f/22
Adams

When you locate a flower, look around. If the background is also interesting, you can include both the flower and the background in your photograph with a wide-angle lens. You won't find many sweeping fields of wildflowers in the southern Appalachians, but scenes like this one are fairly common, particularly in late summer and early autumn.

ated neutral-density filters), there is less likelihood of flare due to fewer elements, and the closest focusing distance is shorter.

Remember the discussion about how to determine the magnification when using extension tubes? The formula is focal length divided by extension equals magnification. So you would think that a great way to achieve a lot of magnification would be to simply add an extension tube to a wide-angle lens. After all, with 28mm of extension on a 28mm lens you're at 1X. The problem is that with wide-angle lenses you have very little working distance. Life-size on a 28mm wide-angle lens puts the lens about ¾ inch away from the subject; not an insurmountable problem when photographing in a studio, but try that with a dew-covered daisy. Not to mention the problems you'll encounter when photographing a bee on that daisy.

Another problem is that a wide-angle lens's angle of view is too great for closeups. You need to narrow the background coverage to give that simplified poster look. Use the wide-angles for sweeping scenics. There are better lenses for closeup work.

NORMAL LENSES

Lenses that fall into the focal-length range of 50mm to 60mm are considered "normal" because that is the focal length that most closely matches the angle of view seen by the human eye. As with wide-angle lenses, we rarely use 50mm lenses for closeups because the working distance is so short and the background coverage is too great. One situation where we do use them is when we photograph several wildflowers growing closely together, whether they be low-growing species like bluets, irises, and phacelia, or larger wildflowers like bee balm and sunflowers. A longer lens isolates a few blossoms, but with the 50mm we can include the whole patch. Occasionally, you will need to add a very short extension tube to allow you to focus closer. Adding a short extension tube to a normal lens is one of the few instances in which we use extension to increase the magnification.

Large round-leaved orchid, page 236
50mm lens, 4 sec. at f/16   Adams

Normal lenses are mostly used to include several flowers growing close together, but they are also useful in cases like this. Here the intent was to include all the flower, along with a little of the surroundings, and to place as much emphasis on the flower as possible. A normal lens positioned close to the subject provided this perspective.

Make sure the normal lens is not picking up too much background coverage, which usually means you need to be shooting straight down or into a dense patch of flowers. Shooting straight down has complications of its own—often there is no way to shoot that way without including a tripod leg. To solve this problem you need some sort of extension arm that projects the camera out from the tripod (see page 12).

Goldenseal fruit, page 213
105mm macro lens, 81A warming filter, 8 sec. at f/22
Adams

The 105mm macro lens was used here, but the 75-300mm zoom, plus diopter, would have worked as well. One advantage to the macro lens in this type of shot is that it is a fixed-focal-length lens, which means it won't "creep," as some zoom lenses do when pointed straight down.

MEDIUM TELEPHOTO LENSES

Falling within this range are lenses with focal lengths from about 85mm to 150mm. When photographing with these lenses, you begin to address some of the drawbacks of wider lenses such as working distance and background coverage. It is a fundamental rule of optics that for any given magnification, the longer the lens, the greater the working distance and the narrower the angle of view. With extension, the working distance with a 28mm lens at 1X is roughly ¾ inch, with a 50mm it is roughly 3 inches, and with a 105mm lens it is roughly 6 inches. Also, with the 105mm lens the narrower angle of view is beginning to give the background a poster effect.

To be honest, we only occasionally use this focal-length range of lenses for closeups. The next category of lenses will do most of what these will, with even greater working distance and narrower background coverage. One situation in which we do use them is when we want to shoot a patch of flowers but can't get close enough with the 50mm lens, or discover that the normal lens's angle of view is too great.

TELEPHOTO LENSES

We use telephotos more than any other lenses for wildflowers. We love the way they isolate a blossom while creating a posterlike background. Also, compared to shorter lenses, the working distance is great when using extension tubes. However, we rarely use extension tubes with telephoto lenses because it requires an unwieldy amount of extension to realize any benefit. This is where the aforementioned two-element closeup diopters come into play. Closeup

Dayflower, page 61
75-300mm lens, 6T diopter, ¼ sec. at f/32   Casstevens

The telephoto lens is perfect for isolating a flower against an out-of-focus background.

diopters are unique in that they make all lenses, regardless of focal length, focus at the same working distance. Mount Nikon's 3T or 5T closeup diopter on a 50mm lens focused at infinity and the working distance is roughly 2 feet. On a 100mm lens it is roughly 2 feet, and on a 300mm lens it is the same 2 feet. Now it seems to reason that if the focusing distance is the same, the diopter will yield more magnification on a telephoto lens. This is true, and it is why we love them. Nikon's 6T diopter mounted on a 75-300mm lens yields about 1X at 300mm when focused at infinity. Rack it out to its closest focusing limit and the magnification is nearly 1.25X. What's more, two-element closeup diopters don't cost precious light like extension tubes, and they don't add a weak mechanical linkage. Remember, while these diopters work very well with long lenses—from about 100mm and up—the increase in magnification with shorter lenses is insignificant.

If we could have only one lens, it would be the 75-300mm zoom. Its focal length ranges from near normal to telephoto, and it is fairly light and compact. We've always wondered why more people don't buy these lenses over the limited-range 80-200mm zooms. When you put a closeup diopter on a 75-300mm zoom you have a closeup *outfit*. Imagine the benefit of being able to zoom from 75mm to 300mm to get the exact cropping you need. You no longer need to change lenses or add other accessories to shoot at a different image size. You no longer need to constantly reposition the tripod to change the cropping. Simply zoom the lens. Also, the Nikon 75-300mm zoom lens has a rotating tripod collar, a decided advantage with closeup photography.

We photograph 75 percent of our wildflower photos with the 75-300mm zoom and a Nikon 5T closeup lens. For more magnification, we use the 6T closeup lens instead, and for even more, we add a teleconverter. That's all there is to it.

MACRO LENSES

Macro lenses cover a broad range of focal lengths, from 50mm to 200mm. Many people think they need one of these lenses to effectively shoot closeups. This is just not true. A macro lens is nothing more than a regular lens that focuses close by itself. With a macro lens you do not need to add extension tubes or closeup diopters to get the lens to focus closer. It is true that they are optimized for flat-field reproduction (sharpness from edge to edge), but this is meaningless for field work. We both have 105mm macro lenses and use them occasionally, but mostly it is for specialized studio work. The biggest drawback of macro lenses, compared to the 75-300mm zoom lens plus diopter, is the inability to crop by zooming the lens. With a macro lens, you have to reposition the tripod nearly every time you change the composition.

OK, let's review what we've learned about making lenses focus closer. First, disregard everything irrelevant. That means bellows, reversing rings, macro lenses (If you already own one certainly use it, just don't go out and buy one because you think you have to have it for wildflowers), stacked lenses, macro converters, enlarging lenses, and short-mount lenses. Now, concentrate on what is relevant for wildflower photography. Wide-angle lenses work well for scenics, nothing more. Normal lenses work well for including a larger area, and long lenses work superbly for isolating flowers against a posterlike background. You can use a short extension tube on a normal lens, but for telephoto closeups it is better to use a two-element closeup diopter. If you need more magnification, add a teleconverter. Everyone shoots in their way with different equipment, but this works for us. The proof is in your hands.

Special Accessories

FOCUSING RAIL

When you photograph a landscape and need to move a little closer, it's no problem to pick up the tripod and move it, but when shooting closeups moving the tripod a few inches can be disastrous. It might mean the difference between a photograph of a dew-covered violet and one without dew because the tripod leg bumped against it. With high magnifications any movement of the tripod not only disturbs the subject, but creates serious problems with composition and focusing. What you need in these situations is a focusing rail. The camera mounts on the rail, which then mounts to the tripod head. A geared track and adjustment knob allow you to precisely focus by moving only the camera back and forth.

A few rails feature both fore-and-aft and side-to-side positioning of the camera. Avoid these. They are bulky, heavy, and a disaster when shooting verticals unless your lens has a tripod collar. One of the neatest rails we've seen is not really a rail at all. It is called a Focusing Slider and is available from Really Right Stuff (see the appendix). It's really nothing more than a long, dovetailed plate that slides back and forth in an Arca-Swiss-style quick-release clamp, but it has two big advantages. It's light and compact compared to regular focusing rails, and since the camera mounts to a quick-release clamp on top of the Slider, there can be slight side-to-side positioning without worrying about bulk. Of course, to use the Slider, you must use the Arca-Swiss quick-release system, but we recommend that you do that anyway. If you already have a regular focusing rail, you can mount an Arca-Swiss quick-release clamp on it to achieve the same side-to-side positioning as the Slider.

Most wildflower situations don't require you to use a focusing rail. Only when magnifications are 1X or greater, or when positioning the tripod could disturb the subject, will you reach for the rail; but on those occasions, you really need it.

EXTENSION ARM

Often, to achieve the composition you want, you need to aim the camera straight down on the subject. If you're using a long lens it isn't much of a problem—just tilt the tripod a little. However, if you're using a normal or wide-angle lens, it is just about impossible to shoot without including a tripod leg in the scene. The only way to solve this problem is to shoot with the camera extended out from the tripod. Several manufacturers make extension arms for this purpose. We use the one made by Bogen, called the Accessory Side Arm, because it is relatively lightweight, sturdy, and inexpensive. Regardless of which model you choose, you'll need to attach a ball head to one end. You can take the head off the tripod and attach the arm directly to the tripod, then attach the head to the end of the arm. However, this setup gives you less flexibility than if

St. John's wort, page 148
75-300mm lens, 5T diopter, 2 sec. at f/22   Adams

This is a photograph of the interior of a large patch of flowers. To shoot this scene using a tripod alone would mean having to tilt the legs to allow the lens to shoot straight down without including a tripod leg in the scene. The tripod would have knocked against the flowers and been very unstable. Using an extension arm allowed the tripod to be securely set up to the side of the patch.

you attach the arm to your head, then attach a second head to the end of the arm.

To use the arm, first determine where to set up the camera and make a mental note of the location. Next, set up the tripod to the side and at the approximate height. Then mount the arm and camera and begin the process of fine-tuning the composition. It's slow, tedious work, but the results are worth it.

Exposure

There's no question about it, exposure is one of the most confusing aspects of photography for all photographers, novice and pro alike. Keep in mind that exposure for closeups is the same as exposure for everything else. Once you learn it, it applies to all photography.

The first thing to clear up concerns meters. We can't think of any reason why a general nature photographer would need to use a separate hand-held meter. Your camera's meter is just as accurate, maybe more so. When you take a meter reading with your camera's meter, you are metering TTL, or "through the lens," and the meter takes into account most variables. Variable-aperture lenses, filters, whether the lens is focused at infinity, the camera's position relative to the subject, and accessories such as teleconverters and extension tubes, all create variables that must be accounted for with hand-held meters.

All reflected-light meters, like the one in your camera, measure the amount of light reaching the film *after* it has reflected off the subject. If the subject is average in tonality, all is well. Photograph a medium-toned jack-in-the-pulpit and the meter will suggest the proper exposure, because it is calibrated to render all subjects medium in tonality. Meters are not capable of determining if the tone of the subject is not average.

Now, let's consider what happens if the subject is not average. Suppose you meter a black bear. The meter thinks it is reading a medium-toned (average)

subject that is receiving very little light—because dark objects absorb most of the light. The meter thinks the subject needs much more light than necessary and will suggest an exposure that will make the bear medium in tonality. You'll end up with a gray bear instead of a black one. What you have to do in these cases is override the meter. Decrease the amount of light and the bear will appear normal. The opposite is true for light subjects. Snow is a good example. When you meter snow, the meter thinks it is reading a medium-toned subject that is receiving a lot of light—because light objects reflect most of the light. The meter thinks the subject needs less light than necessary and will suggest an exposure that will make the snow grayish. You must increase the exposure to make the snow white. This is the foundation for all exposure calculations. Light-toned subjects require more exposure than the meter suggests, dark-toned subjects require less. It's important to remember that it doesn't matter what color the subject is; if it is lighter or darker than average, it requires compensation.

How much should you compensate? We'll discuss a few specifics later on, but there really is no substitute for trial and error. One problem we often hear is that it's difficult to determine exactly when the subject is lighter or darker than medium. Consider this: If something is very dark, a black bear, for instance, you'll instantly recognize that it is darker than medium. If it is very light, such as a large-flowered trillium, you will know that it is lighter than medium. If you look at a subject and have to ask yourself if it is lighter or darker than medium, it's probably medium! This is as precise as you need to be for now. With experience, you'll learn the idiosyncrasies of different subjects.

Some photographers use a special type of meter, called an incident meter, because it measures the light *before* it reflects off the subject. It seems this would be the way to go since you wouldn't have to compensate for the reflectance of light or dark subjects. This is partly true, but you still have to compensate for a host of other variables, such as the ones mentioned earlier. And there are other problems inherent in their use. Stick with the meter in your camera.

One way to avoid having to make compensations for tonality is to meter a medium-toned object in the same lighting. We often do this whenever there is a suitable object available. Some photographers meter their hand and open up one stop (your palm is about one stop lighter than medium) to get the proper exposure setting. We do not. The hand is only two feet from the camera, and if the subject is much farther away, exposure errors can result. If the subject is close to the camera and not medium toned, you can meter a gray card, but be aware that exposure errors can result if you do not precisely place the card. We find that using a gray card usually creates more confusion than it prevents.

Any time you meter a medium-toned object to measure the exposure for a very light or very dark subject, you must make an additional exposure calculation. For light subjects, such as white wildflowers, stop down one-third to two-thirds of a stop after all calculations. For dark subjects, open up one-third to two-thirds of a stop. This will keep the subject from losing detail.

To make compensations, you need a camera that lets you override the meter's chosen setting. A full manual override is preferable, but an exposure compensation dial will suffice. Newer cameras have highly sophisticated metering systems that can compensate for you if the light or dark areas do not take up a large portion of the frame. Canon calls their system evaluative metering, Nikon's is called matrix. Other names include multi-zone and multi-segment metering. These systems will suggest proper exposures in most situations, but remember, if the subject is not medium and occupies most of the frame you still have to compensate.

You probably have heard of the sunny $f/16$ rule. It's a guideline for non-metered exposures on sunny days. Well, it just doesn't work—not for us, anyway. The rule states that when using ISO 50 film on a sunny day, the proper exposure is $1/60$ of a second at $f/16$ (or any equivalent setting). In theory, it should work since the sun's light is consistent. In practice, it's another story. As with using hand-held meters, there are simply too many variables to account for. Variable-aperture lenses, filters, and other accessories must all be compensated for. The sun must be shining brightly, with no haze or clouds. It must be between two hours after sunrise and two hours before sunset. The rule doesn't work with sidelighting, backlighting, or when shooting closeups (exactly the situation we're shooting in). Also, with dark and light subjects, you must compensate in the opposite direction as when taking a meter reading. Why do all this; why not simply take a meter reading? Besides, how often do nature photographers photograph on days that qualify as sunny $f/16$ lighting anyway?

Let's look at what we've learned so far. First, use the meter in your camera, and forget the sunny $f/16$ rule. Much of what you read about exposure concerns these two aspects, so we've simplified things considerably. There's no point cluttering your mind with things that don't apply. Next, remember the basis for all exposure calculations: light-toned subjects require more exposure than medium toned subjects, dark-toned subjects require less.

It's very important to understand how the metering pattern you're using sees the scene and to consider how much of the frame the subject occupies. If you're using the matrix-type metering pattern, the camera is analyzing the entire scene. If the subject is not medium but the surroundings are, it won't make much difference as long as the subject is not occupying a substantial part of the frame. However, in such a case, you will still need to stop down about ½ stop if the subject is white, because the meter is using a scene of predominant medium tone to determine the exposure. If you don't stop down, the white flower will wash out.

If you're using the center-weighted or spot-metering pattern be aware of the tonality of the object within the meter's parameters. These patterns basically disregard everything except what is in the center of the fame. Our usual preference for closeups is the center-weighted pattern. We point the center of the camera at the subject to get a meter reading and work in tones from that. This ensures proper exposure of the subject, the primary interest of our photo. Normally, the subject takes up enough of the frame that we do not need to use the spot meter. To shoot wide-angle scenes, we often switch to the matrix pattern. It usually does a great job of averaging exposure over the entire scene.

It is important to make tests, and don't take ours or anyone else's word for anything. Take notes, but don't confuse things by recording the f-stop and shutter speed information. What you need to record is *why* you felt it necessary to make an exposure compensation. Your notes might read something like this: *On this wildflower scene, I metered off the pink petals and increased exposure ½ stop because I thought they were ½ stop lighter than medium. I also bracketed in ½-stop increments.* When you get the film back, compare it with your notes. You may discover that this particular wildflower is one full stop lighter than medium. You'll then begin to learn how to distinguish tones.

In our experience, we have come to recognize a range of tonalities from one stop under medium, to two stops over. In most situations, you will not photograph a scene that requires more exposure compensation than this. However, with experience, you'll learn to determine tones that vary only by half stops.

DARK

For black bears, crows, and ravens, underexpose 1 stop from the suggested setting. Trailing arbutus, wintergreen, and partridge berry leaves require about $1/3$ to $2/3$ of a stop underexposure.

MEDIUM

For grass, most foliage, most tree bark, average landscape scenes, white-tailed deer, sunrises and sunsets metered to the side of the sun, and 18-percent-reflectance gray card, shoot at the suggested exposure. The foliage of most wildflowers is medium in tonal-

ity, as are the blossoms themselves. The ones that aren't are usually shades of pink, white, and yellow.

LIGHT

For sand on the beach, most white birds, and polar bears, overexpose about 1 stop from the suggested setting. Most pink and white flower blossoms require from ½ to 1 stop overexposure, unless you spot meter directly on the petal (see below).

VERY LIGHT

For snow and white sand beaches, overexpose about 2 stops from the suggested setting. The only time you will need to open 2 stops for wildflowers is if you are spot metering a very white petal, such as large-flowered trillium. Even then, the amount of compensation needed varies from $1^1/3$ to 2 stops. Remember, only experience will teach you the idiosyncrasies of each subject.

Coping with Wind

On a top ten list of problems encountered while photographing wildflowers, dealing with the wind occupies the first seven positions. It is a big, big problem. Occasionally you can incorporate the movement into the photo with good results, but more often any movement will ruin the image. The problem entered a new dimension for us as we began photographing for this book. With over two hundred wildflowers to photograph in one season, we had to develop an innovative approach to dealing with the wind.

The first approach is to photograph early in the morning, before the sun warms the air and creates thermals. Nature is always seeking a balance, and when warm and cool air exist together, the result is wind. Shooting in the morning has another benefit: that's usually when the best lighting occurs.

Using a fast shutter speed is another approach, but one that is rarely applicable. The choice of shutter speed is limited to available light and depth-of-field

Spring beauty, page 196
75-300mm lens, 5T diopter, 2 sec. at f/22   Adams

There are two approaches to properly exposing this scene. You can spot meter the blossoms and open up about 1 stop from the suggested exposure, or you can meter the medium-toned foliage and stop down ½ stop to retain detail in the light-toned blossoms.

Ironweed and ailanthus webworm moth, page 106
75-300mm lens, 5T diopter, ¼ sec. at f/16   Adams

Almost everything in this image is darker than medium. By metering the background and stopping down ½ stop, the correct exposure was obtained. Spot metering the flowers or bracts would have required stopping down even more.

Blue cohosh, page 173
75-300mm lens, 5T diopter, 3 sec. at f/22   Adams

This is an easy subject for exposure—it's all medium. Just meter any part of the scene and shoot at what the meter suggests. If you're uncertain whether the subject is medium, ask yourself "what would this subject look like as a medium tone?" In most cases it will look fine, so even if it was a little light or dark in reality, by shooting at the meter's suggested setting and making it a medium tone you will have a good photo.

Large-flowered trillium, page 220
75-300mm lens, 5T diopter, 1 sec. at f/16   *Adams*

The petals of this trillium are very light toned. If you meter directly off them, you need to compensate by opening up the exposure roughly 2 stops.

Field garlic, page 211
75-300mm lens, 5T diopter, ½ sec. at f/22   *Adams*

Field garlic grows in fields, where the wind is usually blowing during the day. This photograph was made early in the morning, when the wind was calm, the dew had not evaporated, and the light was perfect.

requirements. Of course, when the wind is blowing you should use the fastest speed that you can.

STEM STAKES

If you cannot use a fast shutter speed to stop the wind movement, you need to bring in the heavy artillery. We have a large collection of specialized barriers and stem stakes that allow us to photograph in all but the strongest winds. Each has a specific use depending on the situation at hand.

Rosebud orchid, page 90
75-300mm lens, 5T diopter, 1 sec. at f/16   *Adams*

This wildflower was lightly swaying in a morning breeze. Making a sharp photo required carefully attaching the stem to a stem stake with a pipe cleaner.

The first approach is to stick a wooden stake into the ground so that it intersects the stem at a point just out of the frame. Then carefully twist a pipe cleaner around the stem and the stake. Do not use string or wire as they can damage the stem. Also, be sure to do this before setting up the camera because it always moves the flower a little.

The stakes we use are three-eighths-inch dowel rods from the local home center. We also carry five-foot-long poles made from broom handles. Each dowel and pole is sharpened on one end to stick into the ground.

WIND BARRIERS

Stem stakes alone are often insufficient to stop wind movement, and they are useless when photographing a clump of flowers. Plus, it's sometimes difficult to keep them out of the picture. To solve these problems, we use wind barriers. The setup consists of four, thirty-two-inch wooden dowel rods that we stick in the ground to surround the flower. We then stretch plastic around the dowels to serve as the barrier. We also carry a second system, identical except the poles are five feet long, and the plastic is five feet wide. Using these setups is painstaking and solicits puzzling stares from passersby, but it works.

There is at least one commercially available wind barrier, called the Diffusion Tent. The primary function of the Diffusion Tent is to diffuse the light, but it also blocks the wind. It works well for small scenes on the ground, but it is impracticable for larger flowers that grow several feet high.

A problem you'll quickly notice when using a wind barrier is that it often shows up in the photo. Sometimes you can move the plastic around to get it out of view, but often you cannot. In these cases, you have no choice but to use an artificial background—but more on that later.

USING FLASH TO STOP
WIND MOVEMENT

Sometimes no combination of stem stakes or wind barriers is enough to stop the wind, and you are left with only one option: flash. Because a flash unit exposes the flower very quickly (usually 1/1000 of a second or faster), it prevents almost any movement from being recorded. However, we particularly dislike using flash because of the unnatural lighting that it sometimes produces, and because we never really know exactly just what the result will be. We much prefer the look of diffuse natural light, and only use flash when necessary. It's true that when used properly, today's flash units can produce natural-looking lighting. The problem is that learning how to use them properly requires a tremendous investment of time. Despite what the manufacturers would have you believe, without a lengthy learning period, you can no more make consistently good photos with the latest flash units than you could take a new camera out of the box, point it at something, and expect a great photograph.

We are not qualified to give suggestions for flash use, but the books *Closeups in Nature* and *How To Photograph Insects And Spiders* provide details of closeup flash photography and are highly recommended. By the way, some photographers like to use a subdued flash only to create a little sparkle in their closeups, rather than relying on it for total lighting. We do this with mirrors and reflectors, although admittedly, this is limited to somewhat sunny days.

TILT LENSES FOR
FASTER SHUTTER SPEEDS

Some combination of the above methods will stop minor wind movement in most any situation. There is one situation, however, in which none of them will help: wide-angle scenics. With wide-angle scenes there is simply too much in the photograph to use stem stakes, flash, or surround with a wind barrier. And fast shutter speeds are not an option because you need to stop down to get the most depth of field. You can go ahead and shoot at the slow shutter speed, and the resulting image may be OK. Sometimes, blurring some of the blossoms is effective, but with a wide-angle scenic, you'll need to have some of the blossoms sharply rendered. Of course, anyone who

has tried this on a windy day knows it is an exercise in frustration.

View-camera users have a readily available solution to the problem. Their lenses have front elements that tilt to better align the subject plane to the film plane. This allows a wider open aperture; thus, a faster shutter speed. But 35mm lenses are fixed. So what is the 35mm user to do? Well, there actually are a few 35mm lenses designed specially for this purpose. These lenses have a built-in tilting feature that helps align the planes. With one of these lenses, you can shoot nearly wide open and still have enough depth of field to keep everything in focus from near to far.

As far as we know, Canon is the only company to offer these lenses. They come in four focal lengths: 24mm, 35mm, 45mm, and 90mm. You can have the 35mm lens modified to fit on a different brand camera since it has a manual diaphragm, but the others have electronic diaphragms and require very expensive modification. So if you don't shoot with Canon cameras, you'll not only have to buy a $1,200-plus lens, but also a Canon body to use it.

If you can afford only one of these tilt lenses, you might want to consider the 45mm focal length. We don't recommend the 35mm because it has a manual diaphragm; you have to open the lens to its widest setting for composing, then stop it down to the chosen aperture for metering and shooting. The 90mm lens covers such a narrow field of view that you may be able to use wind barriers to stop the wind movement instead, thus allowing you to stop down for depth of field. The depth of field in a standard 24mm lens is often great enough, even when opened up somewhat, to allow a faster shutter speed. We own the 24mm tilt lens, primarily because it offers an extra feature we consider indispensable for waterfalls and lighthouses: a shift feature (perspective control) that helps keep tall subjects in proper perspective. Canon's other lenses offer this feature as well, as do lenses from several other manufacturers, but it is most useful with the 24mm focal length

These lenses are not cheap, and you'll only

occasionally use them in the tilting mode. Still, for serious landscape work involving wildflowers, they can be indispensable.

PATIENCE

Perhaps the best aid you can have is patience. The saying, "Good things come to those who wait," might be rephrased to say, "Sharp photos come to those who wait." After you've done everything to stop the wind and there is still movement, don't pack up and leave. Breezes rarely continue for hours at a time. Set up all your gear, take hold of the cable release, and carefully watch for a lull. Then fire the shutter. You may not get off many exposures, but you'll at least get the shot. On occasion, we've waited three hours before making an exposure.

Paralleling the Subject

It is a confounding rule of optics that the greater the magnification the less depth of field you have. Thus, camera positioning becomes critical. You can optimize what little depth of field there is by making sure the film plane is parallel to the subject plane. If you're shooting a leaf, for instance, make sure both the leaf plane and film plane (camera back) are parallel. However, you usually won't be shooting a subject with such an obvious flat plane as a leaf. That is when you must determine what portion of the scene *has* to be in focus and align with that. Often, there is no flat plane at all, and there is nothing you can do but focus on the most important part of the scene and watch everything else go soft.

It is often suggested that you should focus one-third of the way into the scene to get the most depth of field. This is technically true, as there is more depth of field behind the point of focus than in front of it. However, it is next to impossible to determine the one-third point when shooting closeups. You can compromise by focusing on the most important part of the scene, then backing off ever so slightly to-

Blue phlox, page 86
75-300mm lens, 5T diopter, 2 sec. at f/16   Adams

Not all of this scene is on the same plane, so there is no way to keep everything in sharp focus. However, by aligning the film plane with the plane of the most important part in the scene—in this case, the two blossoms in the upper right—optimum focus is obtained.

ward foreground focus. This will maximize depth of field while assuring the most critical element is in focus.

Backgrounds

Our pet peeve is cluttered backgrounds. We want our closeup subjects to be the center of attention, not some leaf or twig in the distance. That is a primary reason we love telephoto lenses for closeups. These lenses have an extremely narrow angle of view that effectively isolates the subject against a posterlike background. The important thing to keep in mind is the closer the background is to the subject, the less posterlike it will appear. You could open

20

the lens aperture to help isolate the subject further, but often you need to use smaller apertures just to keep the whole flower in focus. The trick is to look around. Where you see one flower there are probably more, and one of them may present a less-cluttered background.

If you've found the best subject, set up the camera, and there is still too much clutter, there are several things you can do. First, look carefully through the camera while pressing the depth-of-field preview button to see what is causing the distraction. If it is grass blades or dead twigs, you can clip them off. We use the small scissors in a Swiss-Army knife to clip off grass blades without disturbing the subject. If the distraction is from living material other than common grass, you should not cut it. Instead, tie it back or lay sticks over it while you're shooting. Then restore them to their original position.

If this doesn't work, you may have to open the aperture a little, or increase the magnification. The more you magnify the less depth of field you have, resulting in a background that is more out of focus.

If you're using a long lens with the most magnification and widest aperture that is practical, you've eliminated all the clutter you can, and the background is still cluttered, then there is only one option: artificial backgrounds. We prefer the natural look of out-of-focus foliage and don't like to use an artificial background, but sometimes they are necessary. There are several materials you can use for these backgrounds, from poster board to fabric stretched around a frame. We've tried them all, and the only method that results in a natural looking background is a blown-up photograph of an out-of-focus scene. The one we carry is 24 x 30 inches and is mounted on stiff foam-core poster board.

Fruit of jack-in-the-pulpit, page 239
75-300mm lens, 5T diopter, 12 sec. at f/22   Adams

Fruit of doll's eyes, page 185
75-300mm lens, 5T diopter, 4 sec. at f/32   Adams

When shooting at relatively high magnifications, background vegetation that is not close to the subject records as a pleasing poster effect. In the image of doll's eyes fruit, the background vegetation was only inches away, so an artificial background was needed. In the image of jack-in-the-pulpit fruit, the background was a few feet away, so an artificial background was not necessary.

Using and Controlling Natural Light

Lighting is everything in every type of photography. It makes the difference between an OK photograph and a great photograph. Always be aware of the light and how it affects the scene, and be prepared with the proper accessories to control the light to suit your needs.

You almost never want direct, undiffused sunlight in closeup photography. The contrast range is just too much for the film to handle. That is why closeup photographers like to photograph on overcast days, when the cloud layer acts like a giant diffuser. Of course, you can't always shoot on overcast days, so you need to have some sort of diffuser. You can use

many different types depending on the situation. We carry large and small diffusion umbrellas, with homemade aluminum handles that have a ¼-20 thread in the end. The handles screw onto a small ball head attached to a Bogen Super Clamp. The Super Clamp attaches to a second tripod. With this setup there is unlimited flexibility with placement. Also, we carry two 30-inch x 40-inch collapsible diffusers made by Bogen, called Bo-flex. These fold up neatly for stowing but give great coverage in use. Regardless of which method you use make sure to diffuse both the subject and background. And be sure to place the diffuser as close to the subject as possible. If you place it too far away, you'll only be casting a shadow, rather than providing the soft, diffuse light that makes great closeup images. By the way, the clear polyethylene

Gray's lily, page 124
75-300mm lens, 5T diopter, ⅛ sec. at f/22 *Adams*

Overcast days are great for shooting closeups, but only if the sky is not included in the scene. If you need to include the sky, make sure it is blue, as in this case. Make a special effort to look for unique opportunities like this.

Water hemlock, page 175
28mm lens, graduated neutral-density filter, 2 sec. at f/22
Adams

You have to make a planned effort to be in the right place at the right time to make photographs like this. The calm wind allowed the long exposure needed to shoot at this time of day.

plastic that we use for wind barriers makes an effective diffusion material.

After diffusing the scene, you may want to reflect a little light onto the subject for drama. This might seem silly; after all, why diffuse the light in the first place if you're just going to put light back into the scene? The answer is that you will have *control* over the light. You don't have this with normal lighting. You can make a good reflector by covering a piece of cardboard with crumpled gold Christmas foil on one side and crumpled aluminum foil on the other. We like the warm light projected by the gold side, but it occasionally affects the color of white blossoms. In these instances, we use the aluminum side. When you want to cast a direct beam of light onto the subject use a mirror. The best mirrors for field

work are the plastic type (Mirro-flex is one brand name). Check with glass supply houses to see if they have scraps lying around.

You've probably heard photographers talk about a preference for early morning and evening light. We share that preference for most of our photography, but for closeups only the morning is preferred. That is when the light is golden and the flowers are laced in dew. In the evening the wind is usually blowing, and there is no dew. It is important to understand that when we talk about morning and evening lighting for closeups, it is not the same as for landscapes. When shooting closeups, you need to wait until the sun is high enough to provide sufficient illumination. How long you should wait varies. If you're on an east-facing slope in line with the horizon, or on

Pink lady's slipper, page 92
75-300mm lens, 5T diopter, ¼ sec. at f/22 Adams

This beautiful blossom was discovered just as the sun came out after a rain shower. The scene was diffused to remove the harsh contrast, and a mirror was used to direct light on the flower only.

Pinesap, page 207
75-300mm lens, 5T diopter, 8 sec. at f/16 Adams

This flower was growing in a deep, dark forest setting. The lighting was so low that a typical photograph would have required an exposure of 30 seconds, or more. Plus, the quality of the lighting would have been horrible. To compensate, the warm light of a flashlight was used to illuminate the flower.

a mountaintop, the subject receives direct sunlight immediately after sunrise. You can start shooting right away in this case, often with spectacular results. Just keep in mind that the sun quickly becomes too intense and must be diffused.

Rarely, will you be in this situation while shooting wildflowers in the southern Appalachians. More often than not, it is several hours before you see the sun. Don't make the mistake of shooting too early, particularly if you are on a north-facing slope completely shaded from the sun. This is a ready-made prescription for creating a cool, bluish cast to your photographs. And even the strongest warming filter won't help in this case. To get enough warming factor to remove the blue cast will almost certainly alter the color in the flowers. The only solution is to wait until later in the day, when the lighting is more even. In the deep, dark forests of the mountains, this may mean waiting until the sun is directly overhead.

Conversely, once the sun has set behind a ridge on a cloudless day, you can forget making more photographs without a warming filter. And again, with wildflowers this may cause an unnatural color cast to the plant.

Our favorite lighting occurs just after a rain shower when the sun is beginning to break. The flowers are covered in rain drops, the wind is usually calm, and the light is magical. Could anything be better?

As with everything else, the best advice is to get out there and shoot film in all lighting situations and conditions. You'll soon learn when to leave the camera in the pack and when to pull it out.

Composition

Having reviewed thousands of photographs, we are convinced that the vast majority could have been improved if their makers had only followed one rule: simplify the composition. If there is an element in the scene that is not obviously helping the composition, it is taking away from it. Get it out of there. Ask yourself, What am I photographing? What is my subject? Then photograph that and that only. Anything else in the scene should only be included to enhance the subject. Beginning photographers often try to include the mountain, the stream in the foreground, the raven soaring overhead, the mountain climber, the deer drinking out of the stream, the flowers growing along the bank—well, you get the idea. Pick one of these and photograph it. There is nothing wrong with a photograph of a mountain with a babbling brook flowing in the foreground, as long as one enhances the other and doesn't compete for attention.

Wildflower photographers should have no problem identifying their subjects. Obviously, it is the flower. However, it can be difficult to discipline yourself to photograph only the flower and not every-

Wild oats, page 163
75-300mm lens, 5T diopter, ½ sec. at f/22   Adams

This photograph was made during our favorite lighting condition for closeups. It was during the middle of the day, just after a rain shower, and the sun was trying to peek out. The raindrops were still clinging, the wind was calm, and the light level was high enough for a reasonable exposure time. Plus, the bright overcast sky provided beautiful illumination.

thing within wide-angle view of it. That is one of the biggest problems we see with flower photographs. The photographer just didn't get close enough to the subject, and the resulting image includes a lot of unnecessary elements. Study the photographs in this book for an idea of what we mean by simplification.

You've probably heard of the rule of thirds. It states that an image's strongest compositional points are at the intersections of lines drawn to divide the frame into horizontal and vertical thirds. You should place the strongest part of the scene on one of these imaginary intersections. Obviously, this won't work with all subjects, but it often works well with wildflowers.

If possible don't place the subject dead center in the frame. This creates a static image with no emo-tional impact. However, there are a few exceptions to this rule, such as when shooting an extreme closeup of a flower with perfect radial symmetry. In this case, it is sometimes effective to place the blossom in the center of the frame and have everything radiate out from it. Also, when shooting individual flowers that grow in narrow spikes, like lady's tresses and colicroot, it looks funny placing them off-center. Go ahead and center them, even though there is dead space on either side. If it is a good photo, the editor will crop this out before printing. Ideally, you want to look around until you find several specimens growing together and compose the scene to fill the frame.

You can create artsy, moody wildflower images by

Colicroot, page 233
75-300mm lens, 5T diopter,
¹/₈ sec. at f/22   Adams

In the field, the composition is limited to the format of the film. Using 35mm film, there was no way to make this image without a little dead space on both sides, or a lot of dead space on one side of the flower. However, it was simple to crop the image like we wanted during the production phase of this book.

Yellow mandarin, page 163
75-300mm lens, 5T diopter,
½ sec. at f/8   Casstevens

Sometimes it is preferable not to have all of the scene in focus. If much of this scene was sharp, the image would be distracting. However, it's important to have sharp focus on at least a small part of the flower.

Yellow trillium, page 166
75-300mm lens, 5T diopter,
2 sec. at f/22   Adams

The rule of thirds was used to place the flower in this scene.

selectively using soft focus. The trick is to try different points of focus until you find one you like. If you're using a lot of magnification and set the aperture wide open, only a tiny portion of the flower will be in focus, with everything else going soft. This is what you want with soft-focus images, but it is important that some portion of the scene be in focus.

Another method for creating artsy wildflower images is to shoot a double exposure. Make one exposure with the scene sharply focused, and the second with the scene a little out of focus. This creates a soft-focus image that retains a measure of sharpness. To determine the exposure, simply figure out what the proper exposure should be and shoot both exposures one stop less than this. For instance, if the proper exposure is determined to be $^1/_{30}$ at $f/16$, shoot both exposures at $^1/_{60}$ at $f/16$ and the image will be correctly exposed. Of course, to use this method, you need to have a camera that has double-exposure capability.

There really isn't a right or wrong way to shoot soft-focus images because they are so subjective. Everyone has their own ideas as to just what works and what doesn't. However, it is usually better to slightly overexpose the image.

Technique

Proper technique is the single most important factor in producing quality photographs. You hear the term used frequently, but just what is good technique? If you employ every applicable situation listed in the following outline, we promise your photographs will improve. This is assuming up front that you have a sturdy tripod, quality lenses and filters that are clean, and are using a sharp film. Also, this outline applies specifically to closeups; other types of photography require modified approaches. Remember, achieving quality results takes time. It is not unusual for us to spend three hours or more on a single composition.

Pay any bills that are due, make up with your spouse or sweetheart, and return all phone calls before going into the field.

Arrive at the scene before you expect the best light so you are not rushing when you get there.

Don't try to photograph when you need to go to the bathroom.

Make yourself comfortable. If it is hot, wear shorts and a T-shirt. If it is cold, wear a hat. If it is wet, wear a rain suit. This may seem obvious, but it is important.

Set your pack down several feet from the subject to keep from inadvertently jarring it.

Slow down and take a careful, studied approach.

Roughly determine what magnification you need and what the background is like. This will help you decide which lens to use (usually the longest focal length possible).

Try out all possible compositions while hand-holding the camera. Choose the one(s) you like best while making a mental note of where the camera needs to positioned. Then set up the tripod.

If the proper composition requires you to lay on your belly in the cold dew, or step into six inches of muck, so be it. You should prepare for inconveniences like this and not hesitate to endure them.

Be extremely careful not to disturb the subject when setting up the tripod. Watch out for any vegetation that may be against the subject. This is critical on a dewy morning.

Firmly seat the tripod and thoroughly tighten all controls.

Roughly compose the scene, readjusting the tripod if necessary. Check the background with the depth-of-field preview button. Remove any distracting elements by tying back, laying sticks on, or cutting out (never cut anything except common grass). Be very careful that you do not disturb the subject in the process.

Check the depth-of-field preview button again to make sure the background is not distracting.

Set up any necessary diffusers, reflectors, or wind barriers. Stem stakes need to be set up before composing.

Focus on the subject and determine the proper exposure. If you need to meter an object to the side of the subject, do this without refocusing. Fine tune the composition and look around the edges of the frame one last time for distracting elements jutting in.

Just before tripping the shutter, check the lens to make sure it is clean. Occasionally, insects or blowing vegetation will land on the front element. Even dust specks can cause image degradation if there are a lot of them. Carry a large bulb blower and blow off the lens at each new subject. Also, blow out the camera back every time you change film.

Attach a cable release if you have not yet done so, and determine if the subject is still. If so, lock up the mirror (if your camera has this feature) and release the shutter. If the subject is not still, wait until it is. Don't read a book or watch birds while waiting. Look at the flower. When shooting with high magnifications, you should look through the lens for movement, as it is hard to detect with the naked eye.

If you are shooting fairly close to the subject, try not to breathe in its direction throughout the process. Doing so will cause a slight wind.

After making the exposures, look back at the subject and decide if you have photographed the best compositions.

Put the lens cap back on before stuffing the lens in a pack. You'd be surprised at the number of people we see walking around with a bag full of unprotected gear.

Leave the scene as you found it.

When Not to Take a Picture

You may have heard it said that there is always one more way to shoot a subject, or that a really good photographer can always make good photographs. This is nonsense. Very often there is simply no way to make a good photograph, or there may only be one good way to shoot a certain subject. This is particularly true of wildflower photography, when good photographs depend on suitable living subjects. Photographers who do not understand this waste a lot of film and time making bad photographs. Conversely, it's important not to fall into the trap of justifying a lack of desire to photograph by reasoning that every situation "just won't work." At the same time, it's important to know when that is the case. Unfortunately, we can't tell you that because every situation is different. What you should do is go over every possible angle in your mind. If nothing seems to work, think about it some more. If you still can't come up with anything, don't keep torturing yourself. Give up and look somewhere else.

Ethical Considerations

Not many years ago, there were only a handful of nature photographers in the country. Now, millions of people carry cameras into the field hoping to bring back memorable images. One survey estimates there are over fourteen million nature photographers in the United States alone. Imagine the stress on the environment from all these people. If you think no one else is photographing your subject, think again. The southern Appalachians draw more wildflower enthusiasts than perhaps any other region in the country. You may not see another photographer, but you can safely bet another will come along soon. You can minimize impact if you always follow this motto: the subject is more important than the photograph. It's as simple as that. No photograph is worth the destruction of the wildflower to get it.

The most common negative impact we see comes from photographers who are so concerned about positioning themselves that they are oblivious to what is around them. Consequently, they trample everything in the vicinity. If you find a flower that is not approachable without disturbing other flowers, walk away. It is just not worth it. To those who say the end justifies the means if the photographs are used for education, we say nonsense. The world does not need another photograph of anything if that photograph was made at the expense of the subject.

It is common practice among some photographers to pick the wildflower and either take it inside, or mount it in a special device, to make a photograph. Certainly, if these are backyard flowers, there is no harm done; but too often they are uncommon species taken from the wild. Not only is this illegal in many places, but it is quite unethical. For us, the joy of nature photography is finding a subject and photographing it in its natural environment. And it gives us a lot of satisfaction knowing that the wildflower will be there for the enjoyment of the next person that comes along.

Into every discussion of ethics enters the question of subject manipulation. Is it OK to cut out distracting foliage? Is there anything wrong with using mist sprayers to create artificial dew? If you don't like the arrangement of elements in a photograph, what's wrong with moving them around? Everyone answers these questions differently, and each person must photograph within their own personal boundaries of ethics—that is, after agreeing that it is never OK to wantonly cut out or trample vegetation. We follow a philosophy of enhancement without creation. For instance, we will tie back distracting foliage and use filters or reflectors to enhance a scene we have discovered in the wild, but we will not create a scene that did not exist. To do so takes something away. It seems like an attempt to one-up Mother Nature. We're trying to become a part of nature, not to overcome it. A big part of the photographic equation is in the dreaming, the planning, and the search. The click of the shutter is merely the culmination of this process. To shortcut it by overly manipulating the scene removes a part of the equation that we are not prepared to give up.

Today, a discussion on ethical considerations for photographers is not complete without mentioning computer digital manipulation. The technology is now so sophisticated that computer operators can literally create images that did not exist, and manipulate images to any extent. With this technology, photographers don't need to worry about distracting backgrounds, they can just remove the distractions in the computer, or move the flower, or change the color of the flower, or add a second flower, and on and on. Photographers who believe this is ethical, that is. We feel the same way about computer manipulation as we do about manipulating the scene in the wild, at least for editorial work such as this book. This book was produced using digital technology, with each image scanned and "enhanced" in the computer. However, our enhancement consisted only of restoring the true color balance that was lost because of film limitations, removing any dust specs from the scanning process, and cropping. Except for cropping, which is done to almost all printed photographs, every image in this book appears exactly as it did through the viewfinder.

Regardless of whether you are behind a camera or in front of a computer, we ask only that you follow your conscience. We believe if you do that, you will make a better photograph and leave your subjects unharmed. Remember, photography is merely an excuse to spend time in the natural world we all love so much. In the end, that is what truly matters; the photographs are secondary. For those in the minority, those who do not care if they have a negative impact, may we suggest you take up a different hobby?

The Natural Setting

The Appalachian Mountains are the second-largest mountain system in North America. They stretch some two thousand miles along a chain of ridges and valleys, beginning in north-central Alabama and continuing to Newfoundland. The typical tourist traveling these highlands views them in scenic innocence, in awe of the majestic ridges lined up in the distance and the crystal-clear streams flowing through dense forests. But tourists are often oblivious to the ecology of these mountains. The biologist, on the other hand, sees a much broader picture. To be sure, many tourists flock to this region because of the biology: the great spring wildflower displays, the white-tailed deer along the roadways, the splendor of autumn; but only the more acute observer begins to fully appreciate the exceptional natural diversity of the Appalachians.

The scope of this book covers the southern portion of the Appalachians, which also happens to be the most diverse region in the chain. In fact, the southern Appalachians support over half of the flowering plant and fern species found in North America. The specific numbers for flora and fauna are staggering: at least 400 species of moss; 130 species of trees; and over 2,500 species of flowering plants, at least 200 of which are found nowhere else in the world. The Great Smoky Mountains National Park, the largest undeveloped region in the southern Appalachians, and an International Biosphere Reserve, supports incredible numbers of its own. Within the park are more than 100 species of trees (more than all of northern Europe); over 2,000 species of fungi; at least 70 species of fish; 22 species of salamanders; 200 species of birds; 50 species of mammals; 80 species of reptiles and amphibians; and over 1,500 different types of flowering plants.

The obvious question is why the diversity? Several factors combine to make the southern Appalachians the botanical jewel of eastern North America, not the least of which is water. The amount of rainfall in the southern Appalachians is surpassed in this country only in the Pacific Northwest, and perhaps the Florida panhandle. This moisture, along with the generally mild climate, helps create the lush forests that make the region unique. Also, the southern Appalachians were spared during the most recent glacial activity; the glaciers extended only as far south as the Poconos in Pennsylvania. Thus, the region served as a sort of refuge for many species.

Geologists divide the southern Appalachians into three main geological provinces: the Blue Ridge Province—the main ridge of mountains generally along the eastern front; the Valley-and-Ridge Province, which lies just west of the Blue Ridge Province; and the Appalachian Plateau Province, which lies along the western boundary. Within these geologically distinct zones are numerous forest types. Five broad and easily recognized forest types are the spruce-fir, northern hardwood, oak-hickory, pine-oak, and cove forests.

Interspersed within these broad forest types are dozens of distinctive natural communities. There are grassy balds, heath balds, bogs, spray cliffs, rocky summits, and several more specific forest types; all divided and subdivided into categories only a botanist fully understands. North Carolina alone has more than fifty natural communities within its mountain region.

All these communities contribute to the natural diversity of the southern Appalachians, each hosting its own unique assortment of plants and animals, many of which grow only in that environment. Learning at least the broadest definitions of these environments will greatly help in the overall understanding of wildflowers. For one thing, you won't spend time looking for certain wildflowers where they don't grow. Just as learning the name of a wildflower leads to a greater appreciation of it, so does learning about the communities in which it grows.

Butterfly on bleeding heart, page 226
75-300mm lens, 5T diopter, 1 sec. at f/22   Adams

Botanical Exploration of the Southern Appalachians

In the space allotted here, it would be impossible to write a meaningful treatment of the history of botanical exploration in the southern Appalachians, but we felt compelled to mention some of the more notable characters and their contributions to our understanding of the region. This region has been inhabited by humans for at least twelve thousand years, but European expeditions did not begin until 1540. In that year, Hernando De Soto became the first European to explore the Appalachians, which he named after the Appalache Indians of Florida. But his was not a botanical expedition; rather, it was one of conquest, and one in search of gold and other riches. It was more than two centuries later before anyone entered the Appalachians to study its plants. One of the first to do so was John Bartram.

Bartram, the first native-born naturalist of the New World, made several excursions to study plants from his hometown of Philadelphia. On his last expedition, a long trip to Florida, he took his son, William. The elder Bartram never explored the mountains farther south than the Shenandoah Valley, but William did; and in the spring of 1775, he became the first naturalist to study the Cherokee country of the southern Appalachians. The Bartram legacy lives on in a genus of moss named *Bartramia* and the Bartram Trail, a popular hiking trail, in the mountains.

Another famous explorer was André Michaux, who traveled widely in the region and climbed such peaks as Roan Mountain and Grandfather Mountain. Michaux is one of the most recognized names in botanical circles. Several species were named after him including Carolina lily, *Lilium michauxii*, and Michaux's saxifrage.

Michaux's greatest legacy may have been his discovery of a little wildflower resembling galax. In 1839, thirty-seven years after Michaux's death, Dr. Asa Gray was in France studying at the Michaux herbarium when he came across a "low woody plant with saw-toothed leaves" (one translation). This was the little wildflower resembling galax that Michaux had discovered in 1788, but which had not been named. Gray, the best-known botanist in America, then and now, named the plant *Shortia galacifolia* (the common name is shortia or Oconee bells) after his friend Dr. Charles William Short. Gray, and others, spent many fruitless years in search of shortia growing in the wild. Finally, in May 1877, a 17-year-old boy found the plant growing on the banks of the Catawba River—much to Gray's chagrin. Two years later, Gray was able to see the plant himself. His long search over, he exclaimed: "Now let me sing my Nunc Dimittis" (meaning: "Let me depart in peace"). Among Asa Gray's noted accomplishments is the discovery of one of the most beautiful lilies in all the Appalachians, Gray's lily, *Lilium grayi*. Gray's lily grows on the grassy balds of Roan Mountain and on a few other southern Appalachian peaks. Gray was so enamored with Roan Mountain that he called it "without doubt, the most beautiful mountain east of the Rockies."

Accompanying André Michaux on one expedition was the Scottish botanist John Fraser. Fraser receives little mention in botanical history, but he is credited with discovering two well-known southern Appalachian plants: Catawba rhododendron, *Rhododendron catawbiense*, and Fraser fir, *Abies fraseri*.

Although he never visited the southern Appalachians, Karl von Linné—or Carl Linnaeus, as he is generally known in America—had such an impact on botany all over the world that his name merits mention here. A Swedish-born teacher, naturalist, and physician, Linnaeus crowned himself the "Prince of Botany," a title that he would eventually deserve. In the early days of botanical exploration, chaos abounded. Many plants had different names attributed by different botanists, and many of these names were ridiculously long. Linnaeus spent his life working on sensibly classifying and naming the world's plants. Many disciples from all over the world sent him plants for identification or naming, including John Bartram, whom Linnaeus called the "greatest natural botanist in the world." To name these plants, Linnaeus developed a system of classification in which a plant received a one-word generic name and a one-word specific name, both in Latin. The generic name identified a group of plants with common characteristics, and the specific name distinguished those plants within the group. Thus, any plant could be distinguished readily from all others, and since the Latin language was no longer in use, there would be less chance of name corruption.

Not all of Linnaeus's ideas proved sound, but his system of naming became universally accepted and is the same system we use today. We should be thankful for that. Otherwise, we still might be referring to *Rudbeckia hirta*, black-eyed susan, as "Chrysanthemum Marilandicum, caule & foliis hirsutis Hieracii, flore magno, pluribus petalis radiato, disco granti protuberanate." Try to put *that* on a 35mm slide label!

Butterfly on daisy fleabane, page 214
75-300mm lens, 5T diopter, 1 sec. at f/16   Adams

Environmental Concerns

Many plants, animals, and even entire ecosystems are in danger of extinction unless public opinion and influence over government changes. The list of known dangers is far too long to describe in full, but we will point out a few of the problems. It should be emphasized that biologists are only beginning to understand the intricate complexities of species interaction. The decline of a species can rarely be linked to a single cause.

Consider the spruce-fir forests on the region's highest summits. There's no question they are in serious danger; these peaks look more like graveyards—dead tree skeletons everywhere—than healthy forests. Certain groups are quick to suggest that the trees are dying from the balsam woolly adelgid (aphid), a European pest introduced around the turn of the century. The adelgid is killing the Fraser firs, but other plants are dying there as well, including the red spruce, which the adelgid does not attack. Studies have proven that air pollution (acid rain and ozone) is having a direct influence on the ecosystem. At Mount Mitchell, pH levels of 2.12, the acidity of lemon juice, have been registered in fog clouds. The average pH of clouds in the vicinity of the mountain is 3.7, much more acidic than neutral water, which has a pH of 7.0. Simple logic dictates that this is unhealthy for the forest.

This discussion of air pollution should not diminish the effect of introduced pests, which poses a serious threat to the survival of several Appalachian species. No doubt, the worst horror story is the devastation caused by the fungus *Endothia parasitica*. The chestnut blight, as it is known, eventually wiped out every mature chestnut tree in the Appalachians. Only immature specimens sprouting from old rootstock remain, and the blight kills them before they can produce ample crops of nuts. There are a few isolated stands in other parts of the country that do produce good crops, but even these are now showing signs of blight infestation.

Other pests are making headlines. The well-known gypsy moth is now threatening southern forests—particularly oak forests—defoliating just about everything in its path. The hemlock woolly adelgid threatens to do to the East's hemlocks what the balsam woolly adelgid is doing to the Fraser firs. The colorful, red-berried mountain ash is being defoliated by a pest called the mountain ash sawfly. Pitch and Virginia shortleaf pines serve as unwilling hosts to the southern pine beetle. And perhaps most disturbing for wildflower enthusiasts is the devastating dogwood anthracnose, a fungal disease that is killing our beloved flowering dogwood trees.

It is worth noting that most of these pests were introduced from other countries and have no natural defenses here. Also, their destructiveness is aided, in some cases permitted, by weaknesses already present in their hosts—weaknesses caused by such factors as air pollution.

Probably the greatest threat to wildflowers, or any organism that does not live in the ocean or polar regions, is habitat loss. Driving through the mountains, it doesn't take long to realize the threat is real. Second homes and retirement villages are sprouting everywhere, and there seems to be no end to the destructive practices of logging and road building.

Other threats are less obvious, but often nearly as serious. Natural ecosystems are extraordinarily complex, each organism dependent on another. When alien species invade, they often have carte blanche; the usual checks and balances in a healthy ecosystem do not keep the alien under control. Anyone who has seen a stand of kudzu, or a field of wild mustard, knows what can happen. This fact is hardly a new revelation. As early as 1526, Oviedo recorded the destruction caused by a large number of plants and animals that had become naturalized in the New World following Columbus's arrival.

A very real threat to wildflowers is the outright greed and ignorance of many people. Many of our most beautiful and beneficial wildflower species are near extinction because of over-collecting. Orchids, especially, are a sought-after species. This is ridiculous because orchids that have been dug, having been removed from the natural fungal relationship required for their growth, will almost certainly die. Trilliums, too, are taken from the wild in great quantities.

Orchids and trilliums aren't the only wildflowers sought by collectors intent on transplanting them. Indeed, the rarity of a wildflower often makes it desirable. Gray's lily, Oconee bells, monkshood, fringed gentian, and Catawba rhododendron are among some of the species that collectors seek.

Digging up rare wildflowers to transplant in a garden is devastating, no doubt, but it pales in comparison to illegal collecting by poachers for commercial resale. Unfortunately, many of our native wildflowers have reputed medicinal benefits that make them highly marketable. Goldenseal, *Hydrastis canadensis*, is a prime example. Over-collecting has nearly eliminated the species. The best example of over-collecting is ginseng. In 1980, a staggering 575,000 pounds of ginseng roots were exported from eastern America, with most going to Hong Kong. Of this, 30 percent was taken from the wild. No species can continually withstand this much pressure.

All this gloom and doom is certainly bad news for our beloved wildflowers, but we don't have to take it without a fight. There is plenty we can do. One simple thing is to never buy orchids and trilliums from nurseries unless you know that they were not dug from the wild. Because these two species require several years to propagate, it isn't economically feasible for most nurseries to grow them. Similarly, you should never dig a wildflower yourself, unless it will be destroyed by development. Taking seeds is OK,

but remember, those seeds are meant to propagate the species in the wild. Take only a few, and never those of the rarer species. And try to resist the urge to propagate non-native species. Our native flora is unequaled in beauty and has evolved to grow specifically in this region. Even if you manage to have a healthy-growing non-native plant, there is always the possibility of its escape into the wild, creating who knows what peril for the native species.

All national parks and many other public lands prohibit the removal of any plants or animals. If you see someone breaking these rules, politely inform them of their violation. If they are decent people, they'll appreciate being educated about the perils of removing wildflowers. If they refuse to listen, they most definitely need to be stopped, for they will continue poaching. However, it may be dangerous to confront someone who is obviously defiant and intent on breaking the law, so it's better to report them to the authorities. The appendix lists the numbers you should call to contact the proper authorities for certain areas of the southern Appalachians. One thing you can do is carry a cellular phone with you. It's tough to do—one of the joys of visiting the mountains is leaving the entrapments of everyday life behind—but the simple truth is many offenders are never caught because the witnesses do not have access to a phone, or that by the time they report the violation, the perpetrators have left the scene.

Protecting individual wildflower species is commendable, but the well-being of all wildflowers depends upon the protection of entire ecosystems. As stated earlier, everything interrelates; removing one species, plant or animal, affects all. Waiting until a specific species is in trouble before doing anything is comparable to a person who eats unhealthy foods and never gets any exercise. That person will continue to have health problems, and may visit a doctor for each symptom, but the only real cure is to treat the body properly in the first place.

We need to start treating the environment properly. We need to treat it as a whole, and cure it as a

Catesby's trillium, page 220
75-300mm lens, 5T diopter, ½ sec. at f/22   Adams

All species of trilliums are sought by collectors. Although you should not collect any species from the wild, Catesby's trillium is among the more uncommon trilliums and should definitely be left alone.

Dwarf ginseng, page 240
75-300mm lens, 5T diopter, ½ sec. at f/11   Adams

Rare species like this one are in particular danger from collecting for personal use and financial gain.

whole. We need to do this before it's too late, while we still have large, intact ecosystems. You can contribute to the cause by closely following the actions of elected officials, writing letters, and openly expressing your concern. Join one, or more, of the conservation organizations, especially those in your region. A good choice for the southern Appalachians is The Nature Conservancy or the local chapter of the Sierra Club. Also, there are many local conservation groups that are actively working to promote wildflower habitats, such as the Southern Appalachian Highlands Conservancy. Another good choice would be to join an organization specifically chartered to educate members about wildflowers, such as the National Wildflower Research Center. In addition, many local botanical gardens offer members a wide range of information. The well-respected North Carolina Botanical Garden in Chapel Hill is one such facility.

Photographers have a unique opportunity to contribute; indeed, we believe they have an obligation. We should give something back to the natural world that gives us so many beautiful photographs. Consider making a few photos that tell an environmental story. Everyone has seen a pretty picture of a yellow lady's slipper, and another one will do little to secure its future. However, a photograph of them lined up in pots at a nursery tells a story that needs to be heard. Similarly, photographers are able to selectively shoot what they want. We can photograph a flower growing in a dump and make it look good. We should consider also taking a few photos of the dump and use them for education.

Finally, consider the effect your presence has on a wildflower. Species that grow in bogs and other fragile habitats should not be closely approached and photographed because the danger of trampling the habitat is too great. The best thing you can do is to simply stay on the trail. Anytime you leave the trail, you will have some adverse effect on the environment. It might not be a serious impact, but it may destroy a rare species, especially if you do any off-trail hiking in rocky or boggy environments. The problem is that you usually won't know what effect you're having. It's best to expect the worst and act accordingly.

You may think all this concern is unfounded, but look at how many plants are presently listed as rare in the seven-state region encompassed by this book: West Virginia—399; Virginia—602; Tennessee—431; South Carolina—175; Kentucky—263; Georgia—103; and North Carolina—722. Of these, 57 species are listed as endangered or threatened on the national level at the time of this writing. Of course, there is some crossover from state to state, and many of these plants are more common in other areas, but this is still a sobering number. Obviously, there is valid reason for concern. The loss of even one of these species will create a void in the natural world that will forever remind us of our mistreatment of the environment. Not only will we have exterminated a part of the ecosystem—the repercussions of which we can only speculate—but we will have removed a part of ourselves. And just like the extinct species, it is a part of ourselves that can never be replaced. Aldo Leopold, forester and a founder of the Wilderness Society, said it best: "To keep every cog and wheel is the first precaution of intelligent tinkering."

Format

Be sure to read this chapter before taking the book into the field. It will help you to understand the arrangement of the information, as well as provide helpful advice on how to identify wildflowers.

Common Name

Most wildflowers have more than one—and often many— common names, each of which may or may not be recognized throughout its range. Space does not permit us to include all these names—we don't know them all anyway—but we have tried to choose the most widely accepted one. Some wildflowers have more than one widely accepted name, in addition to the lesser-known names, and we have included these beneath the common name. An asterisk after the common name indicates a non-native wildflower that has been introduced to the region.

Scientific Name

The italicized, two-word scientific (Latin) name follows the naming system designed by Carl Linnaeus in the mid-1700s. This system is recognized worldwide as the standard for naming all living things. Students of botany anywhere in the world can communicate with each other and know exactly which plant is being discussed. The capitalized genus name is given first, followed by the species name in lower case. In some plants, the species is further divided into subspecies, varieties, and forms. However, it is not necessary for the beginning student to distinguish beyond the genus and species level. We have included subspecies and variety names for the benefit of the reader who wishes to learn more and needs to know exactly which plant we are referencing.

Even though Latin names are universally accepted, botanists don't always agree on whether certain plants are individual species, subspecies, or varieties. Sometimes there is even debate about the genus or family to which a plant belongs. Therefore, different Latin names are occasionally used for the same plant. Still, the Latin system of naming is far better than any other. The Latin names we used follow those listed in *A Synonymized Checklist Of The Vascular Flora Of The United States, Canada, And Greenland* (*Kartesz*), by John T. Kartesz. This book is widely accepted as the most current taxonomic treatment on plants available.

For years, botanists followed the Latin names given in *Gray's Manual of Botany* (*Gray's*), and most books written for the average wildflower enthusiast, such as the popular *Peterson's* and *Newcomb's* wildflower guides, follow *Gray's* as well. In some instances, the names in Kartesz's book (and therefore in this book) appear differently in *Gray's*. To avoid confusion for those who wish to cross reference with these guides, any names which appear differently in *Gray's* are listed in parenthesis.

Family Name

Genera (plural of genus) having common characteristics are arranged into families. It is beyond the scope of this book to discuss these characteristics, but with a little study of botanical literature, students will begin to recognize a plant as a member of a particular family even before knowing its scientific name. We have given the Latin family name, which is not italicized, and the common family name. As in the genus and species, differences between *Gray's* and *Kartesz* are noted in parenthesis.

Blooming and Fruiting Dates

These should be considered only as general guidelines due to tremendous variance. Typically, wildflowers that grow in the southernmost segment of the southern Appalachians bloom from one to three weeks earlier than those in the north, and sometimes even earlier than that. The same is true for wildflowers that grow in both low and high elevations—the high elevation plants bloom from one to three weeks later. Blooming dates may also vary from year to year depending on climate and other conditions. In general, fruiting dates are thirty to sixty days after blooming dates.

Growth Cycle

Plants are listed as annuals, biennials, or perennials, depending on their life cycle from seed to a mature plant capable of reproducing, and then to death.

Frequency of Occurrence

All frequency ratings are subjective, but these categories may be loosely defined as follows:

Common wildflowers are easily seen without searching.

Frequent wildflowers can be found without special effort, but may be absent from certain areas.

Occasional wildflowers are likely to be encountered by anyone who spends a fair amount of time in the mountains, but a planned effort is necessary to make sure you are in the right habitat. Some wildflowers listed as occasional may be common locally in some places and totally absent from others.

Scarce wildflowers require a definite effort to find. While they may be rather frequent in a few locations, they are mostly absent from much of the range.

To find *Rare* wildflowers requires a great deal of knowledge about growth requirements and a lot of luck. The average person never encounters these flowers in the wild, and you should feel fortunate if you do. You should also feel obligated to leave them where you find them.

Frequency ratings should not be used as an identification factor, as they can vary so much. Non-native wildflowers, especially, are increasing their range and becoming more common on a yearly basis. Some of the non-native wildflowers in this book listed as frequent or common are listed as rare or scarce in books published ten or more years ago.

Habitat and Range

Habitat describes the particular growth requirements of the wildflower. This information can be used for locating and identifying a plant; but you should keep in mind that, as with other characteristics, it can vary.

There are no generally accepted physiographic or political boundaries for the region referred to as the "southern Appalachians." For this book, we define the region as beginning at the northern end of Shenandoah National Park and extending southwesterly along the mountains through Great Smoky Mountains National Park. To the north, the range extends westward to include Shenandoah Valley and enters into West Virginia. To the south, the range is much broader, extending from the foothills in the east to the Cumberland Plateau in the west. We fully realize this range includes non-related physiographic areas, but we have chosen it to include the popular locations where people travel. Most wildflowers included in this book grow well outside the southern Appalachians, so this book will be useful throughout the eastern United States.

Keep in mind that many non-native wildflowers are steadily increasing their range. In literature that is more than ten years old, some of the range listings are no longer accurate. In a few years, some of the information given here may be invalid as well.

Description

Describing a wildflower in a few sentences is not easy, but we have tried to make it as simple as possible without getting too technical. A quick glance at the glossary of a technical botany manual is enough to discourage most people from learning about wildflowers. There are hundreds of special terms describing plants, with many meaning close to the same thing. You do not need to know all of these words, but becoming familiar with a few of them will help considerably in identifying and learning about wildflowers. We have interspersed a few of these terms throughout the book, and we have included a brief glossary following this introduction, which will help you understand these common terms. Those wishing to broaden their knowledge of plants are encouraged to study the descriptions and glossaries of the technical manuals.

As with all living things, variation occurs even between plants of the same species. Although we have given wide ranges in most measurements, you should consider them as guidelines only. These measurements can vary considerably, even outside these ranges. Similarly, it is impossible to define exactly the color of a wildflower. Colors vary in some species, and people perceive color differently. A blue petal to one person may be a purple petal to another. Immature wildflowers are particularly difficult to identify as they can look quite different when they are mature. Even mature plants will vary according to moisture and habitat conditions. The trick is to study several different mature plants of the same species and look for characteristics which all of them share.

Similar and Related Species

While the descriptions in this section are not as detailed as the main listing, it will help to separate the many wildflowers that look similar to one another. Admittedly, in some cases the listings are fairly distinct, but we felt they should be described.

General Information

This section includes information of general interest such as how the plant received its name, whether it is edible, medicinal uses, and folklore associated with the flower. The food and medicinal information is given only as a historical or modern accounting of the plant and is not meant as an endorsement of such use. In fact, we discourage taking flowers from the wild to use as food or medicine for both environmental and safety reasons. Those who do use them should be absolutely certain the identification is correct. Also, remember that in all national parks, and most state parks, it is illegal to collect any plant part except berries used for personal consumption.

In some listings, we have noted plants that are listed as endangered or threatened in a particular state. This information is given using the most current information available at the time of printing. To keep up-to-date on this information, it is recommended that you contact the state agencies listed in the appendix.

Photo Tips

These apply primarily to the main wildflower listed in each entry and refer to the following wildflower categories section. The sun symbol indicates flowers that close at night or on cloudy days. It is included to save you the inconvenience of arriving early in the morning only to discover that the flower has not yet opened.

Wildflower Photography Categories

The following categories correspond to the photo tips under the wildflower listings in the next section of this book. Nature photography is not a science that can be isolated into neat categories, nor will these categories correlate to every situation you will encounter. The photo tips in these categories are meant only to suggest a starting point, to jump-start your thinking process. Each photographic situation you encounter will be different, and some may require entirely different strategies than what we suggest. More importantly, photographers are different and interpret what they see differently.

CATEGORY 1

This category includes very low-growing and sometimes mat-forming species like bluets, stonecrop, and crested dwarf iris. Composition is usually straightforward for this category—shoot straight down on the subject, while aligning the film plane. You can use any lens from wide-angle to telephoto, the only limitation being the size of the patch you are photographing. If you use a lens in the 50mm or wider range, you'll probably need to use an accessory arm like the Bogen Side Arm (see page 12) to get the camera away from the tripod; otherwise, the tripod legs will show up in the photograph. With any lens, be careful that the film plane is aligned with the flattest plane of the subject to maximize depth of field.

A big advantage in this category is that wind is either not a problem or is easily controlled. Also, since you're completely filling the frame with subject matter, you don't need to worry about background coverage. Simply stake off the patch and wrap plastic around the stakes. Some species, like stonecrop and trailing arbutus, only move in the strongest winds, so you rarely need to use a wind shield for them.

CATEGORY 2

This category includes species that grow individually from a few inches to approximately a foot tall. Bloodroot, toothwort, painted trillium, and lousewort fit this category. Unlike the flowers in Category 1, very few species in this category work well with a straight down composition. Usually, the best approach is to shoot at an angle in order to include the whole plant along with a little of the surroundings. This method is not without problems, however. First, you can't use sticks to stake off the stem. Second, depth of field becomes a major concern. You could shoot a straight-ahead profile and increase depth of field in the subject, but this seriously limits focus on the foreground and background. Plus, it will be likely to create problems with distractions in the background. That is why shooting at an angle is the best compromise. It gives moderate depth of field on the subject, foreground, and background, and it makes the farthest background element in the scene only a few feet or so away.

Since the total subject area is rather small, it is easy to stake off plastic as a wind barrier. Also, you can do a little "gardening" on the foreground or background as necessary. For instance, if you're shooting a pink lady's slipper and the background is rather ugly, just take a few surrounding leaves or pine needles and spread them around. Of course, you have to decide for yourself if this is acceptable. We don't have a problem with minor manipulations such as this.

Sometimes it works best to shoot a tight shot of a portion of the flower. Species like lousewort and pink lady's slipper make great closeup photos using just

Roan Mountain bluet, page 53
75-300mm lens, 5T diopter, 1 sec. at f/16   Adams

Category 1 wildflowers are easy to photograph. For this shot, the film plane was aligned with the plane of flowers, and the lens was zoomed to get the exact cropping desired.

Heartleaf H. arifolia *var.* ruthii, *page 113*
75-300mm lens, 5T diopter, ½ sec. at f/22   Adams

This is the typical approach to wildflowers in category 2. The image was made by shooting at an angle to include both flowers and foliage, along with a little of the surroundings.

the blossom. When you make such a photo, you can use a stake to support the stem from the wind. However, the background now becomes a concern. With higher magnifications, it won't be a big problem, but you'll usually need to pick an angle that has a clear area behind the flower.

CATEGORY 3

This category includes flowers that grow up to a few feet tall, singly or in clumps, and those that warrant isolation closeups of the flower alone. They usually do not grow in a manner that allows you to include the whole plant and still make a good photograph. Species like hawkweed, daisy, columbine, and purple fringed orchid fit this category. The best

composition to use when shooting flowers in this category is almost always a portrait of the flower blossom alone, or in the case of species like beardtongue and bellwort, several blossoms. This may or may not require a lot of magnification. Species like daisies and hawkweeds do require a fair amount of magnification to include only the blossom, so background coverage is not a concern; the background usually blurs into a pleasing poster effect. However, when shooting species like goldenrod and bee balm, there may not be enough magnification to get the poster effect. In these cases, you have to choose the angle very carefully and often tie back background foliage. Sometimes, the only solution is to use an artificial background, but for us, this is always a last resort.

Gray beardtongue, page 97
75-300mm lens, 5T diopter, ¹/₁₅ sec. at f/22   Adams

Species in category 3 usually do not allow you to include all of the plant in the composition. Usually, it is best to isolate a section, as in this photograph.

American bugbane, page 181
75-300mm lens, 5T diopter, ½ sec. at f/22   Adams

Flowers in category 4 can be very difficult to photograph. This image of American bugbane would not have worked without the use of an artificial background.

Usually, the best approach is to shoot at the same height as the blossom, although you may want to shoot a little up or down to better align the film and subject planes.

To prevent wind movement, stakes can be used on the stem, but a plastic shield is not practical since the farthest point in the image is so far back. However, it may help to stake a short section of plastic on both sides of the flower, while leaving the front and back open.

CATEGORY 4

This category includes species like sunflowers, iron-weed, Joe-Pye weed, and cow parsnip that are often hard to photograph. They are very tall-growing spe-cies that often prohibit the effective use of stem stakes, even the five-foot stakes we carry. You can stake off the bottom portion of the stem, but this still leaves a considerable amount to blow in the wind. Also, plastic wind barriers are mostly nonef-fective with these flowers. The only real solution is to choose a time when the wind is calm.

Backgrounds are also a problem. It helps that the flowers usually grow above surrounding vegetation, but since you're shooting at low magnifications, even something a hundred feet away shows up as a dis-traction. Sometimes, a wide-angle scenic that uses the plant as a foreground works best, but this re-quires an ideal situation. Some species, like Turk's-cap lily, allow you to photograph only one of the blossoms. This eliminates background distractions by using more magnification. As in category 3, you can use artificial backgrounds as a last resort.

CATEGORY 5

This category includes medium-tall and very tall wildflowers that grow in dense clumps or tangles, allowing a wide-angle approach. Many plants that fit into categories 3 and 4 also fit this category. Joe-Pye weed, sunflowers, black-eyed susan, bee balm, and phlox often grow closely together, either among their own species or with others. The higher elevations of the Blue Ridge Parkway and the Smokies have spectacular displays of these wildflowers dur-

False hellebore, page 238
105mm lens, 1 sec. at f/22   Adams

A somewhat wide-angle approach is often appropriate for category 5 wildflowers. This image includes a fair amount of foliage from an emerging false hellebore plant. It's not always the blossoms that make the best images.

ing the summer. To effectively capture the scene, a lens in the 28mm to 50mm range is usually needed. By including only blossoms and foliage of the immediate plants—not some plant several feet away—you can make great images. In fact, this type of image is highly marketable and is the type often seen in Sierra Club, Audubon, and similar calendars. The trick is to have enough depth of field to keep all blossoms in focus, and to make sure that any out-of-focus foliage does not distract from the scene.

It's important to understand the distinction between this category and category 9. Category 9 is for sweeping, wide-angle scenics that cover a large area. Here, we are using similar lenses, but covering only a small area.

There is not an effective method to prevent wind movement, so you will have to shoot when the wind is calm. Try early in the morning when the flowers are laced with dew.

Remember, individual flowers in this category often make good subjects by themselves, so consider tying back the surrounding plants and making a few isolation shots.

CATEGORY 6

This category is a miniature version of category 5. Flowers in this category include such species as violets, larkspur, trout lily, fringed phacelia, and Dutchman's breeches. These plants are fairly low-growing and may have single stems or be multi-branched. However, they share one common trait: they almost always grow in dense patches, whether it be clumps of blossoms or foliage. Since everything in this category is low-growing, one advantage is having some control over wind by using plastic shields. Choose a composition that has both blossom and foliage on the same plane to maximize depth of field. Isolation images of single blossoms without foliage usually don't work as well in this category.

CATEGORY 7

Plants in this category have showy, individual flowers that grow in narrow spikes or racemes. The category

Wild pink, page 86
50mm lens, 81A warming filter, ¼ sec. at f/22

Adams

As in category 5 flowers, category 6 flowers usually require a moderate wide-angle approach. The difference here is that the flowers are all low-growing, allowing more control over the wind and lighting. A plastic wind barrier was used to keep the wild pink flowers from blowing in the constant breeze.

Common mullein, page 142
75-300mm lens, 5T diopter, ¹/₈ sec. at f/22   *Casstevens*

Flowers in category 7 grow in narrow spikes or racemes and almost always require closeups of part of the plant. A little searching was required to find a spike that had blossoms right at the top, so the top of the spike would not have to be cropped out. Also, careful composing prevented the lower flower from being cut off at the bottom of the frame.

includes species like Venus's looking glass, tall bellflower, and smooth false foxglove. Serious background and clutter problems usually occur when you include all of the plant in the composition, so it's best to isolate part of the flowering stalk with enough magnification to create a posterlike background. The problem is that it is not easy to decide which part to shoot. Typically, it's best not to shoot a section of the spike with the stem cropped at top and bottom, as this creates a very unstable image. It leaves the

viewer wondering what the rest of the plant looks like. Including the top of the spike solves this problem, but the most attractive flowers don't always grow near the top. The trick is to keep searching for the best opportunities. Ideally, you want to find a spike that has the most attractive flowers growing very near the top, and crop it so all of the flower is shown. In other words, the bottom of the frame should cut off the stem, not the flower. Of course, some flowers, like viper's bugloss, grow together so

Early meadow rue, page 173
75-300mm lens, 5T diopter, ¼ sec. at f/11   *Casstevens*

Flowers in category 8 are usually unattractive, large, and grow in less-than-ideal settings. We usually skip these flowers altogether, but a recent rain shower made this a good opportunity.

tightly that it's impossible not to crop off a flower.

If you have to crop off the top of the stem, consider tilting the camera to make the plant look like it is growing at an angle. This is often more effective than a static image of a spike right in the middle of the frame.

By the way, you should never snip the top of the stem off above the flower you're shooting. Not only is this unethical (and illegal in many places), but any naturalist can instantly spot such a circumstance.

CATEGORY 8

This is the toughest category of all for photography. It includes such species as tall meadow rue, goatsbeard, snakeroot, Canada burnet, and false hellebore. The blossom is too large to include all of it without a serious background problem; the plants are too large and branched to permit effective wind control; and they usually grow in an environment that makes wide-angle shots ineffective. Plus, they usually aren't that attractive. We don't have a solution to the problem except to suggest waiting until you find the absolute best opportunity—a situation that has a blossom growing in attractive surroundings on a calm day—and use a wide-angle approach with as much depth of field as possible. In all honesty, most photographers never shoot flowers in this category because of the aforementioned problems, so unless you have a specific need for the image, or happen to find an ideal situation, perhaps you should just forget it.

CATEGORY 9

Flowers in this category sometimes grow over large areas and permit a wide-angle composition, often with a 24mm or even a 20mm lens. The Appalachians don't have the sweeping wildflower fields that are common out west, but they do have a few good wide-angle opportunities. Species like large-flowered trillium, fringed phacelia, spring beauty, hawkweed, daisy, and buttercup often grow in large masses. Choose as wide a lens as possible and get as close as you can to the foreground blossoms. Stop the lens down as far as it will go (unless you have a Canon tilt/shift lens) and pray for a lull in the wind. Even if the wind doesn't die down, go ahead and shoot a few frames. You may be pleasantly surprised with the results.

CATEGORY 10

This category is reserved not only for a particular type of plant, but also for the environment in which it grows. If you discover a plant listed in this category, be careful with your actions because the plant

Fringed phacelia, page 195
28mm lens, 4 sec. at f/16   *Adams*

Category 9 wildflowers often grow over large areas and permit
the use of wide-angle lenses. Fringed phacelia is a prime
example. In places, it can completely cover the ground with
white blossoms.

Bog rose, page 90
75-300mm lens, 5T diopter, 1 sec. at f/22   *Adams*

Bog rose is representative of both definitions of category 10.
It is a very rare plant that should not be disturbed, and it
grows in a fragile environment.

is either rare or is growing in a fragile environment.
Included here are flowers that grow in wetlands, bogs,
rocky slopes, and other places where a careless foot-
step could have serious repercussions. It is recommended that you consider not photographing in such
an environment. Most plants included in this category can usually be located at public or private botanical gardens, where photographing them poses
no threat to the environment or wild populations.

Glossary

Achene
A small, dry, hard, one-seeded fruit that does not open at maturity.

Alternate (leaves)
Leaves that grow alternately along the stem, as opposed to growing directly opposite each other.

Annual
A plant that completes a life cycle in one year or growing season.

Anther
The part of the stamen that produces pollen.

Auriculate
An ear-shaped appendage usually found at the base of a leaf or petal.

Axil
The interior angle formed where the leaf attaches to the stem.

Basal
At the base.

Berry
A single or many-seeded fleshy fruit that develops from the fertilized ovary.

Biennial
A plant that completes a life cycle in two years or growing seasons.

Bract
A small modified leaf or leaflike part, usually located at the base of the flower.

Calyx
The outermost whorl of flower parts (sepals); they are usually green.

Clasping
A leaf whose base partially or entirely surrounds the stem.

Colony
Technically, a group of plants that are connected. Used here in the general sense to refer to any group of plants.

Compound (leaf)
Divided into two or more similar parts.

Cordate
Heart-shaped; usually refers to rounded lobes at the base of a leaf.

Corm
The underground, bulblike, and fleshy portion of a stem.

Corolla
The inner whorl of flower parts (petals) that surround the reproductive plant parts.

Corolla tube
The base of the corolla where the petals are joined wholly or in part.

Corymb
A broad, short, flat-topped inflorescence, with the outer flowers blooming first.

Cross-pollination
Occurs when pollen from one plant is distributed to the stigma of another plant of the same species, which has a different genetic constitution.

Cyme
Broad, flat flower cluster with the flowers maturing from the center outward.

Deciduous
Plants which shed their leaves annually; not evergreen.

Decumbent
Reclining, but with the end upright.

Decurrent
A leafstalk that attaches to the stem and continues down the stem as a winglike ridge. Also refers to a leaf that extends winglike down the leafstalk.

Dioecious
Plants which have male and female flowers on separate plants.

Disc
The central portion of a flower head containing tubular flowers, as in the Asteraceae family.

Elliptic
Tapering at each end with the widest part in the middle.

Endemic
A plant that grows only in a given area or region.

Entire (leaf)
Lacking teeth, divisions, or lobes.

f.
The abbreviation used to refer to a form of a given species.

Fimbriate
With fringes.

Floret
An individual flower of a flower cluster.

Flowerhead
The many flowers that together make up an inflorescence; used mostly in reference to the Asteraceae family.

Fruit
A seed-bearing mature ovary.

Germinate
To begin growth or development, as in seeds sprouting.

Glabrous
Smooth; not hairy.

Glandular
With secreting glands.

Halberd
Arrow-shaped with basal lobes pointed outward.

Herbaceous
Plants which lack an above-ground woody stem and die back to the roots after flowering.

Hybridize
Refers to the cross-breeding of two separate species.

Inflorescence
The flowering portion of a plant and its prescribed arrangement.

Internode
The part of the stem between two nodes.

Lanceolate
Lance-shaped.

Legume
A fruit in the form of a pod that is bilaterally symmetrical, splitting along two lines.

Linear (leaf)
Long and narrow with parallel veins and/or margins.

Midrib
The main, central rib of a leaf or similar structure.

Node
The point on the stem where leaves are borne.

Oblanceolate
Inversely lance-shaped, with the widest section at the apex.

Obovate
Inverted or reversed ovate; ovate with the narrow end at the base.

Opposite (leaves)
Leaves that are directly opposite each other on the stem. Not alternate.

Ovate
Egg-shaped.

Palmate
With lobe divisions resembling an outspread hand.

Panicle
An inflorescence with a loose arrangement of flowers on pedicels.

Parasitic
Growing on and obtaining food from another living organism.

Pedicel
The supporting stalk of any single flower in an inflorescence.

Peduncle
The main flower stalk that supports a single flower or flower cluster.

Perennial
Plants that continue life cycles for three or more years.

Perfoliate
Leaf bases that completely surround the stem so the stem appears to pierce the leaf.

Petal
One of the often-colored segments of the corolla.

Petiole
The leafstalk attaching to the stem and supporting the leaf blade.

Pinnate
With segments or leaflets on both sides of a common central stalk, resembling a feather.

Pinnatifid
Divided in a pinnate manner.

Pistil
The female reproductive portion of the plant made up of stigma, style, and ovary.

Pistillate
A female flower with functional pistil(s) and no (or sterile) stamen(s).

Pollen
Male spores produced in the anther.

Pollination
Transfer of pollen from the anther (male) to the stigma (female).

Procumbent
Lies on the ground but does not take root.

Prostrate
Lies on the ground.

Pubescent
Covered with soft, short hairs.

Raceme
An inflorescence with individual stalked flowers arranged on an elongated central axis.

Radially symmetrical
An arrangement in which similar parts extend outward from a central point at equal angles, as in a wagon wheel.

Ray
The flat, petal-like flowers that surround the central disc flowers in the Asteraceae family. Each branch unit of an umbel.

Reniform
Kidney-shaped.

Rhizome
An underground stem which roots at the nodes.

Rhombic
Diamond-shaped.

Rosette
A compressed circular cluster of leaves, usually basal, at ground level.

Runner
See stolon.

Scale
Tiny leaves or bracts on some stems.

Scape
A stem without leaves.

Self-pollination
The transfer of pollen from the anther to the stigma of the same flower or another flower on the same plant.

Sepal
One unit of the calyx.

Sessile
Attached by the base, or without any distinct projecting support, as a leaf attached directly to the stem.

Simple (leaf)
A leaf that is not divided into distinct leaflets.

Spadix
A fleshy spike with small, crowded flowers.

Spathe
An enlarged bract that partially encloses an inflorescence.

Spatulate
Spoon-shaped.

Spike
An elongated inflorescence with stalkless flowers on a central axis.

sp.
The abbreviation indicating only one species.

spp.
The abbreviation indicating two or more species.

Spur
A hollow tubular extension of petals or sepals that often contains nectar.

ssp.
The abbreviation indicating subspecies.

Stamen
The male reproductive portion of the plant comprised of the filament and anther.

Staminate
A male flower with functional stamen(s) and sterile pistil(s).

Stigma
The tip of the pistil that receives pollen for fertilization.

Stipule
A leaflike appendage at the base of a leaf stalk.

Stolon
A horizontal branch or stem that grows either above or below the ground and extends from the base of the plant. Also called a runner.

Style
The elongated section of the pistil between the stigma and ovary.

Succulent
Plants with fleshy, juicy leaves and stems.

Taproot
The primary central root.

Trichome
Hairlike growth.

Tuber
An enlarged underground stem used for food storage.

Umbel
A flat-topped flower cluster with stalked flowers radiating from a common point.

var.
The abbreviation referring to a variety of a given species.

Villous
With long, soft hairs.

THE
Wildflowers

Thyme-leaved Bluet

Creeping bluet
Houstonia serpyllifolia

Madder Family   Rubiaceae
April-June; May-July
Perennial
Frequent

105mm macro lens, ½ sec. at f/22   Adams

HABITAT AND RANGE

Rich woods, stream banks, damp roadsides; mainly in the higher elevations of the Blue Ridge Parkway and the Smokies—

DESCRIPTION

A solitary flower with 4 pale blue petals and a yellow center, grows on top of a slender stem, 2 to 4 inches high. The stem tends to creep along the ground before becoming erect. The leaves are tiny and rounded. The plant grows in dense colonies.

RELATED SPECIES

H. caerulea, Quaker ladies, eyebright, or bluet, is almost identical except its flowers are paler blue, and its stems do not creep before becoming erect. It is more common at lower elevations and in drier conditions. The flowers of the common *H. purpurea*, houstonia, are light purple and grow in clusters on branching, somewhat hairy stems. Its ovate leaves are 1 to 2¼ inches long. The rare Roan Mountain bluet, *H. purpurea* var. *montana*, (see photo on page 41) is distinguished from the above species by its deep purple flowers, smooth stems, and leaves that are only ³/₈ to 1¹/₈ inches long. It often grows in dense patches, but it is only found on high-elevation rock outcrops in North Carolina and Tennessee. Long-leaved bluet, *H. longifolia*, is similar to *H. purpurea*, except that it has linear or elliptic leaves.

H. longifolia var. *longifolia* has 6 to 13 pairs of leaves that are usually more than an inch wide. *H. longifolia* var. *tenuifolia* (*H. tenuifolia*) has 3 to 9 pairs of leaves that are usually less than ¼ inch wide.

Linnaeus named the genus *Houstonia* in honor of Scottish (one report says English) surgeon William Houston. In the early 1700s, Houston, who was also a botanist, collected plants and seeds—but not those of bluets—during his travels to tropical America, and he sent them to England for study. The species name, *caerulea*, is Latin for "sky blue." The name *eyebright* refers to the yellow center of the flower.

Look closely at bluets and you will see two types of flowers. One has short stamens and long pistils, while the other has long stamens and short pistils. This ensures cross-pollination for healthier plants.

PHOTO TIPS: Category 1 ☼

As a rule, you'll want to shoot straight down on bluets while aligning the film plane with the plane of flowers. The lens choice is determined by the size of the patch, but focal lengths in the range of 100mm usually work well. A side view presents a rarely seen, and often pleasing, view of the plant. H. purpurea and H. longifolia ordinarily require such a shot.

Eastern Blue-eyed Grass

Sisyrinchium atlanticum

Iris Family	Iridaceae

March-June; May-July

Perennial

Occasional

75-300mm lens, 5T diopter, 2 sec. at f/11

Adams

HABITAT AND RANGE

Moist woodlands and meadows, roadsides; throughout—

DESCRIPTION

The small (½- to ¾-inch) blue flowers have yellow centers, and a distinctly pointed tip on each of the 3 petals and the 3 similar sepals. The ⅛-inch-wide stem grows 6 to 20 inches high. The stem branches from the middle and is very slightly winged on the lower portion (flat edges extend from the stem). The leaves closely resemble grass blades.

RELATED SPECIES

The lower stem of common blue-eyed grass, *S. angustifolium*, is ⅛ to ¼ inch wide and has very prominent wings. It, too, has a branching stem. Slender blue-eyed grass, *S. mucronatum*, does not have a branching stem; nor does the rare white blue-eyed grass, *S. albidum*, which has a flower ranging in color from pale blue to white, and fine fibers at the base of the stem.

Blue-eyed grass is not a grass at all, though the grasslike leaves make it appear so. Notice how closely the leaves of this smallest member of the iris family resemble the flat, double-edged leaves of the larger, more commonly known members, like crested dwarf iris. This is especially true of young plants of the species *angustifolium*.

> PHOTO TIPS: Category 6 ☼
>
> *Blue-eyed grass makes a terrific subject for isolating a single blossom against a background of out-of-focus flowers. Occasionally you may find a dense patch without a lot of clutter, allowing for a straight-down composition using a normal or short telephoto lens.*

Crested Dwarf Iris

Iris cristata

> Iris Family   Iridaceae
> April-May; June-July
> Perennial
> Frequent

50mm lens, 1 sec. at f/22   *Adams*

Rich, moist woods, slopes, streambanks; throughout—

DESCRIPTION

This flower ranges in color from blue to purple, although it is sometimes almost white. The 6 divisions of the flower consist of 3 small, upright inner petals, and 3 larger, downcurving outer sepals with a white- or yellow-crested ridge. The flower stem is 3 to 6 inches tall. The swordlike leaves are ½ to 1 inch wide and may grow to 12 inches long. This plant often grows in dense colonies.

RELATED SPECIES

Dwarf iris, *I. verna* var. *smalliana*, is very similar, although it lacks the crest on the sepals and has distinctive yellow or orange bands instead. All other iris species with similar flowers grow to much taller heights, somewhere in the range of 1 to 4 feet. One such species is *I. virginica*, blue flag, which inhabits marshes and the banks of slow-moving streams.

Had we been born to royalty, we would have been familiar with irises long before our interest in wildflowers. They have been a symbol of power and royalty since the Middle Ages. In France, the iris is called *fleur-de-lis*, after King Louis VII. However, being born to lower stations in life does not lessen our appreciation for this beautiful flower. Indeed, each spring we make a pilgrimage to the Smokies in search of crested dwarf iris colonies.

> PHOTO TIPS: Category 1
>
> *Everyone shoots crested dwarf iris from overhead, and for good reason. It depicts the flower beautifully and provides the most depth of field. This species is a favorite of photographers in the Smokies.*

Bird's Foot Violet

Viola pedata (var. *lineariloba*)

Violet Family   Violaceae
Early April-early May; May-June
Perennial
Occasional

HABITAT AND RANGE

Sunny and dry roadsides and woodland edges, especially in clay soils; throughout—

DESCRIPTION

The 5 petals of this showy violet are usually pale lavender-to-purple; however, there is a variety with 2 dark purple upper petals. Occasionally all-white flowers are seen. The flower may be 1 inch wide, with the lower petal wider than the other 4. Conspicuous orange anthers decorate the center of the flower. The leaves are distinctly divided into numerous, deeply lobed, fingerlike segments.

RELATED SPECIES

Arrow-leaved violet, *V. sagittata*, has arrow-shaped leaves (early leaves may be heart shaped) with jagged bases, and dark-blue-to-violet petals. Long-spurred violet, *V. rostrata*, has pale lavender petals, with the lower petal extending into a ½-inch-long spur. It has heart-shaped leaves. Dog violet, *V. conspera*, is very similar to long-spurred violet, but it has a ¼-inch spur and bearded lateral petals. The common blue violet, *V. sororia*, has blue-to-violet flowers, with the lower petal being smooth and longer than the other petals. Its 2 lateral petals are bearded, and all 3 of its lower petals have prominent dark veins. The leaves of *V. sororia* are heart shaped and toothed.

There are possibly 50 species and varieties of violets in the southern Appalachian region, with 75 percent of those colored blue or purple. These violets present a taxonomic nightmare because they often hybridize, producing intermediaries. Bird's foot violet and the spurred violets are easily distinguished species, but the beginner might want to treat other blue and purple violets on the genus level. They would make a great study project for a budding (pun intended) botany student who likes to spend time in the mountains, and who enjoys solving puzzles.

The bi-colored phase of bird's foot violet—with two dark upper petals—is rare in the southern portion of the region, but more common northward, especially in Shenandoah National Park. *Gray's* lists this phase as (var. *pedata*) and the uniformly colored phase as (var. *lineariloba*). *Kartesz* considers the bi-colored phase as only a color phase of the same species, rather than a recognized variety.

It's easy to see how bird's foot violet got its name, as the leaves do indeed resemble a bird's foot (although they have more "toes" than any bird we've seen). It is one of the most showy and popular of all the violets.

PHOTO TIPS: Categories   1   and   6

The serious wildflower photographer will want to locate and photograph all 3 color phases of bird's foot violet.

Sharp-lobed Hepatica

Liverwort, liverleaf
Hepatica nobilis var. *acuta* (*H. acutiloba*)

Crowfoot Family	Ranunculaceae
March-April	
Perennial	
Frequent	

HABITAT AND RANGE
Rich woods; throughout—

DESCRIPTION
The hairy stem supports a solitary flower which may be white, pink, blue, or purple. The flower has 5 to 12 petal-like sepals. Three green bracts are located beneath the flower. The thick leathery leaves are basal, may be mottled, and have 3 sharply pointed lobes.

RELATED SPECIES
Round-lobed hepatica, *H. nobilis* var. *obtusa* (*H. americana*), is almost identical except that the leaves have rounded lobes.

Hepatica is one of the earliest wildflowers to bloom in spring, usually preceded only by the less graceful arrival of skunk cabbage. When you see this delicate wildflower in bloom in early spring, you may be looking at the current year's blossoms and the previous year's leaves. The new spring leaves do not arrive until after the blooming period has begun. They then persist through the summer, turn reddish brown in the fall, and remain until the next season's flowers appear.

Hepatica was once thought to cure liver diseases because of the leaves' resemblance to the human liver. See page 163 for a discussion of the *Doctrine of Signatures.*

PHOTO TIPS: Category   2   ☼

For the best representation of hepatica, be sure to include the familiar foliage in the composition.

75-300mm lens,
5T diopter,
3 sec. at f16

Adams

Purple Phacelia

Loose-flowered phacelia, fern-leaved phacelia
Phacelia bipinnatifida

Waterleaf Family	Hydrophyllaceae
April-May; June	
Biennial	
Occasional	

75-300mm lens, 5T diopter, ½ sec. at f/16   *Adams*

HABITAT AND RANGE

Moist woods and slopes, streambanks; mostly in the southern portion of the region—

DESCRIPTION

A branching, hairy stem (1 to 2 feet tall) supports numerous ½-inch, blue-to-violet flowers that are bell shaped and lobed. Prominent stamens protrude from the flower. The leaves are divided into 3 to 7 lobed segments.

RELATED SPECIES

See other *Phacelias* on page 195.

Purple phacelia is a rather uncommon wildflower, although where it occurs it is quite conspicuous, growing in thick, bushy clumps. A good place to see it is along the road to Cades Cove in the Smokies.

PHOTO TIPS: Category 5
Try to find a situation that has all, or at least some, of the flowers in the same plane to maximize depth of field.

Dwarf Larkspur

Delphinium tricorne

Crowfoot Family	Ranunculaceae
Late March-early May	
Perennial	
Scarce	

Rich woods; throughout—

This plant grows in a raceme of bluish purple (sometimes white) flowers with 5 sepals, the upper sepal extending backwards into an upright spur. The 4 petals are very small, with 2 of them extending into the spur formed by the sepals. The leaves are mostly basal, palmate, and divided into 5 to 7 irregular segments, which are further lobed. The plant stands 1 to 3 feet tall.

The rare tall larkspur, *D. exaltatum*, grows to heights of 2 to 6 feet, has fewer lobes in the leaves, and blooms in the summer. See wild monkshood on page 67.

75-300mm lens, 5T diopter, 2 sec. at f/16   Adams

Larkspur is not frequently encountered in the southern Appalachians, but where it does grow, it is often in large colonies. Roadsides are blanketed by the species in certain localities. All species of larkspur contain poisonous alkaloids which may cause nausea, vomiting, abdominal pain, and death if consumed in sufficient quantity.

PHOTO TIPS: Categories 3, 5, and 10

You can isolate a single raceme, with or without foliage, or back off and use a wide-angle lens. Don't use too much magnification because depth of field on the irregular raceme becomes a serious problem.

Virginia Spiderwort

Tradescantia virginiana

> Spiderwort Family   Commelinaceae
> April-August
> Perennial
> Occasional

HABITAT AND RANGE

Roadsides, meadows, woods; in northern portion only—

DESCRIPTION

Three petals of equal size, ranging in color from blue to purple, and 6 obvious yellow stamens make up these flowers, which grow in a cluster on top of a somewhat zigzagged stalk. The stalk stands between 8 inches and 2 feet. The sepals and stalk are hairy.

75-300mm lens, 5T diopter, ½ sec. at f/16   Adams

The leaves are long, narrow (½ inch), and grasslike. The upper leaf blades are usually less than ¾ inch wide and as narrow, or narrower, than the opened leaf sheaths.

RELATED SPECIES

Ohio spiderwort, *T. ohiensis*, has a smooth flowerstalk, and its sepals are either smooth or have hairs only at the tips. Zigzag spiderwort, *T. subaspera*, has a more obviously zigzagged stem. Its upper leaf blades are usually more than ¾ inch wide and wider than the opened leaf sheaths. It is common in the southern segment of the region. There are 2 varieties of *T. subaspera* based on minute characteristics, such as the less-zigzagged stem of *T. subaspera* var. *montana*. It is better for the beginner to treat *T. subaspera* on the species level only.

Botanists appreciate spiderwort for more than the simple loveliness of its flower. Research has proven it to be important in cell biology because of its large chromosome structure. Also, a high sensitivity to pollution and radiation causes it to mutate quickly, making it a good indicator of environmental problems. Another interesting characteristic of spiderwort is that its spent blossoms do not fall to the ground— they seem to melt off the plant, due to the actions of certain enzymes.

Tradescantia is named for John Tradescant, who was the royal gardener for King Charles I of England.

> PHOTO TIPS: Category   3
>
> *Spiderwort often grows in dense clumps and makes a good subject for moderate closeups which include several flowers. Otherwise, you can always shoot a tight closeup of one flower along with a little foliage. Don't worry about the exposure creating an artificial color. The range of hue in spiderwort is tremendous, from pale blue to deep purple, and an exposure within ²/₃ stop should be OK from a color perspective.*

Dayflower*

Commelina communis

> Spiderwort Family   Commelinaceae
> May-October
> Annual
> Common

75-300mm lens, 5T diopter, 1 sec. at f/22   Adams

(See additional photo on page 10.)

HABITAT AND RANGE

Roadsides, low, moist woods, wasteplaces; throughout—

DESCRIPTION

The small (½- to 1-inch) flowers have 2 blue petals and 1 much smaller white petal. The petals support 3 short stamens and 3 long stamens. The flowers grow out from a conspicuous spathe that contains new buds. The lance-shaped leaves strongly clasp the stem, which tends to recline.

RELATED SPECIES

The lower petal of Virginia dayflower, *C. virginica*, is blue, not white. Slender dayflower, *C. erecta*, grows more upright than *C. communis*, and has white hairs on the leaf sheath.

Linnaeus named this flower for the Commelin brothers, who were botanists. Two of the brothers had works published, but a third brother died young with no publications to his credit. Dayflower, with two prominent petals and one smaller petal, reminded Linnaeus of the two well-known brothers and their one unknown brother.

True to its name, the individual flowers of dayflower last only a day.

> **PHOTO TIPS: Category 6**
>
> *While dayflower often grows in low, tangled mats of foliage and flowers, it is most effective to isolate a single flower along with minimal foliage. The flowers are so interesting and photogenic that it would be a shame not to show them off with a closeup.*

Southern Harebell

Bluebell
Campanula divaricata

Harebell Family   Campanulaceae
July-October; September-October
Perennial
Frequent

75-300mm lens, 6T diopter, 1 sec. at f/32   *Adams*

HABITAT AND RANGE

Rocky woods and roadsides, loose rocky slopes; throughout—

DESCRIPTION

Nodding from slender, horizontally branched stems are tiny, bell-shaped, bluish purple flowers with 5 lobes and a long protruding style. The elliptic, slightly toothed leaves are 2 to 3 inches long and are arranged alternately on the 1- to 3-foot stem. It typically grows in very dense clumps.

RELATED SPECIES

Bedstraw bellflower, *C. aparinoides*, has blue-to-white flowers, a reclining, bristly stem, and a style that does not protrude. It grows in meadows and other wet areas.

As is too often the case with tiny flowers, most people pass by southern harebell without a second glance. But those who do take the time to look closely at its little "bells" will be rewarded with seeing one of the most beautiful and colorful wildflowers in the mountains. The genus name is from the Latin *campana*, "a bell," obviously referring to the shape of the flowers.

PHOTO TIPS: Category 6

Because southern harebell grows in thick clumps, you can shoot a moderate closeup and still include several flowers. However, the flowers are so small that the only way to adequately reveal their beauty is to shoot an extreme closeup of only a few flowers.

75-300mm lens, 5T diopter,
¼ sec. at f/16

Adams

Venus's Looking Glass *

Triodanis perfoliata var. *perfoliata* (*Specularia perfoliata*)

Harebell Family   Campanulaceae
April-June
Annual
Frequent

HABITAT AND RANGE
Roadsides, fields, wasteplaces; throughout—

DESCRIPTION
Violet-blue flowers with 5 flaring sepals grow in the upper leaf axils of this slender plant. The center of the flower has 5 stamens and a prominent stigma with 3 lobes. Small, alternate, heart-shaped leaves clasp the hairy, 6- to 30-inch stem. You may have to use a magnifier to see the stem hairs.

SIMILAR SPECIES
See tall bellflower, page 64.

It is uncertain just how this plant received such an interesting name. One possible explanation is revealed in its previous scientific name, *Specularia perfoliata*. *Specularia* is derived from the Latin word *specularius*, which means "pertaining to mirrors." It may refer to the plant's shiny seeds.

> PHOTO TIPS: Categories 3 and 7 ☼
>
> *If you try to shoot the whole plant, the small blossoms will be lost in the image, and you'll probably get terrible background clutter. Instead, make a tight vertical composition that includes only a few flowers. Try to find a plant that has flowers near the top of the stem, so you don't have to crop it off.*

Tall Bellflower

Campanulastrum americanum
(*Campanula americana*)

Carolina ruellia
75-300mm lens,
5T diopter, 2 sec. at f/22
Adams

> Harebell Family   Campanulaceae
> June-September; August-October
> Biennial
> Frequent

75-300mm lens,
5T diopter,
½ sec. at f/16
Adams

HABITAT AND RANGE
Rich, moist woods; throughout—

DESCRIPTION
The blue flowers grow on a leafy spike off a 3- to 6-foot, branching stem. Individual flowers have 5 flatish, flaring lobes, and a long style in the center that is downcurving, then upturned at the tip. The lance-shaped or elliptic leaves are toothed and 3 to 6 inches long.

SIMILAR SPECIES
The often-cultivated creeping bellflower, *Campanula rapunculoides*, is very similar, except its flowers are bell shaped and grow along one side of the 1- to 3-foot stem. It only grows in the northern segment.

Carolina ruellia, *Ruellia caroliniensis*, is a scarce plant that grows in Cades Cove and surrounding areas of the Smokies, as well as a few other scattered locales. Its funnel-like flowers have 5 lobes and occur in clusters of 2 or 3. The leaves are ovate, lanceolate or elliptic, and have a stalk ⅛ inch long or longer. There are a number of subspecies, varieties, and synonyms of this species for those who wish to study it in further detail. At least 3 other *Ruellia* species grow in the region; however, all are very rare and unlikely to be encountered.

Tall bellflower has beautiful individual flowers, though they may be somewhat indistinguishable among all the other midsummer wildflowers. However, in a few places along the Blue Ridge Parkway, it is a very common and conspicuous roadside plant, sometimes growing out and above the surrounding foliage.

> PHOTO TIPS: Category 7
>
> *Tall bellflower is very susceptible to exposure errors; a half stop off can completely alter the color from what is perceived. This is especially true in the overexposure direction. If in doubt, shoot at the presumed correct exposure and bracket (shoot at a different exposure) toward underexposure.*

Chicory*

Ragged sailors, wild succory
Cichorium intybus

Sunflower Family   Asteraceae
June-October
Perennial
Common

75-300mm lens, 5T diopter, ½ sec. at f/22

Adams

HABITAT AND RANGE
Fields, roadsides, wasteplaces; throughout—

DESCRIPTION
Numerous blue flowerheads (sometimes white, rarely pinkish red) with 12 to 20 square-tipped, minutely saw-toothed rays, grow on a rigid, and often multibranched, stem. The basal leaves are large and toothed, resembling those of dandelion. The stem leaves are similar but greatly reduced in size, and nearly absent near the top.

The flowerheads of this perennial only last one day, but they only remain open for part of that day, often closing around noon. On cloudy or rainy days, they may stay closed all day.

The leaves are edible in salads or as cooked greens, much like those of dandelion. To make coffee, the roots are roasted and ground. One folk remedy uses a poultice from the roots for skin infections. Experimental work with the plant does show some antibacterial effects. Also in the experimental stage are root extracts that have lowered heart rates in laboratory animals.

An interesting feature is the plant's ability to change color when exposed to mild acid. We have heard that if you hold a chicory flower over a disturbed ant colony, the ants will release formic acid as a protective defense, changing the flower to pink. This is intriguing, but we would never purposely disturb an ant colony to see for ourselves.

PHOTO TIPS: Category 3 ☼

Without question, the best approach here is a tight closeup of 1 or 2 blossoms. Even if you did find a plant suitable for a wide-angle shot, a likely background of highways, telephone poles, and junked cars would rule out any hope for a tasteful image. In fact, because of the plant's tendency to grow within inches of roadsides, you may have a difficult time making any sort of image.

Monkey Flower

Mimulus ringens var. *ringens* (var. *minthodes*)

Figwort Family Scrophulariaceae
June-September
Perennial
Occasional

75-300mm lens, 5T diopter, 2 sec. at f/11 Adams

HABITAT AND RANGE

Bogs, marshes, streamsides, wet woods; throughout—

DESCRIPTION

Violet or pinkish (rarely white), long-stalked, tubular flowers grow in pairs in the leaf axils. The blossoms have 2 lips, with 3 wide lobes on the lower lip. There are 2 yellow ridges in the throat. The lance-shaped leaves are sessile (often clasping) and the squarish stem grows 1 to 3 feet tall.

RELATED SPECIES

Winged monkey flower, *M. alatus*, has a similar flower but on a much shorter stalk. Its leaves have definite stalks, and it has a winged stem. *M. moschatus* has a yellow flower and is occasionally found in the more northern range of the southern Appalachians.

The genus name derives from *mimus*, "buffoon," and refers to the somewhat "grinning" flower. The flower is said to look like a monkey's face, thus the common name, but we have a hard time seeing the similarity. This flower is not too plentiful, especially in the southern portion, but it may be locally common in some places. The small, slow-moving streams at Cades Cove in the Smokies are good places to find it.

PHOTO TIPS: Category 3
Most of the time, due to the nature of the plant, the only suitable approach is to shoot an isolation closeup of 1 or 2 blossoms, often using a horizontal composition. This makes for a rather ordinary and dull image, that necessarily shows the stem running right through the frame—not a good idea. Keep looking and you might find a plant that has a flower blooming close to the top of the stem. This makes for a better image, and you may be able to use a vertical composition.

Wild Monkshood

Wolfsbane

Aconitum uncinatum ssp. *ringens uncinatum*
(*A. uncinatum* var. *acutidens*)

> Crowfoot Family   Ranunculaceae
> Late July–September
> Perennial
> Scarce

105mm macro lens, 4 sec. at f/16   Adams

HABITAT AND RANGE
Moist, rich woods; throughout—

DESCRIPTION
The deep purple or purplish blue flowers have an unusual shape—the upper sepal forms a rounded hood, concealing part of the 2 clawlike petals. The 2- to 4-foot stem is slender and leans as it supports the weight of the flowers. The leaves are divided into 3 to 5 lobes, which are coarsely toothed.

RELATED SPECIES
The very rare trailing wolfsbane, *A. reclinatum*, is similar in most respects, except its flower is white-to-yellowish.

When examined closely, wild monkshood is one of our loveliest wildflowers. It is always a treat to discover this species in the wild. Unfortunately, some people who discover it also pick it, or dig it up, further contributing to its scarcity. It is now listed as a threatened species in South Carolina and Kentucky.

Monkshood is extremely poisonous; a small nibble is enough to cause a reaction. At one time, it was used to poison bait left for wolves, thus the name wolfsbane. Interestingly, the poisonous substance in monkshood also provides a drug used as a sedative and pain reliever.

> PHOTO TIPS: Categories   3   and   10
>
> The erratic, spindly nature of monkshood is such that an overall shot of the plant is rarely appropriate. Concentrate your efforts on shooting a closeup of one or two blossoms, possibly along with a little foliage. You will have to stake off the stem—the flower has a hard time supporting itself when the wind isn't blowing, much less when it is. Just be careful not to damage the stem, and wash your hands afterward.
>
> Be aware that errors in exposure will noticeably alter the color of the flowers. It's a good idea to bracket exposures, especially in the direction of underexposure.

 Skullcap

Scutellaria spp.

> Mint Family   Lamiaceae
> April-September
> Perennial
> Frequent to rare

75-300mm lens, 5T diopter, ¹/₁₅ sec. at f/22   Casstevens

HABITAT AND RANGE

Varies from moist or dry openings to woodlands and sandy, rocky soils; throughout—

DESCRIPTION

The *Scutellaria* genus is characterized by blue-to-violet (rarely white) flowers with 2 lips. The hooded upper lip arches over the flaring lower lip. As is typical with most members of the mint family, skullcaps have square stems and paired leaves. However, they do not have a minty aroma. There are more than a dozen southern Appalachian species of *Scutellaria*, which vary in the orientation of their racemes and leaf structure, among less obvious distinctions. Correct identification is complex, requiring familiarity with the keys in a technical manual.

The skullcaps are handsome members of the mint family, though they are often overlooked. Certain species have been used as a folk remedy for rabies and as a sedative for nervous conditions like epilepsy, insomnia, and neuralgia. A compound isolated from skullcap is a proven sedative and anti-spasmodic.

All the skullcaps have a small projection on the calyx which is the origin of both the common and Latin names. *Scutellaria* is from *scutella*, which means "a dish," in allusion to the shape of the appendage.

> PHOTO TIPS: Category 3
>
> There are usually at least two possible approaches to shooting skullcap. One is to back up and shoot a moderate closeup of all or part of the flowering portion. The other approach is a tight closeup of only a single raceme, or part of a raceme. The condition of the plant and background circumstances will dictate which is best.

Obedient Plant

False dragonhead
Physostegia virginiana, ssp. *virginiana*
(var. *speciosa;* var. *granulosa*)

Mint Family   Lamiaceae
July-October
Perennial
Occasional

75-300mm lens, 5T diopter, 1 sec. at f/16   Adams

HABITAT AND RANGE

Bogs, streambanks, balds, meadows, openings in rich woods; throughout—

DESCRIPTION

Rose-pink flowers (¾ to 1 inch) with a spotted tri-lobed lower lip grow in 4 rows on a terminal spike. The leaves are opposite, lance shaped, and sharply toothed. The stem is square—typical of the mint family—and grows 1 to 4 feet tall.

The mint family is noted for the square stems and flowers with 2 lips found on most of its members. These characteristics and other similar ones often create headaches for identification. But you should have no trouble identifying obedient plant. Just nudge one of its flowers; if it remains in the new position—if it is "obedient"—it is obedient plant.

PHOTO TIPS: Category 3

Obedient plant is typical of wildflowers that grow in compact spikes or racemes, with some flowers growing on the side and others projecting toward the camera. When shooting closeups, there is not enough depth of field to keep everything in focus so you have to choose what is most important. We normally opt for complete focus on the flowers (especially the petal edges) that grow on each side of the spike, while letting those that project toward the camera go soft.

Great Lobelia

Lobelia siphilitica

Bluebell Family   Campanulaceae
Late July-October
Perennial
Occasional

75-300mm lens, 5T diopter, ½ sec. at f/22
Casstevens

HABITAT AND RANGE

Open moist or wet woods, wet meadows, streambanks; throughout—

DESCRIPTION

The stout stem stands 1 to 3 feet tall and supports a leafy spike of pale-to-dark blue (rarely white) flowers. Each 1-inch flower has an upper lip with 2 lobes and a lower lip with 3 lobes. The lower lip is white striped, as is the underneath of the inflated corolla tube. The alternate leaves are elliptic or lance shaped.

RELATED SPECIES

Indian tobacco, *L. inflata*, the most common lobelia, has very small (¼-inch) pale blue flowers growing from the leaf axils, and is in a looser raceme than those of the densely packed great lobelia. Its leaves are milky, ovate, and toothed, and the stem is hairy. Spiked lobelia, *L. spicata* var. *scaposa*, has pale-blue-to-white flowers in a leafless spike, slightly toothed or entire leaves, and a mostly smooth stem. Downy lobelia, *L. puberula* var. *simulans*, has blue flowers with a white center. The flowers of downy lobelia usually grow on only one side of the spike. The leaves have soft, downy hairs.

Exact identification between these, and a few unlisted species, can be difficult. Consult a technical manual for more information.

Although it may not be as showy as cardinal flower, its scarlet relative, great lobelia is a strikingly beautiful plant, and it is one of our favorite wildflowers of late summer.

The species name, *siphilitica*, comes from its use by Indians for treatment of syphilis and gonorrhea. The related species, Indian tobacco, produces an alkaloid which has been used commercially as a non-addictive nicotine substitute to help smokers kick the habit.

PHOTO TIPS: Categories 3 and 7

Direct, diffused sunshine (or undiffused if at sunrise) is the best lighting for shooting great lobelia. We have tried shooting in other conditions—open shade, late evening, early morning, dark overcast— but the flower recorded as a horrible shade of cool blue every time. A slight warming filter might help in these situations, but you need to be careful about the filter adding a yellow cast.

75-300mm lens,
5T diopter, 81A warming filter,
¼ sec. at f/16
Casstevens

*Viper's Bugloss**

Blueweed
Echium vulgare

Borage Family   Boraginaceae
June-September
Biennial
Occasional

HABITAT AND RANGE
Roadsides, fields and wasteplaces; throughout, but mostly in the northern section—

DESCRIPTION
Bright blue flowers grow on short, curly branches. The bristly, leafy plant stands 1 to 3 feet high. The funnel-shaped flowers have protruding red stamens, and an upper lip that exceeds the lower lip. The alternate, lance-shaped leaves are larger and slightly stalked near the base of the stem. The leaves become smaller and sessile toward the top.

A widespread "weed," viper's bugloss gets its unusual name from the seed's supposed resemblance to the head of a viper. If you handle the plant, be sure to wash your hands afterward, as the bristly hairs can cause skin irritation.

PHOTO TIPS: Category 7
Viper's bugloss sometimes grows so closely together that it is difficult to isolate a single plant. However, if you shoot a tight closeup, you can render any background flowers as an out-of-focus blue backdrop.

Heal All*

Self heal
Prunella vulgaris

Mint Family   Lamiaceae
May-October
Perennial
Common

75-300mm lens, 5T diopter, $^1/_8$ sec. at f/22

Casstevens

HABITAT AND RANGE
Roadsides, fields, wasteplaces; throughout—

DESCRIPTION
This is a low-growing species (3 to 12 inches high), with small violet or blue flowers set among many bracts in a crowded, squarish spike. The flowers have 2 lips, with the lower lip fringed. The leaves may be ovate or lance shaped, toothed or entire, and are arranged in pairs on the square stem.

SIMILAR SPECIES
Two species of wood mints, genus *Blephilia*, are occasionally encountered. Both are similar to heal all but grow much taller (1 to 3 feet) and have flowers that grow in whorls separated by colored, fringed bracts. *B. hirsuta*, hairy wood mint, has a conspicuous hairy stem and leaf stalks that are usually longer than $^3/_8$ inch. *B. ciliata*, downy wood mint, has a downy stem and leaf stalks that are usually less than ¼ inch long. It is found only in the northern segment.

See henbit and purple dead nettle under the listing for lyre-leaved sage, page 110.

With a name like *heal all*, it is not surprising that this herb has a long history of medicinal use. The most common use was for mouth and throat problems, perhaps because the flowers suggest a mouth and throat, and the *Doctrine of Signatures* (see page 163) would imply its use for these ailments. Research on the plant indicates that it may lower blood pressure. It may also have astringent, antibacterial, and anticancer properties.

PHOTO TIPS: Category 2

Heal all is a good subject for tight closeups of the flowerhead. Just be careful; as the flowering nears completion, the individual flowers fall off at the slightest touch.

Hedge Nettle

Stachys spp.

Mint Family   Lamiaceae
June-August; September-October
Perennial
Frequent

HABITAT AND RANGE

Meadows, roadsides, clearings, rich woods; throughout—

DESCRIPTION

Hedge nettles are characterized by pink-to-pinkish-purple flowers, often spotted, growing in interrupted spikes or racemes. As with most members of the mint family, the stems are square, and on most *Stachys* species, the stems have some degree of pubescence. A few have distinct bristles. While the number of species of hedge nettle in the southern Appalachian area is only about half a dozen, exact identification can be difficult. It may be preferable to treat this genus as a whole until you master the key system of the technical manuals.

RELATED SPECIES

American germander, *Teucrium canadense*, is similar in most respects to the hedge nettles, but it is easily distinguished by its distinctive lower lip.

American germander

Stachys comes from the Greek word of the same spelling and means an "ear of wheat." The name refers to the characteristic shape of the flower cluster. The flowers are common in certain areas of the region, particularly along some stretches of the Blue Ridge Parkway and in the Smokies—the road to Clingmans Dome in the Smokies is an especially good spot to look for it. In fact, one species, *S. clingmanii*, Clingman's hedge nettle, was named for General Thomas L. Clingman, for whom Clingmans Dome was also named.

PHOTO TIPS: Category   3

Hedge nettle always seems to grow amidst other vegetation, creating serious background problems. Isolate a flower cluster and shoot with as much magnification as possible to help minimize distractions. You may have to gently push back the background foliage and lay a stick over it or prop it behind something rigid. We carry extra wooden stakes just for this purpose. Be sure to restore everything to its original position when finished.

75-300mm lens, 5T diopter, 1 sec. at f/22   Casstevens

Small Purple Fringed Orchid

Butterfly orchid

Platanthera psycodes (Habenaria psycodes)

Orchid Family   Orchidaceae
June-July
Perennial
Occasional

HABITAT AND RANGE

Wet woods, meadows, swamp borders; throughout—

DESCRIPTION

A compact raceme (1 to 1½ inches in diameter) of fragrant, lavender-to-pinkish-purple flowers tops the 1- to 3-foot stem. The lower lip of the flower has 3 finely fringed lobes. A thin tubular spur, with a dumbbell-shaped opening, extends backwards from the lip. The leaves are sessile and elliptical.

RELATED SPECIES

P. grandiflora (*H. fimbriata*), large purple fringed orchid, is a bigger version of *P. psycodes* with a larger raceme of flowers, more prominently fringed lobes, and a rounded opening to the spur. It grows to 4 feet. True to its name, the tri-lobed lower lip of the beautiful and rare purple fringeless orchid, *P. peramoena* (*H. peramoena*), is not fringed, but slightly toothed instead.

Some authorities regard the large and small purple fringed orchids as varieties of one species, while others list them as distinct species. They do hybridize with one another, so varieties of the two species may also be seen. Regardless of the species, *Platanthera* is one of our loveliest genera of orchids.

Small purple fringed orchid is a threatened species in Tennessee and an endangered species in Kentucky.

PHOTO TIPS: Category 3

You'll have to shoot a closeup of just the flower to keep background distractions under control. Choose the smallest aperture possible to keep the fringes sharp.

75-300mm lens, 5T diopter, 3 sec. at f/16   Adams

Blazing Star

Gay feather
Liatris spp.

Sunflower Family	Asteraceae
June-September; September-October	
Perennial	
Scarce	

75-300mm lens, 5T diopter, ¼ sec. at f/16 Adams

HABITAT AND RANGE

Bogs, wet meadows, open woodlands, rocky slopes; throughout—

DESCRIPTION

The genus *Liatris* is characterized by long, dense spikes or racemes of lavender-purple flowerheads supported by scaly bracts. The leaves are usually long and grasslike. There are nearly a dozen southern Appalachian species, none of which are common, though some may be frequent locally. Precise identification is often difficult, especially since they hybridize so easily. You may find it preferable to reference them on the genus level.

Blazing star is one of few members of the Asteraceae family that grows in spikes. The spike itself is unique as the blooms open from the top down, unlike most spiked plants that bloom from the bottom up. It is a popular garden wildflower, creating an interesting and beautiful contrast to goldenrods, black-eyed susans, and other late-summer species. Gardeners also like it because it is a good choice for attracting butterflies.

PHOTO TIPS: Categories 5 and 7

The entire plant of blazing star is so beautiful that it's a shame to shoot a tight closeup of the flowers alone. Unfortunately, all too often that is the only good choice. Perhaps you can find the plants growing in a photogenic meadow and use a wide-angle lens. At least one species grows in ditches at the base of wet rocky slopes, allowing you to use a wide-angle lens with the rock as a background. Remember, as with any wide-angle scene, you must shoot on an overcast day because the lens's coverage is too great to diffuse the light.

Teasel*

Dipsacus fullonum ssp. *sylvestris* (*D. sylvestris*)

> Teasel Family   Dipsacaceae
> July-September; September-October
> Biennial
> Occasional

spindle—to comb or "tease" the wool. It actually worked better than some machinery of the period.

PHOTO TIPS: Category   4

It should be relatively easy to make a good closeup of the flowerhead. Teasel doesn't blow around too much in the wind—assuming you stake off the stem—and it often grows above everything in the field, making backgrounds appear posterlike. You need a tall tripod to shoot the taller plants, otherwise, the sky shows up in the background when you tilt the lens up.

HABITAT AND RANGE

Roadsides, meadows, wasteplaces; continually spreading, but currently rare in the southern portion. Common in West Virginia—

DESCRIPTION

The single flowerhead is egg shaped and covered with spines. Tiny lavender or nearly white flowers grow between the spines, beginning as a band in the middle of the flowerhead and expanding up and down. Stiff, pointed bracts beneath the flowerhead may grow upward to exceed the length of the flowerhead. The stem stands 2 to 10 feet high and is also covered with spines. The paired leaves are lance shaped and prickly on the edges and midrib.

"Do not touch" seems to be the message from teasel, as every part of the plant is prickly. However, the message is ignored frequently as it is commonly used in dried arrangements. The egg-shaped flowerhead holds its shape long after the tiny flowers have bloomed and can be seen standing in the fields well into the winter months.

Teasel was brought to America by wool manufacturers, who used the flowerheads—fastened to a

75-300mm lens, 5T diopter, ¼ sec. at f/16   Casstevens

Fringed Gentian

Gentianopsis crinita (Gentiana crinita)

75-300mm lens, 5T diopter,
81A warming filter, ¼ sec. at f/22   *Casstevens*

Gentian Family   Gentianaceae
September-October
Annual or biennial
Rare

HABITAT AND RANGE

Moist meadows, wet woods, seepage slopes; A few isolated localities—

DESCRIPTION

The intensely blue (rarely white) tubular flowers have 4 flaring lobes that are finely fringed on the margins. The flowers are solitary and grow on long stalks that branch from 1- to 3-foot stems. The opposite leaves are lance shaped, entire, and sessile.

Mother Nature saves one of her best for last with the late-blooming fringed gentian. It is considered by many to be not only the most beautiful member of the gentian family, but of any family. In the right conditions, dozens of flowers grow on a single plant. In fact, one specimen was supposedly discovered with an incredible 176 flowers!

Unfortunately, the beauty and popularity of fringed gentian has contributed to its decline, as people pick and dig up the flower. Persons who wish to have the wildflower in their garden are encouraged to propagate their own, with seeds from other garden plants.

PHOTO TIPS: Categories 3 and 10 ☼

Closeups of individual flowers usually make the best images and are relatively easy to make. Extreme care should be exercised, however, and not just in the treatment of the plant. Conscientious photographers will have no problem making their photos and leaving the flower unharmed, but their actions could attract other people who would do harm. Remember, a nature photographer with a lot of gear can attract as many people as a movie crew. You should give serious consideration to passing by any locality that might draw a crowd.

Bottle Gentian

Closed gentian
Gentiana clausa

Gentian Family Gentianaceae
August-November
Perennial
Scarce

HABITAT AND RANGE

Bogs, moist roadbanks and moist, open woodlands; throughout—

DESCRIPTION

A terminal cluster of tightly closed, swollen-tubular, blue-to-purple (sometimes bluish white) flowers tops the 1- to 2½-foot stem. Smaller clusters may also grow below the terminal cluster. The tips of the flowers have short fringes between the lobes, but you must pull the lobes apart to see them. The elliptic to lanceolate leaves are sessile or have very short stalks. The stem is glabrous.

RELATED SPECIES

G. decora is very similar except its stem is densely pubescent; however the pubescence may not be visible to the naked eye. Soapwort gentian, *Gentiana saponaria*, has lobes that are either open or only loosely closed. Closed gentian, *G. andrewsii*, has visible fringes at the tip of its closed flower. It is a very rare plant of the northern segment of the southern Appalachians, though it is more common in the northeast United States. Sampson's snakeroot, *G. villosa*, has greenish white flowers. Correct identification of these, and a few other very rare species that occur in the region, can be difficult. Consult a technical manual.

It is interesting how certain things remind you of your childhood. Every time we see the blue flowers of bottle gentian it reminds us of the large, old-fashioned Christmas tree lights that we used to string on our trees.

Gentians were used by Indians and pioneers as a general health tonic to stimulate appetite and aid digestion. The pioneers added gentian to their gin or brandy, which probably made the bitter taste a bit more palatable. One species of gentian, not found in the Appalachians, is still used today to flavor some liquors.

PHOTO TIPS: Categories 3 and 10

This is a tough one. The basic approach is the same as for pink turtlehead, page 96. Also, keep in mind that with blue and purple flowers, even slight exposure variances result in dramatic color shifts. It's best to bracket exposures and pick the best one later.

75-300 mm lens, 5T diopter, 2 sec. at f/16   Adams

Stiff Gentian

Ague weed
Gentianella quinquefolia ssp.
quinquefolia (*Gentiana quinquefolia*)

Gentian Family	Gentianaceae
August–October	
Annual	
Frequent	

75-300mm lens, 5T diopter, 1 sec. at f/22   *Adams*

HABITAT AND RANGE
Roadsides, wet fields, bogs; throughout—

DESCRIPTION
Violet-to-white flowers grow in multiple clusters on the 6- to 30-inch stem. Dozens of tubular, ½- to 1-inch flowers, each with bristly tipped lobes, may be found on a single plant. We counted 300 flowers on one plant! The leaves are opposite and sessile on a stem that is branched and winged.

RELATED SPECIES
See other gentians on pages 77 and 78.

Stiff gentian is quite common in certain locations throughout the southern Appalachians. In places along the Blue Ridge Parkway, it is one of the most showy and prominent wildflowers during September. There, it holds its own amidst the more well known goldenrods and asters. Particularly good viewing locations are near Devils Courthouse, Richland Balsam, and Waterrock Knob.

PHOTO TIPS: Category 3

Stiff gentian makes a very good photo subject because it is attractive and doesn't blow around much in the wind. If you can find a suitable setting, you can include all of the plant in the composition, but you should watch out for distracting backgrounds. Otherwise, you can always shoot a closeup of only a portion of the plant. You might get lucky and find a plant growing among other late-summer flowers like goldenrods and asters, permitting you to use a wide-angle lens.

75-300mm lens,
5T diopter,
1 sec. at f/16
Adams

75-300mm lens, 5T diopter, ½ sec. at f/16
Adams

Aster

Aster spp.

Sunflower Family Asteraceae
July–October
Perennial or annual
Common to rare

HABITAT AND RANGE

Practically every possible habitat except submerged areas; throughout—

DESCRIPTION

The genus *Aster* includes nearly 4 dozen southern Appalachian species, with most colored blue to purple. A white species, white wood aster, is listed on page 193. The asters represent one of the most difficult genera in terms of identification. Even professional botanists must sometimes compare herbarium specimens for positive identification. Unless you wish to spend time at an herbarium, or seek out specialists, labeling plants as *Aster* sp. will be sufficient.

The asters are one of our favorite wildflowers for a variety of reasons. They have beautiful blue or purple flowers that blend well with the goldenrods often found growing among them, and they attract a variety of insects. Perhaps the best thing we like about them is that they bloom during our favorite time of the year—late summer and early autumn, when the nights are chilly and the mornings are dewy.

PHOTO TIPS: Categories 3 and 5

Asters make great photo subjects as they are usually so plentiful that you have unlimited choices with composition and angle of view. This allows you to maximize the lighting and background conditions to your benefit. Since asters are late bloomers, another advantage is the possibility of photographing them covered in an early frost.

Robin's Plantain

Fleabane
Erigeron pulchellus

Sunflower Family	Asteraceae
March-June	
Perennial	
Frequent	

75-300mm lens, 5T diopter, 3 sec. at f/22   Adams

HABITAT AND RANGE
Rich woods, roadsides; throughout—

DESCRIPTION
The flowerheads are 1 to 1½ inches wide and have as many as 50 very thin, violet or pink (occasionally white), rays surrounding a flat, yellow central disc. The basal leaves may be slightly lobed or toothed and are broadest at the tip, while the stem leaves are smaller and clasping at the base. The plant is covered with soft hairs and grows 6 to 20 inches tall on a hollow stem.

SIMILAR AND RELATED SPECIES
The daisy fleabanes on page 214 are similar. Robin's plantain may be confused with certain aster species, but most asters do not bloom until well after robin's plantain has finished blooming.

Robin's plantain is unusual in that it is a spring-blooming species of the sunflower family. Most members of the family, like asters and goldenrods, are late bloomers. The name *fleabane* comes from its use by pioneers as mattress stuffing in an attempt to keep away fleas and other insects. But don't bother trying this at home because it doesn't work.

> PHOTO TIPS: Category 3
>
> *Since robin's plantain often grows in colonies, try composing a scene that sharply renders one or two foreground flowers against a background of out-of-focus flowers.*

Purple-flowering Raspberry

Thimbleberry

Rubus odoratus

> Rose Family   Rosaceae
> June-August; July-October
> Perennial
> Common

75-300mm lens, 5T diopter, ½ sec. at f/16   Adams

HABITAT AND RANGE
Woodland borders, streambanks, roadsides; throughout—

DESCRIPTION
This bushy, 1- to 4-foot plant has bright, magenta flowers that are 1 to 2 inches wide and usually have 5 petals. The reddish brown branches are covered with bristly hairs. The maplelike leaves are large, with 3 to 5 lobes.

The genus *Rubus*, which includes over 200 species of raspberries, blackberries, and dewberries, is collectively referred to as brambles. However, purple-flowering raspberry is the only one in the region with simple leaves, and without the customary prickles that can make the work of picking the juicy fruits of most of these plants quite painful.

We've admittedly strayed from our format by including this plant, which is technically a shrub. However, most people probably never associate it with the shrubs since it doesn't have a true, bark-covered, woody stem; and since much of the plant dies back after producing fruits.

> PHOTO TIPS: Category 5
>
> *Many possibilities for good compositions exist with raspberry plants, limited only by your imagination. However, inadequate depth of field ruins most of them. Look for a few blossoms and 1 or 2 leaves that are on roughly the same plane.*

Waterleaf

Scorpion weed

Hydrophyllum virginianum

> Waterleaf Family   Hydrophyllaceae
> May-June; July-August
> Perennial
> Occasional

75-300mm lens, 5T diopter, 4 sec. at f/22

Adams

HABITAT AND RANGE
Rich, moist woods, streambanks; throughout—

DESCRIPTION
These tiny ($^1/_3$-inch) white or violet, bell-shaped flowers have 5 lobes and very long stamens. They grow in clusters on smooth, slender, 1- to 2-foot stems. The leaves are divided into 3 to 7 ovate, toothed segments. They have a somewhat mottled appearance, as if a white powder had been sprinkled on them. These splotches may disappear around the time of flowering.

Broad-leaved waterleaf

Large-leaved waterleaf

Waterleaf

RELATED SPECIES
The scarce large-leaved waterleaf, *H. macrophyllum*, is a rough, hairy species with whitish pink flowers that have prominent protruding stamens and leaves divided into 9 to 13 segments. The leaves have conspicuous white splotches on the upper surface and brown splotches on the lower surface. The overall appearance of the plant is that it has been sprayed with a powdery chemical and is shriveling up and dying. The broad, maplelike leaves of broad-leaved waterleaf, *H. canadense*, distinguish the species from the other two. Its white or pale purple flowers are hidden underneath the leaves. It is the most frequently seen species, especially in the low-elevation rocky woods of the Smokies.

Indians chewed the roots of waterleaf to relieve cracked lips and mouth sores, and the young leaves are said to make an excellent cooked green. The common name *waterleaf* supposedly relates to the leaves' water-stained appearance. The name *scorpion weed* refers to the shape of the buds, which are curled over like a scorpion's tail.

> PHOTO TIPS: Category 6
>
> *As with most wildflowers in this category, the best approach is usually to choose a picturesque set of flowers and frame them with foliage. Try to keep everything on the same plane to maximize depth of field.*

Wild Geranium

Cranesbill
Geranium maculatum

Geranium Family   Geraniaceae
April-June
Perennial
Common

75-300mm lens, 5T diopter, ¼ sec. at f/22

Casstevens

HABITAT AND RANGE
Rich woods, thickets, roadsides; throughout—

DESCRIPTION
The 1- to 1½-inch-wide flowers have 5 pinkish purple (sometimes light pink to nearly white) petals and 10 stamens. The minutely hairy leaves, 2 to 4 inches wide, are deeply lobed into 3 to 5 toothed segments. The lower leaves are on longer stalks than those farther up the stem.

Four other *Geranium* species are frequently encountered in the southern Appalachians. All have similar leaf and flower structures, but the flowers on these other species are much smaller than wild geranium's, usually ¼ inch wide or less. See a technical manual for distinctions.

Because wild geranium cannot self-pollinate and is entirely dependent on insects for pollination, it makes a good candidate for studying the interaction of insects with plants. Look closely at the flower petals. You will see light-colored lines that run from the outer edge of the petal toward the center of the flower. These are thought to guide insects to the nectar. After pollination, the pistil becomes long and thin as it develops into a fruit resembling a bird's beak, thus, the common name *cranesbill*.

Used in a poultice, the tannin-rich roots act as a coagulant to help stop bleeding. Diarrhea, hemorrhoids, gum diseases, and stomach disorders are among the many ailments that have been treated with the plant. At one time, geranium was listed in the United States Pharmacopoeia.

> PHOTO TIPS: Category 6
>
> *You should have no trouble locating a few flowers close together and on the same plane to include in a closeup composition. Often, the plant grows so densely you can shoot a wide-angle view that includes some of the distinctive foliage.*

ose Pink

Bitterbloom
Sabatia angularis

Gentian Family	Gentianaceae
July-August; September-October	
Annual	
Occasional	

75-300mm lens, 5T diopter, $^1/_{15}$ sec. at f/22   Casstevens

HABITAT AND RANGE
Moist woods, meadows and marshes; throughout—

DESCRIPTION
The pink flowers (rarely white) have 5 petals and grow on paired flower branches. The flower has a greenish yellow center with borders that are deep pink. Paired, ovate leaves clasp the squarish, winged, 1- to 3-foot stem.

RELATED SPECIES
Although most other members of the *Sabatia* genus grow on the coastal plain, slender marsh pink, *S. campanulata*, does sometimes occur in the mountains. It has narrow, elliptical leaves and long, thin calyx lobes equal in length to the petals.

Rose pink is a delightfully beautiful wildflower with a delicate fragrance. Its genus name honors the Italian botanist Liberato Sabbati, while the species name refers to the angled stem. The plant has often been used as a tonic for general health.

PHOTO TIPS: Category 3

Rose pink is rather easy to photograph, offering good opportunities for tight closeups and for overall views that include several blossoms. Be careful not to overexpose the passion pink petals, as this will cause them to appear faded.

Creeping Phlox

Phlox stolonifera

HABITAT AND RANGE

Rich woods, roadsides, streambanks; throughout—

DESCRIPTION

The pinkish blue flowers stand erect and are supported by low (8- to 10-inch), creeping stems. Each flower has 5 rounded, entire lobes that flare out from a slender tube. The stamens protrude slightly from the tube. The leaves are ovate or lanceolate, with the basal leaves slightly larger than the stem leaves.

SIMILAR AND RELATED SPECIES

The only other phlox species commonly encountered during April is blue phlox, *P. divaricata* (see photo on page 20). Its petals are various shades of sky blue, wedge shaped, sometimes notched, and the stamens are recessed. The often-cultivated *P. subulata*, moss pink, also blooms in April, but it is rather uncommon and inhabits dry, rocky slopes. It is different from other phloxes—except the rare *P. nivalis* of dry, sandy woodlands—in that it has woody stems, needlelike leaves, and grows in low, dense mats. Most other phlox species bloom later in the year, but can be recognized by the 5 rounded or wedge-shaped petals that vary in color from pink to blue or purple. The leaves in most species are simple, entire, and opposite. A characteristic of all phlox species is that the petals are united into a slender tube. Because of the extreme difficulty in differentiating between most phlox species, their subspecies, and hybrids, it may be best to treat them on the genus level, except for those specified above.

A very similar plant that is sometimes confused with phlox is wild pink, *Silene caroliniana* ssp. *pensylvanica* (var. *pensylvanica*) [see photo on page 44]. It grows in dry, rocky woodlands, mostly in the northern portion of the southern Appalachians. It is differentiated by petals that are separate, and sepals—not petals—united into a slender, sticky tube.

Dame's rocket, *Hesperis matronalis*, resembles phlox, except that it has 4 petals, and its leaves vary from ovate to lanceolate. It is particularly common along the Skyline Drive.

Fireweed, *Epilobium angustifolium* ssp. *angustifolium*, is a summer-blooming plant found in recently burned areas and has flowers that resemble dame's rocket in color and petal number. However, the flowers of fireweed grow in spikelike racemes, and its leaves are linear to lanceolate.

Creeping phlox is a welcome sight in early spring, as its flowers carpet the ground in dense patches. The flowers are equally as beautiful even before they open, when they are tightly rolled into pointed, bluish purple cones. Blue phlox often grows in association with creeping phlox, and a good place to see both is the lower elevations of the Smokies along Newfound Gap Road.

PHOTO TIPS: Category 6

Both creeping phlox and blue phlox make excellent photo subjects, providing compositions limited only by the photographer's imagination. Blue phlox, especially, grows so densely that tight, artsy closeups are quiet effective. Like many blue flowers, phlox is susceptible to color variance from overexposure or underexposure, as well as the inability of most films to accurately portray the perceived color. It's best to try different films and bracket exposures. Then pick the combination you like best.

75-300mm lens, 5T diopter, 1 sec. at f/16

Adams

Virginia Meadow Beauty

Deergrass

Rhexia virginica

Melastoma Family   Melastomataceae
May-September
Perennial
Occasional

75-300mm lens, 5T diopter, 1 sec. at f/22   Adams

HABITAT AND RANGE

Sandy soil of low-altitude bogs, wet ditches, and meadows; throughout—

DESCRIPTION

The flower has 4 rose-purple petals and 8 bright yellow, curved anthers. The leaves are opposite, hairy, and elliptical, with 3 to 5 prominent veins. The 1- to 2-foot-tall stem is round, but it has 4 prominent wings that make it appear square. All parts of the plant are hairy.

SIMILAR SPECIES

The flowers of Maryland meadow beauty, *R. mariana* var. *mariana* (*R. mariana* var. *leiosperma*) are pale pink. Interestingly, the stem has 2 broad convex sides and 2 narrow concave sides. You may need to use a magnifier to see this fully. This species usually has more hairs than Virginia meadow beauty.

Meadow beauty is one of only a few northern species in this tropical flower family, and it is much more at home on the warmer coastal plain. Its flowers are short-lived, often lasting only a few hours, although the seed capsule that remains after the petals fall is conspicuous and contributes to the beauty of the plant. Thoreau once compared the shape of the fruit to that of a cream pitcher.

PHOTO TIPS: Category 3

It's tough to make a good photograph of the entire plant, so you should concentrate on isolating 1 or 2 blossoms. Try to find blossoms that are on roughly the same plane to maximize depth of field.

Deptford Pink

Dianthus armeria

Pink Family   Caryophyllaceae
May-September
Biennial
Common

105mm macro lens, ½ sec. at f/16   Adams

HABITAT AND RANGE
Fields, roadsides, wasteplaces; throughout—

DESCRIPTION
The slender, rigid stem is 8 to 24 inches tall and supports a small cluster of pink flowers with white spots. The flowers have 5 petals and toothed margins. Long, thin bracts occur at the base of the flowers. The leaves are narrow, grasslike, and arranged in pairs on the stem.

Deptford pink is a common, but beautiful, wildflower that is often overlooked. The name refers to Deptford, England, where the flower once grew in profusion. Deptford is now a part of London.

PHOTO TIPS: Category 3

A fair amount of magnification is required to make the flowers show up well. With such a closeup, the only way to keep all of the petals in focus is to shoot straight down to align the film plane with the subject plane, but this may not be a good option from a compositional standpoint.

Grass Pink

Rose wings

Calopogon tuberosus var. *tuberosus* (*C. pulchellus*)

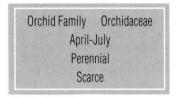

Orchid Family   Orchidaceae
April-July
Perennial
Scarce

HABITAT AND RANGE
Bogs and wet meadows; throughout—

DESCRIPTION
The magenta-pink (occasionally white) flowers open successively upward in a loose raceme. The raceme is on a slender stem that may reach 4 feet in height. An erect lip located at the top of the flower has a squarish tip with a tufted yellow crest. Petals and sepals flare out below the lip, and a downcurved column is in the center of the flower. A single 8- to 12-inch, grasslike leaf sheaths the stem at the base.

SIMILAR SPECIES
The following 4 species are also members of the orchid family, though smaller than grass pink:

Bog rose, *Arethusa bulbosa*, (see photo on page 46) is an extremely rare inhabitant of sphagnum bogs. It has a solitary flower with 3 upright, lanceolate sepals, and a hood covering the downcurved lip. The lip has magenta spots, a notch at the tip, and 3 to 5 fringed, yellow or white crests. A single grasslike leaf appears after the flower opens. It blooms in late May and early June. Bog rose is a relict of the last ice age. As glaciers dipped as far south as Pennsylvania, traditional northern species, such as bog rose, migrated southward in response to the cooling of high-elevation peaks and valleys. As the glaciers retreated northward, so did the plants, leaving behind relict populations scattered over the southern Appalachians. In the southern Appalachians, bog rose is found in only a few isolated high-elevation bogs.

Rose pogonia, *Pogonia ophioglossoides*, is similar to bog rose except that it has a single leaf midway up the stem and a leaflike bract just under the flower. Occasionally, 1 or 2 basal leaves are present. Two or 3 flowers sometimes grow on a single stem. It blooms in May and June.

Rosebud orchid, or spreading pogonia, *Cleistes bifaria* (*C. divaricata* var. *bifaria*), (see photo on page 18) is easily distinguished by its 3 purplish brown sepals that radiate out from a pinkish purple or white tube. As in rose pogonia, there is a single leaf about midway up the stem and a leaflike bract below the flower. It often invades after fire and grows in drier sites, especially pine ridges. It blooms in June.

The flowers of nodding pogonia, or three-birds orchid, *Triphora trianthophora*, look like a cross between the 3 species mentioned above. One to 7 flowers grow on a plant, but as the common name suggests, the number is usually 3. This orchid is easily distinguished by the small, oval to heart-shaped leaves that sheath the stem. It blooms in August in rich woods.

All five of these orchids are rare and, with the exception of bog rose, are much more common on the coastal plain. Remember, most orchid species rarely live when transplanted from the wild and collection of any plant part, including the seeds, is prohibited in the national parks and most state parks.

PHOTO TIPS: Categories 2 and 10

These species should be approached with extreme care, not only for their rarity, but for the sensitive environment in which some of them grow. Bog rose should be left completely alone if discovered, and its location reported to the state's natural heritage program or a similar organization.

Grass pink
75-300mm lens, 5T diopter, 2 sec. at f/22   *Adams*

Rose pogonia
75-300mm lens, 5T diopter, ½ sec. at f/22   *Adams*

Pink Lady's Slipper

Moccasin flower
Cypripedium acaule

> Orchid Family   Orchidaceae
> Mid-April–mid-June
> Perennial
> Occasional

Showy lady's slipper, *C. reginae*, has a rose-colored pouch, white sepals and petals, and leaves along the entire stem. One of our most striking orchids, it is, sadly, exceedingly rare. Currently, it is only known in 4 sites in Virginia and 1 in Tennessee. Fortunately, it is more common, though not necessarily secure, in northern swamps and bogs, especially in the Great Lakes states.

Pink lady's slippers prefer the dry, acid soil of pine and oak forests. They, and other slipper orchids, require the presence of a special fungus of the genus *Rhizoctonia* to grow. The fungus forms a symbiotic relationship with the plant that enables the plant to absorb nutrients from the soil. This adaptation makes the plant very difficult to propagate outside its natural environment. Unfortunately, that makes it a candidate for heavy harvesting from the wild. You should never purchase any of the slipper orchids from a nursery, unless you are certain they were not taken from the wild. Likewise, you should never dig one for yourself, as transplanted orchids rarely live more than a year or two.

HABITAT AND RANGE
Dry woodlands, especially pine forests; throughout—

DESCRIPTION
The lower petal of this flower forms a hollow, pink pouch with heavy veining and a center groove. The remaining sepals and petals are greenish brown and lance shaped. Two oval, smooth-edged, ribbed leaves grow at the base. The stem has no leaves. There is a rare white form of pink lady's slipper (*C. acaule* f. *albiflorum*) that occurs in association with the pink form.

PHOTO TIPS: Category 2

Pink lady's slipper is one of the most photogenic of our native wildflowers. It makes great closeups, as well as compositions that include the whole plant along with a little of the surroundings. The best time to shoot closeups of the slipper is on a sunny day. Use a diffusion umbrella or plastic to diffuse the harsh sunlight, then use a mirror to direct light only onto the slipper. Since it is somewhat translucent, it reproduces well in such situations.

75-300mm lens, ½ sec. at f/22

(See additional photo on page 23.)

Adams

Showy Orchis

Purple-hooded orchid
Galearis spectabilis (Orchis spectabilis)

> Orchid Family   Orchidaceae
> April-early June
> Perennial
> Occasional

HABITAT AND RANGE
Cove hardwood forests, streambanks; throughout—

DESCRIPTION
This beautiful orchid produces a loose raceme of 2 to 15 flowers. Each flower is about an inch long and has a white lip. The pink-to-purple sepals and lateral petals form a hood above the lip. Occasional color variations occur where the lip is pink or the whole flower is white. Two egg-shaped basal leaves sheathe the stem; they are glossy, slightly sticky, and 3 to 8 inches in length. The plant is 4 to 12 inches tall.

While several orchids in the southern Appalachians are in danger of becoming threatened or endangered, the endemic showy orchis is rather frequently encountered. It is one of our most attractive orchids, but like so many wildflowers, a close examination is required to fully appreciate its beauty.

75-300mm lens, 5T diopter, 1 sec. at f/16   *Adams*

PHOTO TIPS: Category 2

Don't be satisfied with photographing the first plant you see. Where you see one showy orchis, you are likely to find several more, and one of them may present a better opportunity. The biggest problem with photographing showy orchis is that any composition that doesn't chop off the leaves is necessarily shot from a distance, and tends to be stale and boring. It's better to find a plant that has more erect leaves and try an up-close vertical composition.

105mm macro lens, 1 sec. at f/32   *Casstevens*

Fringed Polygala

Gaywings
Polygala paucifolia

Milkwort Family   Polygalaceae
April-May; June-September
Perennial
Scarce

tered at the top of the stem; lower stem leaves are small and bractlike.

The tiny, delicate fringed polygala is often mistaken as a member of the orchid or pea family. Perhaps a more fitting name would be "planeflower," as the bloom looks very much like a tailless, single-engine airplane. It was once believed that eating plants of the milkwort family would increase milk production in cows and nursing women.

HABITAT AND RANGE
Moist woods, often on banks; throughout—

DESCRIPTION
This low-growing plant, 3 to 6 inches high, bears a cluster of 1 to 5 rose-purple flowers. The flowers are 1 inch across, with 2 flaring sepals, and petals that are rolled together into a tube with a bushy fringe at the tip. Oval, evergreen leaves are clus-

PHOTO TIPS: Categories 1 and 2

Depending on the circumstances, you can shoot straight down and include several flowers, or close in on a single flower from above or at an angle. Fringed polygala usually grows in colonies, sometimes large ones, so you have several possible settings from which to choose.

Pink Turtlehead

Chelone lyonii

Figwort Family   Scrophulariaceae
July-September; October
Perennial
Occasional

75-300mm lens, 5T diopter, 4 sec. at f/32   Adams

HABITAT AND RANGE

Mostly higher altitude rich woods, ditches, and streambanks; throughout—

DESCRIPTION

The rose-pink flowers have 2 lips and grow in a short spike on the 1- to 3-foot stem. The flower's upper lip arches over the lower lip, and the inflated throat is woolly inside. Ovate to lanceolate, toothed leaves, with ½-inch or longer petioles (leaf stalks), are arranged oppositely on the stem.

RELATED SPECIES

Red turtlehead, *C. obliqua*, is similar but with lance-shaped leaves and petioles less than ½ inch. The rare *C. cuthbertii* is similar to both red and pink turtlehead, but it has flowers arranged in 4 distinct rows and its leaves are sessile. White turtlehead, *C. glabra* (var. *dilata*; var. *elatior*), has white flowers that may be tinged with pink.

Take one close look at the flowers of turtlehead and you will instantly see how it got its name. Both the common and Latin name reflect its resemblance to the reptile; *Chelone* is Greek for "tortoise." The flowers are quite attractive, often occurring in rather dense patches. Two good places to see it are Mount Mitchell State Park along the Blue Ridge Parkway and Clingmans Dome in the Smokies.

PHOTO TIPS: Categories 3 and 6
If you want to make a closeup of just one flowerhead, try to find one that has several flowers stacked in the cluster. Otherwise, the image will appear funny in both vertical and horizontal compositions: the horizontal composition leaves dead space on each side; the vertical composition, if you back up enough to include all the flower, leaves dead space at the top or clutter at the bottom. Often you will find patches that allow for a moderate wide-angle composition.

Gray Beardtongue

Penstemon canescens

Figwort Family Scrophulariaceae
May-July
Perennial
Common

75-300mm lens, 5T diopter, 1/8 sec. at f/16   *Adams*

(See additional photo on page 42.)

HABITAT AND RANGE
Roadsides, rocky slopes and woodlands; throughout—

DESCRIPTION
The violet-purple-to-pinkish flowers have 2 lips. The upper lip has 2 lobes, and the lower lip has 3 lobes. Lines in the throat are purple and white, and one sterile stamen is obvious with its beard of yellow hairs. The stem leaves are paired, lance shaped, and clasp the flower stem, while the larger rosette leaves have leaf stems. The flower stem and leaves are covered with fine, gray hairs. The plant grows 1 to 3 feet tall.

RELATED SPECIES
Gray beardtongue is the most common *Penstemon* in the region; but there are 4 other species that occur rather frequently, along with several others that are scarce. The 4 most common species are: *P. digitalis, P. laevigatus, P. smallii,* and *P. pallidus.* Most of these species are very similar and difficult to distinguish. Consult a technical manual for exact identification.

PHOTO TIPS: Category 3

The beardtongues make excellent subjects for early morning backlighting. For added emphasis with this type of image, try to find a plant that has a dark, shaded background.

Wild Bergamot

Monarda fistulosa ssp. fistulosa var. mollis
(M. fistulosa var. mossis)

Mint Family   Lamiaceae
July-August; August-October
Perennial
Frequent

HABITAT AND RANGE

Dry open woods, meadows, and roadside banks; throughout—

DESCRIPTION

The flowerhead has numerous lilac-to-purple (sometimes pink) tubular flowers, with a tuft of hairs on the tip of the upper lip of each flower. The bracts may be tinged with pink. Triangular leaves grow in pairs on the 1- to 4-foot stem.

RELATED SPECIES

Basil balm, *M. clinopodia*, has spotted white-to-pinkish flowers and white bracts. *M. media* has reddish purple flowers. See bee balm, page 122.

Tremendous variability occurs within the *Monarda* genus, with colors ranging from deep red to pink, purple, and white. Various species, subspecies, forms, and hybrids have been defined in the past by different authors, making the whole picture quite confusing for the beginning student of botany. Perhaps the best method is to label any *Monarda* that has a tuft of hairs on the tip of the flowers as "bergamot, *M. fistulosa*," and to label any deep red *Monarda* as "bee balm, *M. didyma*" (page 122). Anything else can be labeled simply as *Monarda*. Remember, it is perfectly acceptable to not specify species, subspecies, and varieties, but if you do, they should be accurate.

75-300mm lens, 5T diopter, ½ sec. at f/16   Adams

75-300mm lens, 5T diopter, 3 sec. at f/32   *Adams*

Helonias bullata

> Lily Family   Liliaceae
> Early April–early May; June–July
> Perennial
> Rare

DESCRIPTION

The pink flowers, with showy blue anthers, are borne in a tight cluster on the 1- to 2-foot, hollow stem. Stem leaves are small and scalelike; basal leaves are evergreen, oblong to lance shaped, and grow in a rosette.

The bright pink color of swamp pink stands in stark contrast to the greens and browns of the bogs where it grows. The plant seems out of place, like it should be growing in a coastal-plain marsh instead of a mountain environment. Unfortunately, this uniqueness may contribute to its decline, as unenlightened people approach and pick the flower. Currently, it is a threatened species in Georgia, South Carolina, and North Carolina. The boggy habitat where swamp pink grows is very fragile so people should not walk on it. However, one place where you can see and photograph the plant with a clean conscience is the Highlands Botanical Garden (see the appendix).

The flower is interesting in that it begins flowering while the stem is only a foot or so high, but it continues to grow. By the time flowering has finished and fruiting begins, it may be 3 feet tall or higher.

PHOTO TIPS: Categories 3 and 10

Swamp pink should not be approached closely in the wild due to the fragility of its environment, though you may get lucky and discover a plant near the edge of the bog that allows you to use a telephoto lens without causing undue harm. However, the best advice is to photograph this species at a botanical garden, as we did.

Bull Thistle*

Lightning plant
Cirsium vulgare

Sunflower Family	Asteraceae
June-September	
Biennial	
Frequent	

HABITAT AND RANGE
Pastures, roadsides, wasteplaces; throughout—

DESCRIPTION
A purple-pink flowerhead resembling a man's shaving brush sits on top of a series of stiff, spiny bracts. The leaves are very spiny, have irregular, deep lobes, and have bases that extend as wings along the stem. The prickly stems are 3 to 6 feet high and usually contain several flowerheads.

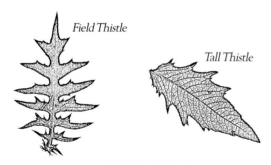

Field Thistle

Tall Thistle

RELATED SPECIES
The fragrant Canada thistle, *C. arvense*, has numerous, clustered flowerheads and smooth, branching stems. The flowerheads are an inch or less across. The leaves of tall thistle, *C. altissimum*, are toothed, but without the deeper lobes of most other thistles.

Underneath the leaves is a dense white downy covering. The spineless stems are multibranched and can grow to 10 feet tall. Pasture thistle, *C. pumilum*, very closely resembles bull thistle, but it has larger flowerheads, and very hairy, unwinged stems. The underside of its leaves are villous. Field thistle, *C. discolor*, has deeply cut leaves that have a white, woolly covering underneath and long colorless spines on the tips of the bracts.

See spotted knapweed, page 102.

Most people consider thistle an annoying weed. While it may be a pest to some, to us it is a beautiful wildflower, and it is very beneficial to birds and many insects. Painted lady butterflies feed and lay eggs on the plant, and goldfinches are frequent visitors, eating the seeds and using the fluffy white seed dispersal filaments to line their nests.

An old legend says that when the Danes invaded Scotland they tried to sneak up on the Scots by taking off their boots and creeping through the fields. However, a cry of pain from an unfortunate soldier who stepped on a thistle warned the Scots, who were then able to defend themselves successfully. The thistle is now Scotland's national emblem.

Young leaves of thistle can be eaten in salads or cooked after removing the spines, though we can't imagine someone with that much patience. The new stems can be peeled and eaten raw like celery.

PHOTO TIPS: Category 3

If you are lucky enough to discover a suitable wide-angle situation, by all means use a wide-angle lens. Usually, you'll have to shoot a tight closeup of 1 or 2 flowerheads. You should make a special effort to visit thistle early in the morning to search for lethargic insects and crab spiders.

75-300mm lens, 5T diopter, 1 sec. at f/16

Adams

Spotted Knapweed*

Star thistle

Centaurea biebersteinii (C. maculosa)

Sunflower Family	Asteraceae
June-October	
Perennial	
Common	

HABITAT AND RANGE

Roadsides, fields, and wasteplaces; mostly in the northern segment—

DESCRIPTION

The 1-inch flowerheads have a tuft of pinkish purple (sometimes white) disc flowers. The flowerheads grow on a slender, multibranched stem that stands up to 4 feet tall. The bracts have black-fringed tips, and the lower leaves are deeply divided into narrow lobes.

RELATED SPECIES

Bachelor's button, *C. cyanus*, usually has deep blue flowers, but they may be pink or white. The bracts

are fringed over half their length, not just at the tips, as in spotted knapweed.

Knapweeds, genus *Centaurea*, are often confused with the true thistles of the genus *Cirsium*, to which they are closely related. Generally, thistles have spiny-tipped leaves and a more densely compacted flowerhead. Plus, many thistles are covered in sharp spines or bristles, while knapweeds are smooth.

PHOTO TIPS: Category 3

Like the true thistles, spotted knapweed benefits from a closeup representation. Shoot 1 blossom, or 2 growing close together, and use as much magnification as possible to eliminate background clutter. Remember, there is no way to get complete depth of field on the flower, so focus on what you consider to be the most important part.

75-300mm lens, 5T diopter, $^1/_{15}$ sec. at f/22 Casstevens

50mm lens, ½ sec. at f/16   *Adams*

Queen of the meadow
Eupatorium fistulosum

Sunflower Family	Asteraceae
July-October	
Perennial	
Common	

HABITAT AND RANGE

Moist woods, roadsides, meadows; throughout—

DESCRIPTION

The flower cluster is a large, fuzzy dome of pale-pink-to-purplish flowers. Each individual head contains roughly 4 to 7 flowers. The elliptic to lanceolate leaves occur in whorls of 4 to 7. The leaves are on a hollow, sometimes white-waxy stem with conspicuous purple coloration. This species grows to 8 feet or more. You do not have to destroy the stem to see if it is hollow. If it depresses even a little when you squeeze it, it's hollow.

RELATED SPECIES

E. maculatum is distinguished by its solid stem and flatter flower cluster containing 9 to 22 flowers per individual head. The stem of *E. purpureum* is also solid, but is uniformly green, being purple only at the leaf joints. Its leaves are said to smell of vanilla when crushed. It is a shorter species, more at home in woodlands than in the open.

In mid- to late summer, you can see why this impressive plant earned its Appalachian nickname of queen of the meadow. It does have a rather regal presence, towering above other summer bloomers like white wood aster and jewelweed. It is such an impressive sight on a drive along the Blue Ridge Parkway that it makes one wonder how it ever became known as a "weed."

The widely accepted story on the common name is that it was named for an Indian medicine man named Joe Pye. He used the plant to cure typhus fever and several other ailments.

PHOTO TIPS: Categories 4 and 5

Telephoto lenses are usually necessary to photograph individual flowers; that is, unless you make a habit of carrying a step ladder with you. A better option is to find a good situation for shooting a cluster of several flowers. This shouldn't be too hard, as this species tends to grow in photogenic arrangements.

75-300mm lens, 5T diopter, 1 sec. at f/16   Adams

*Common Milkweed**

Asclepias syriaca

Milkweed Family   Asclepiadaceae
June-August; July-September
Perennial
Common

Fields and roadsides; throughout—

DESCRIPTION
This is a tall (4- to 6-foot), stout plant, with 2- to 3-inch-wide umbels of dusty rose flowers growing in the leaf axils. The 3- to 12-inch leaves are opposite and oblong. There is a warty appearance to the seedpods.

RELATED SPECIES
A. incarnata, swamp milkweed, has deep rose-colored flowers and, as the name suggests, grows in a wet environment. There are two subspecies of swamp milkweed based on slight differences. Consult a technical manual for distinctions. White milkweed, *A. variegata*, has white flowers with a purple center. *A. exaltata*, poke milkweed, also has white flowers, but they are tinged with lavender or green and are droopy. This species is common in the forest margins along the Blue Ridge Parkway. Blunt-leaved milkweed, *A. amplexicaulis*, has distinctive, wavy-edged leaves that clasp the stem. Whorled milkweed, *A. verticillata*, has distinctive whorled, linear leaves. Green milkweed, *A. viridiflora*, has sessile umbels of green flowers. The spring flowering *A. quadrifolia*, four-leaved milkweed, has middle leaves in whorls of four and grows in woodlands.

Although each of these species is distinctive in one way or another, exact identification can sometimes be difficult. It's best to consult a technical manual.

Most people are familiar with milkweed because of its seedpods that split open in the fall, exposing silky, parachuted seeds for the wind to disperse (see photo on page xii). The common name describes the milky sap present in the stems. During World War II, an attempt was made to produce rubber from this sap, but the time and expense outweighed the benefit and the project was abandoned.

The sap has been used as chewing gum, a dangerous practice since it contains cardiac glycosides, which adversely affect the heart. The butterflies, caterpillars, and milkweed bugs that feed on milkweed absorb the glycosides into their bodies without harmful side effects, but they do become foul tasting to their predators. To remind these predators of their bad taste, most of these insects have bright orange, red, and black markings. Some insects, who aren't foul tasting themselves, exploit this situation by mimicking these warning colors. Viceroy butterflies, for instance, enjoy relative immunity from bird attacks because of their close resemblance to the monarch butterfly, which feeds and lays eggs exclusively on milkweed.

PHOTO TIPS: Category 5

The various species of milkweeds are among the most photogenic of all wildflowers. However, it's not the flowers that photographers like about milkweed, but the seed pods and the continuous parade of insects on the plants. Be sure to visit early in the morning, when the cool temperatures and dew keep the critters from crawling or flying away.

75-300mm lens, 5T diopter, ¼ sec. at f/22   Casstevens

New York Ironweed

Vernonia noveboracensis

Sunflower Family	Asteraceae
July-September; August-October	
Perennial	
Common	

The genus name honors William Vernon, an English botanist who traveled to Maryland in 1698 to collect plants.

PHOTO TIPS: Category 4

Ironweed makes a good photo subject, but you need to be at the same level with the flowers or slightly above them. It is visited by numerous insects, so be sure to make your visit early in the morning, when the cool temperatures make insects sluggish.

75-300mm lens, 5T diopter, 2 sec. at f/11   *Adams*
(See additional photo on page 16.)

HABITAT AND RANGE

Wet fields, streambanks, roadsides, low woodlands; throughout—

DESCRIPTION

Deep purple (sometimes blue or white), loosely compacted flowerheads, with 30 to 65 individual flowers, grow on top of a stem that is 3 to 8 feet high. The bracts have long, hairlike tips. The alternate leaves are lance shaped and finely toothed.

SIMILAR SPECIES

Though it is rare in the mountains, mistflower or ageratum, *Eupatorium coelestinum*, has a corymb of blue (rarely white) flowerheads on a hairy, branching stem that is 1 to 3 feet high. The leaves are ovate to narrowly ovate and opposite.

Ironweed blooms at the same time as milkweed, Joe-Pye weed, sunflowers, and many other members of the sunflower family, as well as other flowers like jewelweed and evening primrose. These species often grow together on roadsides and in meadows along the Blue Ridge Mountains, providing a mid- to late summer show of color that, to a wildflower lover, rivals that of the approaching autumn season.

35-70mm lens, 81A warming filter, 1 sec. at f/32

Casstevens

Wild Live-forever

Allegheny stonecrop
Sedum telephioides

Orpine Family   Crassulaceae
July-September; August-October
Perennial
Occasional

HABITAT AND RANGE
Cliffs, rock crevices, rocky woods; throughout—

DESCRIPTION
A cluster of small pinkish-purple-to-white flowers with 5 pointed petals tops the slender stem. The leaves are ovate, thick and fleshy, and may be entire or slightly toothed. The plant is 12 to 18 inches tall.

The genus name is from *sedere*, "to sit," and refers to the manner in which the plant attaches to rocks. The common name alludes to the plant's ability to regenerate from almost any fragment.

PHOTO TIPS: Category 6

This plant often grows in rock crevices, making it highly photogenic. Compose the scene to include all the plant and as much of the rock background as the composition allows. Choose the smallest aperture on the lens to sharply render both flower and rock.

Soapwort *

Bouncing bet
Saponaria officinalis

> Pink Family   Caryophyllaceae
> May-October
> Perennial
> Frequent

SIMILAR SPECIES
See the *Phlox* genus on page 86.

A distinguishing feature of this plant is the soapy lather that forms when the bruised roots or leaves are placed in water. This lather has been used as far back as the Middle Ages by monks who believed its cleansing traits were sent by God. Early pioneers used the plant's lather as a substitute for soap, and it has been used to clean cloth in textile mills. Poison ivy, eczema, and other skin disorders were treated with poultices of the lather. Some chemicals have been isolated in the plant which are useful for the treatment of syphilis and jaundice; however, large doses may be toxic.

HABITAT AND RANGE
Fields, roadsides, wasteplaces; throughout—

DESCRIPTION
Pink or nearly white flowers grow in terminal clusters on the 1- to 2-foot, smooth, stout stem. Individual flowers have 5 reflexed petals that are notched at the tip. The opposite, clasping leaves are elliptic to lanceolate with 3 to 5 prominent veins. The stem is swollen where the leaves join.

PHOTO TIPS: Category   3

The best approach probably is to isolate several of the blossoms in a closeup composition. But don't decide upon a compostion until you look through the camera. It's hard to prejudge a closeup composition until you do. You may be pleasantly surprised by what you thought would be a dull composition.

*75-300mm lens,
5T diopter,
2 sec. at f/16*
Casstevens

ℋorse Nettle

Solanum carolinense

Nightshade Family   Solanaceae
May-July; August-September
Perennial
Common

75-300mm lens, 5T diopter, ¼ sec. at f/22   *Casstevens*

HABITAT AND RANGE
Roadsides, fields, wasteplaces; throughout—

DESCRIPTION
The star-shaped flowers are white to violet with 5 wide lobes. Protruding yellow anthers form a beak in the center of the flower. The branched stem (1 to 4 feet tall) and the rough, irregularly lobed leaves are prickly. The fruit is an orange or yellow berry.

RELATED SPECIES
Bittersweet nightshade, *S. dulcamara*, has flowers with 5 reflexed violet petals and yellow anthers that form a beak. It grows as a vine and has oval leaves with 2 small lobes at their base.

The highly toxic horse nettle and bittersweet nightshade come from the same family as tomatoes, potatoes, and eggplants. Horse nettle, which grows in grazing pastures, has frequently been associated with livestock poisoning. Cattle will not knowingly eat it, but it often gets mixed in with their hay. Prickles on the plant can cause painful wounds and should be avoided. The berries of horse nettle were once considered useful as an antispasmodic for the treatment of epilepsy.

PHOTO TIPS: Categories 2 and 3

We don't expect to see too many photographers plunge through a cow pasture at 6:00 A.M. to photograph horse nettle, but those who do will be rewarded with a surprisingly photogenic wildflower. Of course, shooting while it is still covered in morning dew makes it even better. Two pieces of advice: watch where you step, and look out for bulls! Trust us on this, folks.

Lyre-leaved Sage

Cancer weed
Salvia lyrata

> Mint Family   Lamiaceae
> Mid-April–May; May–July
> Perennial
> Common

HABITAT AND RANGE

Roadsides, paths and borders, meadows, wasteplaces; throughout—

DESCRIPTION

The blue-to-violet flowers grow in whorls on a hairy, 1- to 2-foot, square stem. Each flower is 1 inch long and has 2 lips, the upper lip being smaller than the lower lip. The leaves are usually lyre shaped, irregularly lobed, and grow in a basal rosette. The stem may have 1 or 2 pairs of small, oblong to ellip-tic leaves, but they are often absent.

SIMILAR AND RELATED SPECIES

Nettle-leaved sage, *S. urticifolia*, does not have basal leaves, but instead has paired stem leaves that are ovate and toothed. The smaller henbit, *Lamium amplexicaule*, a common weed of fields and wasteplaces, and with similar flowers, has paired leaves that are rounded and scalloped. Its flowers grow from the leaf axils intermittently up the stem. The lower leaves are on stalks, while the upper leaves are sessile and clasping. The flowers of purple dead nettle, *Lamium purpureum*, are mostly located towards the top of the stem. Its uppermost leaves are heart shaped with short stalks, and they are so crowded they overlap. See page 73 for the hedge nettles and page 68 for the skullcaps.

Lyre-leaved sage is a very common roadside herb that is frequently encountered by picnickers along the Blue Ridge Parkway and in the Smokies. It has lovely bluish purple flowers, and like most members of the mint family, it has a square stem.

The roots have been used as a folk remedy for cancer (thus the common name *cancer weed*). In the Appalachian Mountains, a tea is made from the leaves that is said to soothe stomach disorders.

> PHOTO TIPS: Category 3
>
> *If you see this wildflower along the roadsides, go ahead and shoot it. On several occasions, we've scouted a subject such as this one, only to return in better lighting and find it mowed down. Keep this in mind with all roadside species.*

75-300mm lens, 5T diopter, ¼ sec. at f/16   Adams

Speedwell

Gypsyweed
Veronica officinalis

Figwort Family   Scrophulariaceae
May-September
Perennial
Occasional

Roadsides, meadows, open woods; throughout—

DESCRIPTION
Small (¹/₈- to ¹/₂-inch) pale-blue-to-violet flowers, often striped with purple, grow in short racemes that stand erect from the prostrate, hairy stems. Each flower has 3 rounded petals and a lower petal that is narrower than the others. The hairy leaves are oval or elliptic, evenly toothed, and short stalked.

RELATED SPECIES
There are nearly a dozen species of *Veronica* found in the southern Appalachian region. Several are infrequent to rare, while some are quite common. Most are similar to speedwell and may be difficult to distinguish. It's best to consult a technical manual for exact identification.

Speedwell is one of those low-growing, inconspicuous plants that rarely gets noticed, even by wildflower enthusiasts. Even those who do notice it must look very closely to appreciate its delicate beauty. The species name means "of the shops," probably referring to the fact it has been sold for medicinal purposes. The plant contains a compound that may be toxic to grazing animals.

PHOTO TIPS: Category 2

Speedwell is so small that it requires a great deal of magnification to adequately portray it, so background clutter is not a problem. Often, 2 racemes grow closely together, and you should include both if possible. This helps to keep the image from appearing static, as it does with one narrow raceme in the middle of the frame.

105mm macro lens, 1 sec. at f/22
Adams

Lily-leaved Twayblade

Large twayblade
Liparis liliifolia (*L. lilifolia*)

Orchid Family	Orchidaceae
Mid-May–early July	
Perennial	
Scarce	

75-300mm lens, 5T diopter, 4 sec. at f/32   *Adams*

HABITAT AND RANGE
Rich woods and streambanks; throughout—

DESCRIPTION
The pale purple, 1-inch flowers grow in a loose cluster on the 2- to 10-inch stem. Quite delicate in appearance, the flowers have pale green, slender sepals; threadlike, downcurving purple petals; and a rounded, pale purple lip with pointed tips on the edge. A pair of shiny, broadly elliptical leaves with a prominent midrib clasp the base of the stem.

SIMILAR AND RELATED SPECIES
Yellow twayblade, *L. loeselii*, has very similar basal leaves and grows in the same habitat; but it is a smaller plant, with yellowish green or pale yellow flowers that have threadlike petals and sepals, and an oblong, downcurved lip. Appalachian twayblade, *Listera smallii*, has a pair of kidney-shaped leaves midway up the stem, and brownish green (sometimes yellowish green) flowers with a cleft lip. It is a dainty little plant, easily overlooked, that often grows in colonies under rhododendron—especially along stream banks. Southern twayblade, *Listera australis*, is a very rare plant that is similar in most aspects, including habitats, to Appalachian twayblade. It is distinguished by the lower lip of the greenish purple or reddish purple flower, which is deeply divided into 2 long prongs.

The orchid species listed here are not as showy and popular as some of the other orchids, but they are elegant nonetheless. You just have to look a little closer to appreciate them, as they are small and rather inconspicuous. In fact, most people probably never notice the Appalachian and southern twayblades, even though the former is sometimes frequent. However, none of these plants are so common that it is OK to dig them up. As with most other orchids, those that are dug will likely die—it is nearly impossible to duplicate the conditions required for their growth.

PHOTO TIPS: Categories 2 and 10

To make these inconspicuous orchids stand out in your photos you need a dark, contrasting background. You might try removing some of the dead leaves or pine needles to expose the darker soil. Just be extremely careful that you do not disturb the soil itself, and that you put the surrounding leaves back when finished.

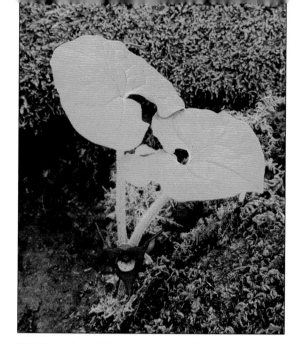

75-300mm lens, 5T diopter, 2 sec. at f/22   Adams

Asarum canadense

Birthwort Family   Aristolochiaceae
April-May
Perennial
Occasional

HABITAT AND RANGE
Rich woods; throughout—

DESCRIPTION
The most noticeable characteristic of this wild-flower is the pair of kidney-shaped or cordate, deciduous leaves. These leaves are 3 to 6 inches long and are covered with fine hairs. Look for the solitary flower at ground level, between the 2 leafstalks. It is a cup-shaped, brownish purple calyx with 3 pointed lobes. The roots taste and smell like ginger.

SIMILAR SPECIES
There are 4 species of heartleaf, or little brown jugs, *Hexastylis* (*Asarum*), that resemble wild ginger. They are distinguished from wild ginger by their leathery, smooth, dark, evergreen leaves. *H. shuttleworthii* (*A. shuttleworthii*), has large, 1- to 2-inch, urn-shaped flowers that are lined on the inside with raised ridges, and it has cordate leaves. *H. arifolia* has much smaller flowers than *H. shuttleworthii*. They are basically smooth on the inside, and the leaves are mostly triangular. *H. arifolia* var. *arifolia* (*A. arifolium*) has spreading flower lobes up to ¼ inch long. *H. arifolia* var. *ruthii* (*A. ruthii*) [see photo on page 41] has erect flower lobes less than ⅛ inch long. *H. heterophylla* (*A. virginicum*) also has a much smaller flower than *H. shuttleworthii*, but it is similar because its leaves are usually cordated and the inside of the flower is lined with an open network of low-relief ridges. Its flower lobes are up to ⅜ inch long. The flower of *H. virginica* (*A. virginicum*) is similar to *H. heterophylla*, except that it has a close network of high-relief ridges and its flower lobes are less than 3/16 inch long.

It will be all too easy to miss the flowers of wild ginger and heartleaf during a walk in the woods—they are hidden under the leaf litter of the forest floor. However, the leaves are quite distinctive and should enable you to easily locate all the species.

The leaves of wild ginger smell of ginger when crushed. The root, when cooked with sugar, has been used as substitute for ginger.

PHOTO TIPS: Category 2

To adequately portray both wild ginger and heartleaf, you'll want to include both the flowers and the leaves in the composition. This requires stopping the lens down as far as it will go to gain enough depth of field.

Puttyroot

Adam-and-Eve
Aplectrum hyemale

Orchid Family   Orchidaceae
May-June
Perennial
Occasional

HABITAT AND RANGE
Rich woods, swamps; throughout—

DESCRIPTION
The slender, leafless stem (1 to 2 feet high), holds a loose cluster of 8 to 20 flowers, each with 2 lips. The flowers are usually greenish purple, but may be yellow or white, tinged with purple. The lower lip is white with purple spots, wavy at the front edge, and has a small lobe on each side. A single, oval basal leaf, with conspicuous white veins, appears in the fall and withers before flowering.

SIMILAR SPECIES
Three species of coralroot, *Corallorrhiza maculata* (*Corallorhiza*), *C. odontorhiza*, and *C. wisteriana*, may be encountered. Each species has flowers similar to puttyroot, but they are distinguished by the lack of green color in the plants. *C. odontorhiza* has flowers that do not fully open. Also, these 3 species do not have the characteristic basal leaf of puttyroot. See a technical manual for specific distinctions.

Cranefly orchid, *Tipularia discolor*, is somewhat similar in most respects, but its basal leaf does not have the white veins and the underside is purple. Also, its flowers are smaller, more numerous, and in a longer, narrower column. The blooming season is different as well, with cranefly orchid blooming from July to September, long after puttyroot is finished.

Puttyroot is a rather inconspicuous herb, blending well with the woodland floor; thus, it is often overlooked. However, like all wildflowers, you only need to look closely to appreciate its beauty. Bend down and observe the delicate lower lip, and see how the purple edges blend into the green of the sepals and petals surrounding the tiny, open throat. Look for the lone leaf in winter, as its bright green color is a refreshing addition to winter's muted tones.

PHOTO TIPS: Category 2

The best approach is to shoot a profile of only the flowering portion of the plant. You can stake off the stem just out of view and keep it from blowing in all but the strongest winds. However, since you're shooting in a forest setting, background clutter becomes a major problem. Choose a plant and angle of view that has a long, open corridor behind it, which will keep the background as simple as possible. You need to shoot on an overcast day regardless of whether you choose an open corridor, as the lens's coverage is too much to use diffusers.

Puttyroot
75-300mm lens, 5T diopter, 1 sec. at f/11

Adams

Cranefly orchid
75-300mm lens, 5T diopter, ½ sec. at f/11

Casstevens

115

Wake Robin

Red trillium, stinking willie, stinking benjamin
Trillium erectum

> Lily Family   Liliaceae
> April-early June; July-August
> Perennial
> Occasional

HABITAT AND RANGE
Rich, moist woods; throughout—

DESCRIPTION
The flower has 3 green sepals and 3 maroon-to-dark-purple petals. The unpleasantly scented petals are lanceolate and 1 to 2 inches long. A whorl of 3 ovate or rhombic leaves grows beneath the flower, on the short, 6- to 20-inch-long stalk.

RELATED SPECIES
Wake robin exhibits a wide range of color forms, often making identification difficult. See page 220 for a discussion of the white form. Southern red trillium, *T. sulcatum*, has been recognized only recently as a distinct species from *T. erectum*. It is distinguished by its long pedicel and by its petals. The petals form a somewhat cup-shaped base and are only slightly longer than the sepals (*T. erectum* has spreading petals that are much longer than the sepals). *T. sulcatum* is an uncommon species, found primarily within the New River drainage. Sweet betsy, *T. cuneatum*, is also uncommon. It has sessile, maroon flowers with erect petals and sepals, mottled leaves, and a spicy odor. Toadshade, *T. sessile*, a rare species found in the northern portion of the southern Appalachians, is very similar to sweet betsy but with reflexed sepals. One of the largest and most spectacular of all Appalachian trilliums is Vasey's trillium, *T. vaseyi*, a species endemic to the southern Appalachians, mostly in the vicinity of the Smokies. It is very similar to southern nodding trillium (page 218) except that its petals are maroon (only rarely white). The petals of southern nodding trillium are usually white, but there is a form with dark purple or brown petals.

Imagine strolling through the woods and spotting a beautiful, deep maroon wildflower. You bend down to inhale its fragrance and flinch at the smell of rotten meat—that is how some people describe the odor of wake robin. Several plant species with maroon flowers, such as wake robin and skunk cabbage, make up for their lack of showiness by producing a foul odor that attracts carrion flies, who pollinate the plant. The foul odor may serve another useful purpose, though probably not an intentional one: it might keep people from picking it.

> PHOTO TIPS: Category   2
>
> *Wake robin is typical of many spring woodland flowers: to make the best photograph you have to kneel, sit, or lay on the ground. It looks much better shot from a ground-level perspective than from a few feet above. It's no coincidence that many nature photographers suffer from back pain.*

75-300mm lens, 5T diopter, 2 sec. at f/11

Adams

Skunk Cabbage

Polecat weed
Symplocarpus foetidus

> Arum Family   Araceae
> February-March; September
> Perennial
> Occasional

75-300mm lens, 5T diopter,
81A warming filter, 8 sec. at f/22   *Adams*

HABITAT AND RANGE

Bogs, swamps, wet meadows, very wet woods; northwest portion of North Carolina and northward. Rare to the south—

DESCRIPTION

The purple or reddish brown spathe wraps around and curves over a heavy, round spadix. The tiny flowers grow on the spadix. The large ovate-cordate leaves are ribbed, broad at the base, and appear after the flowers have bloomed. The plant has a foul, skunklike odor.

Mother Nature shows a sense of humor when the earliest wildflower to bloom gives off the foulest of odors. Skunk cabbage breaks through the ground before the snows melt, but it is uniquely adapted to cope with the cold conditions as the plant produces heat when the flowerbuds emerge. In addition to protecting the flower, the heat also makes the odor of the plant stronger, attracting the carrion flies and other insects that pollinate it. In turn, the carrion flies are often eaten by spiders who build webs over the opening of the spathe. It is likely that the heat, which can be a constant temperature of just over 70 degrees Fahrenheit, also provides a comfortable stopover for other species of insects.

The leaves appear after the flowers and persist throughout the summer. They are quite prominent in early spring before other foliage appears. If you want a good sampling of skunk cabbage odor, just break off a portion of a leaf and crush it in your hands.

Like its relative, jack-in-the-pulpit, skunk cabbage contains calcium oxalate crystals throughout the plant. The leaves and roots are edible only after thorough drying, and after you become so hungry you can ignore the odor.

A good place to see the plant is along the Blue Ridge Parkway in the vicinity of Mabry Mill and Rocky Knob.

> PHOTO TIPS: Categories 2 and 10
>
> *Skunk cabbage is easy to photograph while in flower, as it remains still in the strongest of winds. To make a unique image, locate an emerging plant in the snow, or return after a snowfall. The heat generated by the plant will melt the surrounding snow and provide a one-of-a-kind photo opportunity.*

75-300mm lens, 5T diopter, 1/8 sec. at f/22

Casstevens

Fire Pink

Catch fly
Silene virginica

Pink Family	Caryophyllaceae
April-July	
Perennial	
Frequent	

HABITAT AND RANGE
Rocky, open woods, roadsides, and hillsides; throughout—

DESCRIPTION
The crimson red flowers have yellow stamens and 5 narrow petals that are often deeply notched at the end. A sticky, tubular calyx is at the base of the flower. The opposite, lance-shaped leaves are mostly basal, though the slender, 1- to 2-foot stem does have a few leaves.

RELATED SPECIES
See the discussion of wild pink under creeping phlox, page 86.

Like most red flowers, hummingbirds are attracted to the blossom of fire pink. The red, star-shaped flower stands out boldly against the gray rocks and soil of the banks where it usually grows.

Most members of the pink family have variously notched petals at the tips, as if cut by pinking shears. The sticky calyx and sap from the stems provide the common name *catch fly*.

PHOTO TIPS: Category 3

Most photographers shoot a closeup of 1 or 2 flowers, and this is quite effective. It helps if the background is a little darker, as the bright red flowers stand out in stark contrast. Be sure to choose blossoms that are on roughly the same plane to maximize depth of field.

Cardinal Flower

Lobelia cardinalis

Harebell Family   Campanulaceae
Late July-September; September-October
Perennial
Occasional

PHOTO TIPS: Categories 3 and 7

You might think cardinal flower would be a prime candidate for trying out a Tiffen Enhancing Filter, considering that it is reputed to do a great job of enhancing red tones without unduly affecting other tones. This is only partly true. Yes, the filter does a very good job of enhancing reds, oranges, and russets, but it is at the expense of adding a magenta bias to other shades as well. Even if no other tones are present, such as in an extreme closeup of cardinal flower, using this filter often produces unbelievable, garish color. There is nothing at all wrong with using filters and films to enhance and saturate an existing color, but be careful about creating new tones when photographing wildflowers.

HABITAT AND RANGE

Lower altitude stream banks, ditches, swamps, and wet meadows; throughout—

DESCRIPTION

The vivid red, tubular flowers grow on an erect stem. Like all lobelias, cardinal flower has 2 prominent lips. The lower lip has 3 lobes, and the upper lip has 2 lobes. The stamens project through a division in the upper lip. Dark green leaves beneath the flower spike are tapered at both ends. Plants are usually 2 to 5 feet high.

One of the most popular and beloved of all our wildflower species, cardinal flower was named for its resemblance to the colors worn by cardinals of the Catholic Church. The brilliant red flower was one of the first plants sent back to France by the French colonists.

Cardinal flower is principally pollinated by hummingbirds. This is not surprising considering the bird's partiality to other red wildflowers such as columbine and Gray's lily, and the fact that hummingbirds are ideally adapted to navigate tubular flowers.

75-300mm lens, 5T diopter, 3 sec. at f/22   Adams

Indian Pink

Spigelia marilandica

> Logania Family   Loganiaceae
> Late May–mid-June; June-July
> Perennial
> Scarce

75-300mm lens, 5T diopter, 1 sec. at f/16   *Adams*

HABITAT AND RANGE
Rich woods, usually in association with limestone; southern portion of region—

DESCRIPTION
These unusual flowers occur in clusters of 2 to 12 at the end of the flower stem. The tubular corolla is red outside and yellow inside, and has 5 spreading lobes at the tip. The stamens and style project from inside the flower tube. Paired, sessile leaves are ovate and entire. The plant is 15 to 20 inches tall.

Indian pink is generally rare in the southern Appalachians and absent from the northern portion of the region. Interestingly, the plant was first discovered in Maryland in the 1690s by Hugh Jones. Jones apparently collected the entire Maryland population (a lesson in the need for restraint by botanists, as well as others), and it has not been found in the state since.

Half a century later, Alexander Garden, an avid collector of flora, studied the plant, which by then was well known for its importance in treating intestinal worms. Garden was certain that the plant had been incorrectly placed in the genus *Solanum* by Mark Catesby and in the genus *Lonicera* by Carl Linnaeus. Garden. sent a description and a discussion of the plant and its virtues to London physician John Huxham, who read the letter before the Royal Society. In 1767, Linnaeus acknowledged his mistake and named the plant *Spigelia marilandica*, the name it is known by today.

> PHOTO TIPS: Categories 3 and 10
>
> *This striking plant makes great closeups, especially if you can catch it at its peak. If you're too early, the lobes won't be fully opened, and if you're too late, the stamens and style might be missing.*

ee Balm

Oswego tea
Monarda didyma

Mint Family Lamiaceae
Late June-early September; September-October
Perennial
Frequent

HABITAT AND RANGE
Rich woods and streambanks; more or less throughout—

DESCRIPTION
The showy ragged flowerhead has numerous tubular, scarlet flowers and reddish bracts. The leaves are in pairs on a square, 2- to 3-foot stem. Bee balm often grows in dense colonies, and, as with most members of the mint family, the plant has a distinctive aroma.

RELATED SPECIES
See the listings and comments under wild bergamot, page 98.

Bee balm looks like Mother Nature's pin cushion, and it is a favorite of humans and hummingbirds alike. The name *Oswego tea* derives from a soothing hot drink that is made from the dried leaves and flowers. John Bartram learned of the tea while visiting the Oswego Indians near Lake Ontario. They used it to treat a number of ailments, including colds, fevers, stomach disorders, insomnia, and measles. Early colonists used the tea as a substitute for the English tea dumped into Boston Harbor.

> PHOTO TIPS: Categories 3 and 5
>
> *Along the roadsides of the Blue Ridge Parkway, bee balm often grows so densely that wide-angle lenses used up close are very effective. You can always shoot a closeup of just one flower, but choose the flower carefully. Try to find one that is comparatively tall and slender, as opposed to short and squatty. Also, shoot at an angle that places the leaves just under the flowerhead in a fore-and-aft position, not on the right and left of the frame. This approach lets you use the most magnification possible, resulting in an uncluttered, posterlike background. Use a vertical composition, which is more effective than a horizontal placement.*

75-300mm lens, 5T diopter, 1 sec. at f/22   Adams

50mm lens, ½ sec. at f/22

Adams

Gray's Lily

Bell lily
Lilium grayi

Lily Family   Liliaceae
Mid-June–July
Perennial
Scarce

HABITAT AND RANGE

Balds and meadows; limited to a few high-elevation areas of northwestern North Carolina, northeastern Tennessee, and southwestern Virginia—

DESCRIPTION

The nodding, 2½-inch, reddish orange flowers of this attractive lily are bell shaped. The sepals and petals of the flower have purple spots and are slightly flared. The flowers grow in groups of 1 to 12. The lance-shaped leaves are arranged in several whorls along the 2- to 5-foot stem.

RELATED SPECIES

Canada lily, *L. canadense*, has spotted, yellow or orange-red, nodding flowers. The sepals and petals of the flower are strongly flared, and the leaves are arranged in whorls. Plants with red flowers are separated into ssp. *editorum* (var. *editorum*). The purple-spotted, orange-red flowers of the beautiful and rare wood lily, *L. philadelphicum*, stand erect on a 1- to 2-foot flowerstalk.

Gray's lily, named for its discoverer—the eminent botanist Asa Gray—is considered by some to be the most beautiful lily, and one of the most beautiful wildflowers in all the southern Appalachians. Perhaps part of its appeal is that some of the locations where it grows are also beautiful, such as the high-elevation grassy balds and meadows along the North Carolina-Tennessee border. Unfortunately, its appeal also contributes to its decline, as ignorant people pick and dig the flower. Another threat is from livestock, who enjoy grazing it. Perhaps the greatest threat of all—indeed, the greatest threat to all flora—is habitat loss.

Tennessee lists Gray's lily and wood lily as endangered and Canada lily as threatened. Canada lily is threatened in South Carolina, Gray's lily is threatened in North Carolina, and wood lily is threatened in Kentucky. Gray's lily is a candidate for federal listing as endangered.

PHOTO TIPS: Category 10

Closeup shots of individual flowers are always effective, but other opportunities usually exist. On sunny days, shoot up at the flowers, using the blue sky as a background, or search out a plant in a landscape setting. On overcast days, you can also shoot wide-angle scenes using the flower in the foreground, but don't include any part of the sky in the composition. Remember to be extremely careful with the flower and the fragile environment in which it grows.

75-300mm lens, ½ sec. at f/22   Adams

(See additional photo on page 22.)

Turk's-cap Lily

Lilium superbum

Lily Family   Liliaceae
July-August
Perennial
Frequent

HABITAT AND RANGE

Moist meadows, borders, rocky seepage areas; throughout at higher elevations—

DESCRIPTION

This plant has conspicuous, nodding orange flowers with brown spots, and petals and sepals that curve backwards almost to the point of touching. The stamens have dark brown anthers, and the inside base of the sepals and petals has an obvious green zone in the shape of a star. The pointed, elliptic to lanceolate leaves are 3 to 7 inches long, smooth, and grow in whorls. The plant is 3 to 8 feet tall and supports up to 30 or more flowers.

RELATED SPECIES

Michaux's lily, *L. michauxii*, closely resembles Turk's-cap lily, but its flowers are smaller and fewer in number; and they lack the obvious green central coloring, though there may be a faint green area. The leaves of Michaux's lily are shorter and wider towards the rounded tip.

Turk's-cap is the largest and showiest lily in the southern Appalachians, and a favorite wildflower of nature lovers and photographers alike. When conditions are right, it has been reported to produce 40 to 50 blossoms on a single plant. Turk's-cap and Michaux's lily occur somewhat frequently in most

75-300mm lens, 5T diopter, ¼ sec. at f/16   Adams

of the region; however, Turk's-cap is on the endangered species list in Kentucky. A good place to see both is along the Blue Ridge Parkway, particularly towards the southern end.

PHOTO TIPS: Category 4

Turk's-cap lily is such a bold and imposing wildflower that it makes a good foreground subject for wide-angle scenes; that is, if you can find a plant in an interesting setting. Otherwise, you can always make a closeup of just one flower. One possibility is to shoot a portion of the plant from underneath, using the blue sky as a background.

When shooting closeups, it's important to have the pistil and some of the stamens in focus, even if parts of the petals and sepals are soft.

 Columbine

Rock bells, meetinghouses
Aquilegia canadensis

Crowfoot Family   Ranunculaceae
April–mid-July
Perennial
Frequent

HABITAT AND RANGE
Rocky or wooded slopes, roadsides; throughout—

DESCRIPTION
Nodding scarlet flowers (1 to 2 inches) with 5 long, curved spurs, a yellow center, and protruding stamens grow on very slender, 1- to 2-foot stems. The leaves have 2 to 3 leaflets that are divided into 3 segments.

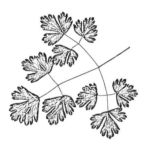

If anyone presents you with a bouquet of columbine, you should think twice before saying thanks. The wildflower is a symbol of unfaithfulness and deceit, and receiving it is considered an insult.

Aquilegia derives from Latin for "eagle," as the long spurs resemble an eagle's talons. The common name *columbine* is also from the Latin, *columbinus*, meaning "dovelike," although the flower looks nothing like a dove to us.

If you look closely at the flowers, you may see tiny holes in the spurs. These were made by bees who were unable to reach the nectar through the long tube, so they punched a hole in the spur to give them access. Hummingbirds, with their longer mouth parts, are better adapted to retrieve the nectar, pollinating the plant in the process.

PHOTO TIPS: Category 3

Columbine is ideal for including only one blossom in the composition. Be aware, however, that the flowers dangle in the slightest breeze. The flowers are somewhat translucent and photograph well in direct sun as long as the background is dark.

75-300mm lens, 5T diopter, $^1/_{15}$ sec. at f/22   Adams

75-300mm lens, 5T diopter, ¹/₈ sec. at f/22   *Adams*

Touch-me-not, snapweed
Impatiens capensis

Touch-Me-Not Family   Balsaminaceae
Mid-June–September; July–October
Annual
Common

Streambanks and moist, shady places; throughout—

DESCRIPTION
Orange blossoms with reddish brown spots hang at the end of long stems. Three petals surround the opening to a small, hollow tube made up of 1 of the sepals. This tube forms a curved spur at the back. The leaves are 2 to 5 inches long, oval, and toothed. The densely growing, shrublike plant grows to heights of 5 feet.

RELATED SPECIES
Pale touch-me-not, *I. pallida*, (see photo on page viii) is nearly identical but has yellow flowers.

When you see this flower in the early morning as it dangles like an earring covered with dew, you will understand why it is called jewelweed. The dew also beads up on the teeth of the leaves, sparkling like diamonds.

Following pollination, fruits take about a month to ripen, after which the slightest touch or breeze will cause the seedpod to burst, shooting the seeds several feet into the air.

The use of crushed jewelweed leaves and stem juices as a relief for poison ivy rash is a well-known folk remedy.

PHOTO TIPS: Category 5

You can isolate 1 or 2 blossoms and shoot a closeup, or use a wide-angle lens to capture a larger area. Either way works well, but you need to shoot on a very calm day, as the flowers dangle in the slightest breeze. Certainly, the best time to shoot is when the leaves are beaded in dew. Photographers who use spray bottles to create artificial dew will be frustrated—the leaves repel water like a freshly waxed car. Only real dew beads up on the leaf surface, but the slightest touch knocks it off.

Indian Paint Brush

Painted cup
Castilleja coccinea

75-300mm lens, 5T diopter, 2 sec. at f/22   *Adams*

Figwort Family	Scrophulariaceae

Mid-April–June; May–July
Annual or biennial
Occasional

HABITAT AND RANGE
Roadsides, meadows, woodland edges; throughout—

DESCRIPTION
Showy scarlet, red-tipped, tri-lobed bracts surround tubular, yellow-green flowers with 2 lips and 4 stamens. The basal leaves are entire, and the stem leaves have 3 to 5 deep lobes. The plant is 1 to 2 feet tall. Yellow plants occur rarely.

Most species of *Castilleja* are associated with midwestern and western states; however, this species lends its color to the southern Appalachians. Hummingbirds, as well as humans, enjoy this bright red wildflower. Unlike most species, the most colorful part of the plant is the bracts, not the petals. It may be partially parasitic upon certain plants.

The name comes from an Indian legend that tells of an Indian brave who was given colored paint brushes by the Great Spirit to paint the sunset. When the brave finished painting, he tossed the brushes aside, and Indian paint brush grew wherever a brush landed.

This species is rare to uncommon in Virginia, threatened in South Carolina, and endangered in Kentucky.

PHOTO TIPS: Category 3

Indian paint brush makes a good subject for early-morning backlighting. Remember to explore all angles of the subjects you photograph.

Lousewort

Wood betony
Pedicularis canadensis

Figwort Family   Scrophulariaceae
April-June; May-July
Perennial
Common

HABITAT AND RANGE
Open woods, roadsides; throughout—

DESCRIPTION
The flowers of lousewort may be yellow, red, or a combination of both colors. They are hooded, with a tri-lobed lower lip, and grow in a short, dense spike. The leaves are fernlike, deeply lobed, and arranged alternately. The 6- to 18-inch stem is densely hairy.

RELATED SPECIES
Swamp lousewort, *P. lanceolata*, is an uncommon inhabitant of wet environments. This species, which blooms in the fall, has yellow flowers and a mostly smooth stem that is 1 to 3 feet high. The mostly opposite leaves aren't as deeply lobed as in *P. canadensis*.

Although this herb is somewhat scruffy and unusual in appearance, it certainly doesn't deserve a name as undignified as lousewort. Apparently it comes from a misbelief that animals who graze the plant will soon be covered with lice. Wood betony is a kinder name.

Indians used the ground roots of lousewort as aphrodisiacs. Today it is used in the treatment of Bell's palsy, a disease that affects facial nerves.

PHOTO TIPS: Category 2

Lousewort, and similar flowers with cylindrical flowerheads, present a depth-of-field dilemma. It is impossible to achieve sharp focus on all the flowerhead, so what is the most important part to focus on? Typically, it is better for the blossoms that are projecting toward you to be slightly out of focus than for those on the right and left margins of the image to be blurry. A trick we use is to focus on the most important part—in this case the right and left sides of the flowerhead—then back off just a smidge toward the front. Remember, a lens renders more depth of field behind the point of focus than it does in front of it.

75-300mm lens, 5T diopter, ½ sec. at f/16   Adams

Butterfly Weed

Pleurisy root, chiggerweed
Asclepias tuberosa

> Milkweed Family   Asclepiadaceae
> May-August; August-October
> Perennial
> Frequent

75-300mm lens, 5T diopter, 1 sec. at f/16   *Adams*

HABITAT AND RANGE
Dry soil of roadsides and fields; throughout—

DESCRIPTION
Umbels of orange (rarely yellow or red) flowers grow on a 1- to 2-foot, hairy stem. The dark green leaves are lance shaped, 2 to 5 inches long, and grow alternately on the stem. The plant does not have a milky sap, as in most other milkweeds.

Visit this plant on a sunny day and you will surely see why it is called butterfly weed. Swallowtails, in particular, visit the flower in numbers. Seeing such a show makes you wonder why there are so few true orange flowers.

The common name *pleurisy root* comes from its use by Indians and pioneers to treat lung ailments. Like many other plants used for medicinal purposes, the root is poisonous if used in large amounts.

PHOTO TIPS: Category 3

Butterfly weed is highly photogenic, providing photographic opportunities in various lighting situations. Early-morning visits result in images of dew-covered flowers and insects, all in beautiful lighting. Visiting later in the day, especially on sunny days, provides the photographer with wonderful opportunities for shooting butterflies.

Yellow Fringed Orchid

Orange plume

Platanthera ciliaris (Habenaria ciliaris)

Orchid Family   Orchidaceae
July-September
Perennial
Occasional

HABITAT AND RANGE

Dry uplands, meadows, sandy woods; throughout—

DESCRIPTION

A 1- to 2-foot stem holds a cluster of orange-to-yellow-orange flowers. Each flower has a ½-inch-long, deeply fringed lower lip. A long, slender spur curves downward from the base, exceeding the length of the lip. The lower leaves are lance shaped and may be 12 inches long, while the upper leaves are much smaller.

RELATED SPECIES

The rare crested fringed orchid, *P. cristata* (*H. cristata*), is very similar. However, it has smaller flowers and much shorter spurs, and only a few narrow, pointed leaves.

Yellow fringed orchid is relatively common as orchids go, often growing in small colonies along roadways. As with many wildflower species, its true beauty can only be appreciated by close examination. The next time you spot a blur of orange while tooling down the highway in mid- to late summer, why not stop and investigate? You might be rewarded with a close look at one of the most charming of our native orchids.

75-300mm lens, 5T diopter, ½ sec. at f/16   *Adams*

Cresses and Mustards*

Mustard Family   Brassicaceae (Cruciferae)
Throughout the season
Annual, biennial, and perennial
Common

28mm lens, polarizing filter, ¼ sec. at f/22   *Adams*

HABITAT AND RANGE

Roadsides, wasteplaces, fields, disturbed sites; throughout—

DESCRIPTION

Numerous non-native, yellow-flowered (some have white or pink flowers) members of the mustard family grow throughout the southern Appalachian region. They are generally characterized by having 4 small petals and having slender seedpods that, in many species, angle upward. They usually have 6 stamens, with the 2 outer stamens being shorter than the inner 4. The leaves (especially basal) are often deeply dissected. Specific identification is sometimes difficult, but many species can be determined by consulting technical manuals.

Field mustard, *Brassica napus*, (pictured) is distinguished by its grayish green, somewhat succulent leaves that strongly clasp the stem. The leaves have a white coating and ear-shaped appendages (auriculate) at the base, and the tips often curl. It grows throughout the region, but is especially common in the northern portion, such as the northern half of Shenandoah National Park.

Most yellow members of the mustard family are considered troublesome weeds, but at least they add a splash of color to the otherwise bland fields and disturbed sites they prefer. Some species, such as the cresses, *Barbarea* spp., are gathered for cooked greens

or salads. The mustard family as a whole is important economically, providing vegetables like broccoli, cauliflower, and cabbage, as well as table mustard. Dyer's woad, *Isatis tinctoria*, found in Shenandoah National Park, is a member of the mustard family that was used to make an indigo dye.

PHOTO TIPS: Categories 5 and 9

Most photographers pass these wildflowers by without a second glance. Granted, they usually aren't photogenic, but sometimes they completely cover fields and make good wide-angle scenics. Perhaps the best approach in the southern Appalachians is to search out plants at the overlooks along the Blue Ridge Parkway and Skyline Drive, and use them as foregrounds in a landscape composition.

Goldenrod

Solidago spp.

> Sunflower Family   Asteraceae
> August-October
> Perennial
> Common to rare

75-300mm lens, 5T diopter, ¹/30 sec. at f/16   *Casstevens*

HABITAT AND RANGE

Practically all habitats except very wet areas; throughout—

DESCRIPTION

Goldenrods have alternate leaves and yellow, tuftlike, wandlike, or plumelike flowers. Species of the genus *Solidago* are perhaps the most difficult wild-flowers to identify, both for the layperson and the botanist. Roughly 3 dozen species occur in the southern Appalachians. While most of these species can be placed into crude categories based on general plant structure, it can be exceedingly difficult to further distinguish between them. Adequate classifica-tion is only possible after becoming very familiar with the genus and studying entire plants, including the root system. Contributing to the confusion is the fact that some species hybridize. Labeling all plants as *Solidago* sp. is sufficient.

During late summer and autumn, the goldenrods are the most common and familiar wildflowers of the southern Appalachians. They can be seen just about everywhere, sometimes in large masses. Unfortunately, this abundance makes many wildflower enthusiasts take them for granted. Insects and birds, however, know a good thing when they see it. Sev-

75-300mm lens, polarizing filter, ¹/₈ sec. at f/16   Adams

eral bird species eat the seeds, including goldfinches and juncos, and insects visit the plants in great abundance.

Several of these insects serve as pollinators, picking up the sticky pollen from one plant and transferring it to another. Because goldenrod is pollinated this way, as opposed to relying on wind-blown pollen, it does not cause hay fever, as is commonly believed. That distinction belongs to ragweed, a plant with inconspicuous greenish yellow flowers that bloom at the same time as goldenrod.

PHOTO TIPS: Categories 3, 4, 5, 7, and 9

The photographic possibilities are seemingly endless, limited only by your imagination and the particular species you photograph. However, one possibility holds true for almost all goldenrods: they make great subjects for insect photography. A favorite visitor of ours is the black-and-yellow, cross-striped locust borer beetle. The best time to photograph the beetles, and other insects on the flowers, is early morning, when the cool temperatures and dew prevent them from crawling around. See additional photo on page 8.

Rattlesnake Root

Tall white lettuce
Prenanthes altissima

Sunflower Family   Asteraceae
August-October
Biennial
Frequent

HABITAT AND RANGE
Dry (mainly oak) woods; throughout—

DESCRIPTION
This is a tall plant (3 to 7 feet) with clusters of nodding, greenish white or yellow, trumpet-shaped flowers with protruding styles. A series of short, smooth bracts tops a second series of longer bracts. The leaves vary in shape and may be triangular, heart shaped, lobed, or entire. A milky sap is present in the stems and leaves.

RELATED SPECIES
Lion's foot, *P. serpentaria*, has hairy bracts and the lower leaves are bluntly lobed. Gall-of-the-earth, *P. trifoliolata*, has pale-green-to-pink bracts, a reddish stem, and the lower leaves have 3 distinct segments.

136

White lettuce, *P. alba*, occurs infrequently and its smooth, purple stem has a white coating. The hairs beneath its bracts are cinnamon brown.

As the common name suggests, this plant was used by Indians as a treatment for rattlesnake bites. The descriptive genus name is from the Greek *prenes*, "drooping," and *anthe*, "flower."

PHOTO TIPS: Category 8
You won't find a situation that allows you to effectively include all of the plant, so look for closeup opportunities with a few individual flowers.

75-300mm lens, 5T diopter, ½ sec. at f/22   Adams

Wingstem

Verbesina alternifolia (Actinomeris alternifolia)

75-300mm lens, polarizing filter, ¼ sec. at f/22   *Adams*

Sunflower Family   Asteraceae
August-September
Perennial
Frequent

HABITAT AND RANGE

Woods, fields, and wasteplaces; throughout—

DESCRIPTION

This branching, 4- to 12-foot plant has an unkempt appearance. The many yellow flowerheads grow in a loose arrangement, and the few (2 to 8) rays are reflexed backward around the yellow disc center. The alternate, lance-shaped leaves flow into wings that run down the stem.

SIMILAR AND RELATED SPECIES

V. virginica var. *virginica* also has alternate leaves. However, the ray flowers are white in this species, and the flowerheads grow in a more compact arrangement. Crownbeard, *V. occidentalis*, has opposite, ovate leaves. It has fewer rays (1 to 5), and the flowers are more ragged and moplike in appearance. See the sneezeweeds, page 156.

PHOTO TIPS: Category 4

These plants have such a disheveled appearance that a moderate wide-angle image looks disorderly and lacks a point of view. Try backing up and using a telephoto lens to isolate a few flower clusters. Don't use a wider lens up close for the same image size because it will include too much background coverage. Of course, if you find a good landscape opportunity, a wide-angle lens works fine.

Golden Ragwort

Groundsel, squaw weed
Senecio aureus

Sunflower Family   Asteraceae
August-October
Perennial
Frequent

75-300mm lens, 5T diopter, 2 sec. at f/16

Adams

HABITAT AND RANGE
Meadows, pastures, wet woods; throughout—

DESCRIPTION
Numerous yellow flowerheads grow on a 1- to 3-foot, branching stem. The rays are sparsely scattered around the central disc. The long-stalked basal leaves are ovate, with a cordate base, and are often purple tinged beneath. The elliptic to lanceolate stem leaves are few and often pinnatifid.

Golden ragwort

Small's ragwort

Robbin's ragwort

RELATED SPECIES
Most species of ragwort have very similar flowers and are best differentiated by the basal leaves. Small's ragwort, *S. anonymus* (*S. smallii*), has elliptic to lance-shaped basal leaves which may be pinnately lobed and toothed. The stem is densely woolly near the base. It blooms a little later and prefers drier, open fields and meadows. Roundleaf ragwort, *S. obovatus*, has an ovate basal leaf. However, it is re-versed (obovate), with the widest portion located above the middle, and the lower portion tapering into a slender stalk. It is an uncommon resident of wooded slopes, especially those with basic soils. Robbins' ragwort, *S. schweinitzianus*, is a disjunct species from the Northeast. It is found only on a few high balds, where it can be quite conspicuous from late May into July. It is distinguished by its long, slender basal leaves that are 2 to 3½ times longer than wide.

The ragworts can often be seen growing in masses, filling meadows with a sea of gold. Most species are poisonous and may cause liver damage if consumed. Despite this fact, it was used by Indians to relieve the pain of childbirth.

PHOTO TIPS: Categories 3 and 9

Except in places where ragwort grows in large patches, a telephoto portrait works best. Be sure that the camera is at the same height as the flower when shooting portraits.

Butter and Eggs *

Yellow toadflax
Linaria vulgaris

Figwort Family	Scrophulariaceae
June-August	
Perennial	
Occasional	

HABITAT AND RANGE
Roadsides, fields, wasteplaces; throughout—

DESCRIPTION
Yellow flowers with an orange throat and thin spurs at the base grow in a crowded raceme. The numerous leaves are very slender, pointed at each end, and uniformly distributed on the 1- to 3-foot stems. The plant has a slight medicinal odor.

Butter and eggs is an Asian wildflower, first introduced into Europe, then America. It was used to produce a yellow dye until sources for commercial dyes improved. The leaves resemble flax, giving the plant its genus name—*linum* is Latin for "flax." If you squeeze a flower on both sides, it will open like a toad's mouth, thus the common name *toadflax*.

The orange and yellow colors make the flower very attractive to pollinators. Bumblebees are strong enough to push open the mouth of the flower and reach inside. In the process they pick up pollen from male flowers to transfer to female flowers. Other insects, like butterflies, have long mouth parts that reach through the opening, bypassing the pollen. They rob the plant of its nectar, providing no benefit in return.

Ointment from the flowers has been used for skin irritations and infections. Tea from the leaves was used as a diuretic and a laxative, and to treat jaundice and pinkeye. An insecticide was made by mixing the plant's juice with milk.

PHOTO TIPS: Category 7

With any shot of a raceme using moderate magnification, the depth of field is too shallow to keep all of each flower in focus. You must decide which part is most important. We usually try to keep any petal edges sharp that show on each side of the raceme, while letting flowers that project toward the camera go soft.

75-300mm lens, 5T diopter, ½ sec. at f/22   Casstevems

Whorled Loosestrife

Four-leaved loosestrife
Lysimachia quadrifolia

> Primrose Family   Primulaceae
> May-July
> Perennial
> Common

HABITAT AND RANGE
Dry or wet open woods and clearings, in full sun; throughout—

DESCRIPTION
Elliptic to lanceolate leaves and yellow, 5-petaled flowers with red-dotted centers grow in whorls of 3 to 6 on the 1- to 3-foot stem. The flowers are on long, slender stalks and occur singly in the leaf axils. The uppermost whorls may be without flowers. The leaves are sessile or on very short stalks.

RELATED SPECIES
The flowers and leaves of fringed loosestrife, *L. ciliata*, do not grow in whorls, and they have lightly fringed petals and leafstalks. Lance-leaved loosestrife, *L. lanceolata*, also has flowers and leaves that are not in whorls. The narrower leaves are lance shaped to linear. The flowers of swamp candles, *L. terrestris*, grow in a terminal spike, and the leaves are usually paired. It is a plant of wet meadows and swamps. Moneywort, *L. nummularia*, has very similar flowers, but it is a trailing vine with small, ovate, shiny, opposite leaves.

One version of the origin of the genus name *Lysimachia*, tells of Lysimachus, a king of ancient Sicily, who was chased by an angered bull. In a desperate attempt to pacify the animal, Lysimachus seized a member of the *Lysimachia* genus and waved it at the bull.

> PHOTO TIPS: Category 3
>
> *You will probably want to include all the flowers in the whorl, so background clutter is a real problem. Choose the plant and angle of view carefully.*

75-300mm lens, 5T diopter, ½ sec. at f/16   Adams

Smooth False Foxglove

Smooth gerardia

Aureolaria laevigata (*Gerardia laevigata*)

Figwort Family   Scrophulariaceae
July-September; September-October
Perennial
Common

75-300mm lens, 5T diopter, ¼ sec. at f/22   *Adams*

HABITAT AND RANGE

Woodlands, open areas, often under oak trees; throughout—

DESCRIPTION

Bright yellow, funnel-shaped flowers with 5 lobes grow in a leafy raceme on the smooth, green, 2- to 4-foot stem. Most of the lance-shaped leaves are entire, though the lower ones may be lobed.

SIMILAR AND RELATED SPECIES

A few other species of *Aureolaria* with similar yellow flowers grow in the southern Appalachians. Downy false foxglove, *A. virginica* (*G. virginica*), has downy hairs on the stem and leaves. The leaves are more deeply lobed than *A. laevigata*. Yellow false foxglove, *A. flava* (*G. flava*), has deeply lobed, smooth leaves, and a stem that is sometimes purple. Fern-leaved false foxglove, *A. pedicularia* (*G. pedicularia*), has fernlike leaves and sticky stems. This species has numerous varieties and may be indistinguishable from another species, *A. pectinata* (*G. pectinata*). Consult a technical manual.

Wild indigo, *Baptisia tinctoria* (*B. tinctoria* var. *crebra* and var. *projecta*) has yellow, pealike flowers; smooth, bluish green stems; and 3-part, cloverlike leaves that turn black when dried. Several similar *Agalinis* species with purple flowers also grow in the Appalachian region.

Smooth false foxglove and other members of the genus *Aureolaria* are partially parasitic upon the roots of certain oak trees, mainly white oaks.

PHOTO TIPS: Category   7

The flowers open from the bottom up on the rather long stem. Keep looking until you find one that has open flowers near the top in order to avoid a shot which crops the stem at the top and bottom of the frame.

Common Mullein *

Flannel leaf, velvet plant, Quaker rouge
Verbascum thapsus

Figwort Family	Scrophulariaceae
June-September	
Biennial	
Common	

Moth mullein
75-300mm lens, 5T diopter, ¹/8 sec. at f/16   Casstevens

HABITAT AND RANGE
Roadsides, fields, wasteplaces; throughout—

DESCRIPTION
Fragrant yellow flowers, with 5 lobes and 5 protruding stamens, grow sporadically on a thick, 2- to 6-foot stem. Large, woolly basal leaves form an obvious rosette. The stem leaves become progressively smaller up the stem, and the bases extend into wings down the stem (decurrent).

RELATED SPECIES
The uncommon *V. phlomoides*, clasping-leaved mullein, has darker, larger leaves, a more frequently branched stem, and larger flowers. Its leaves are not decurrent. *V. blattaria*, moth mullein, is much more slender with fewer leaves. Its flowers can be white or yellow, and are on loosely clustered racemes along the branching stems.

It is hard to miss this tall plant, as it stands along roadsides or in fields like a soldier at post. Perhaps this prominence has contributed to its many uses over time. Roman soldiers dipped the thick stalks in fat to make long-burning torches. In cold weather, peasants lined their shoes with the thick leaves. Quaker women used to make their cheeks red by rubbing them with mullein leaves, since their religion forbade the use of makeup. Mullein tea, made from the leaves or flowers, is a highly regarded folk remedy for coughs and congestion. The seeds are eaten by birds, and in winter the rosette of soft, velvety leaves makes a cozy home for many insects.

PHOTO TIPS: Categories 4 and 7

You can always shoot a closeup of the flowering spike alone, but this does not represent the plant well. Instead, try to find a plant that allows a wide-angle approach. Mullein is common along the Blue Ridge Parkway, and perhaps you could include the scenic highway or a backdrop of mountains in your photos.

28mm lens, polarizing filter, ¼ sec. at f/22   *Adams*

(See additional photo on page 44.)

Field Hawkweed*

King devil

Hieracium caespitosum (H. pratense)

Sunflower Family   Asteraceae
May–September
Perennial
Common

HABITAT AND RANGE

Fields, roadsides, sparse woodlands; throughout—

DESCRIPTION

Yellow, dandelion-like flowerheads grow in tight clusters, with 5 to 40 heads per plant. The stems, leaves, and bracts are covered with dense, blackish hairs. Stem leaves are usually absent; basal leaves are lance shaped. The plant grows 1 to 3 feet tall, often in large colonies.

SIMILAR AND RELATED SPECIES

Roughly a dozen species of *Hieracium* occur in the southern Appalachian region. Six species are listed below. Although they are all somewhat similar, most have distinguishing characteristics. Still, you may wish to consult a technical manual, or simply label all species as "hawkweed, *Hieracium* sp."

Like field hawkweed, rattlesnake weed, *H. venosum*, has no stem leaves, but it is easily distinguished by its prominent, purple-veined basal leaves. Rough hawkweed, *H. scabrum*, has elliptical stem leaves that get smaller as they ascend the rough, hairy, reddish stem. It usually has no basal leaves. Hairy hawkweed, *H. gronovii*, is slender with a flower cluster (con-

taining 40 to 100 blooms) that stretches from top to bottom along the plant. The leaves only grow on the lower half of the stem. Panicled hawkweed, *H. paniculatum*, is a hairless species with flowerheads that grow on stalks horizontal to the main stalk. Its stem is leafy, but there are few, if any, basal leaves. Orange hawkweed, *H. aurantiacum*, is the only species in our area with orange flowerheads. It is a common plant north and east of the southern Appalachians, but here it is scarce and unlikely to be encountered. Mouse ear hawkweed, *H. pilosella*, is only 10 inches tall, has no stem leaves, and bears a single (rarely 2 or 3) blossom. It often grows in very large colonies and is distinguished by its solitary flowerhead. Other hawkweeds have a few to several flowerheads.

Smooth hawk's beard, *Crepis capillaris*, is similar in most respects to the hawkweeds. It is distinguished

75-300mm lens, 5T diopter, ¼ sec. at f/16   Adams

Orange hawkweed
75-300mm lens, 6T diopter, ½ sec. at f/22
Casstevens

by its smooth stem, large basal leaves, and narrow upper leaves that clasp the stem with arrowlike lobes. Like many alien species, it was once rare in the region, but now is encountered rather frequently.

See the listings under dandelion, page 146.

Field hawkweed

Rattlesnake weed

Smooth hawk's beard

Hawkweed is another one of those prolific plants that many farmers call weeds. Cattle avoid eating it, so it can overrun pastureland in a short time. This is often the case when non-native plants are introduced. The hawkweeds were brought to America by doctors who used the plant to cure eye diseases. It was believed that hawks drank the plant's juices to improve their eyesight, thus the common name. This is certainly not true, and most likely the folk remedy is false as well.

In *Gray's Manual of Botany* (1950), Fernald, with witty sarcasm, suggested that technical specialists in Europe had eyesight "stimulated beyond that of the ancient hawks," referring to the seemingly absurd number of species, subspecies, varieties, and forms they attributed to the genus *Hieracium*. For example, mouse ear hawkweed, *H. pilosella*, was divided into 624 "subspecies."

PHOTO TIPS: Category 3

Some species, like mouse ear hawkweed, often provide great wide-angle opportunities. Usually, however, the best approach for hawkweeds is to shoot a tight closeup of the flowerheads.

75-300mm lens, 5T diopter, ½ sec. at f/22   *Adams*

*Dandelion**

Lion's tooth, puffball
Taraxacum officinale

Sunflower Family   Asteraceae
March-October; March-October
Perennial
Common

HABITAT AND RANGE

Roadsides, open fields, wasteplaces; throughout—

DESCRIPTION

Almost everyone recognizes this bright yellow,

multirayed wildflower. The plant has lobed, jagged-edged leaves that are 2 to 20 inches long, a hollow stem with milky sap, and reflexed outer bracts. The fluffy ball of white seeds that develops after pollination further distinguishes the species.

SIMILAR AND RELATED SPECIES

An infrequent relative, *T. laevigatum* (*T. erythrospermum*), red-seeded dandelion, has shorter leaves (2 to 7 inches) with deeper lobes, and bracts that are not reflexed. Coltsfoot, *Tussilago farfara*, grows to 18 inches and has a very similar flower; however, its leaves are heart shaped and appear after the flowers, and the stem has reddish, scalelike leaves. While it is more common in the northern region, it is steadily advancing southward and becoming common. Two species of yellow goat's beard, genus *Tragopogon*, have similar, but paler yellow, flowers and grow to 3 feet. *T. dubius* has grasslike leaves on a smooth, milky stem. Its distinctive pointed bracts extend beyond the rays. *T. pratensis* is similar, but its bracts do not extend beyond the rays. Four species of *Krigia*, dwarf dandelion, may be encountered. *K. biflora*, *K. dandelion*, *K. montana*, and *K. virginica* all have slender, milky, mostly smooth stems (with or without leaves) and basal rosettes of long, narrow, and variously lobed leaves. See a technical manual for exact distinctions. Cat's ear, *Hypochaeris radicata* (*Hypochoeris radicata*), has pale yellow flowerheads and a mostly smooth, often branched, milky stem with scale-like bracts. It has a basal rosette of dissected, densely hairy leaves.

See the hawkweeds on page 144.

Dandelion grows nearly everywhere in the world. Known to most people as a "weed" and the enemy

105mm macro lens, 1 sec. at f/32   *Adams*

of well-manicured lawns, the hardy perennial is highly adapted for survival. Its large taproot must be destroyed entirely to keep the plant from growing back. The leaves contribute to the plant's success by growing up and out, competing with nearby vegetation.

Young leaves, high in vitamins A and C, can be cooked or eaten raw as salad greens. Roots are roasted and ground as coffee, and the flowerheads are used to make wine. Tea made by steeping the leaves makes a good tonic for general health.

Dandelion is from the French meaning "the tooth of the lion," though there is some difference of opinion whether the "teeth" are the flowerheads or the jagged leaves. Any child can tell you why these flowers are called puffballs. For that matter, what adult hasn't occasionally tried to blow off the seed head in one breath, hoping to fulfill a wish?

PHOTO TIPS: Categories 1, 2, and 9 ☼

When the flowerhead grows close to the ground, an overhead vantage point is best, but if it is a few inches high you can shoot a near-ground-level portrait, producing a seldom-seen view of dandelion. Sometimes, the plant grows so dense and over such a large area that a wide-angle view is appropriate.

St. John's-wort

Hypericum spp.

St. John's-wort Family   Clusiaceae
June-September
Perennial
Common

75-300mm lens, 5T diopter, ¹/₁₅ sec. at f/11   Casstevens
(See additional photo on page 12.)

HABITAT AND RANGE

Roadsides, fields, open woods, balds, meadows; throughout—

DESCRIPTION

Many of the 20 or so species of *Hypericum* in the southern Appalachians are shrubs. The herbaceous members of the genus are characterized by bright yellow petals, and few-to-many stamens. Many species have leaves and petals with black or translucent dots, or a combination of both. The leaves are usually simple, entire, and opposite. Although several species have distinguishing characteristics, they may not always be obvious. Consult a technical manual for exact identification.

The yellow flowers of St. John's-wort are so bright they seem to have stolen their color directly from the sun. Blooming at the time of the summer solstice—the supposed birthday of St. John the Baptist—the flowers were often used in ceremonies to welcome the summer season. They have also been used to ward off evil spirits. Medicinally, the plant was used for both internal and external ailments. Two compounds in the plant show some antiviral qualities and have been considered in AIDS research. The plant also contains compounds that create photosensitivity in animals and some people.

PHOTO TIPS: Categories 3 and 6

These flowers often grow in clumps. You can isolate a single blossom against a background of out-of-focus blossoms, or include several flowers in the frame.

Sundrops

Oenothera fruticosa ssp. glauca (see below)

> Evening Primrose Family   Onagraceae
> May-July
> Perennial
> Frequent

75-300mm lens, 5T diopter, ¼ sec. at f/22   Adams

HABITAT AND RANGE
Meadows, open woods, roadsides; throughout—

DESCRIPTION
Typical of most members of the *Oenothera* genus, sundrops has 4 yellow petals and long, slender calyx tubes. The alternate leaves are elliptic to lanceolate, and the fruit is a small, glabrous (or with glandular hairs), obovoid, 4-winged capsule.

RELATED SPECIES
O. fruticosa ssp. *fruticosa* is differentiated by a fruit capsule that is widest above the middle and has mostly nonglandular hairs. However, if these distinctions are not enough for correct identification by the beginner, label all plants as *O. fruticosa*. Both species have many synonyms in *Gray's* under both *O. fruticosa* and *O. tetragona*.

The common evening primrose, *O. biennis*, is similar in most respects, except it has a longer, cylindrical seedpod that is not winged. Cut-leaved evening primrose, *O. laciniata*, has larger, deeply lobed leaves.

Several other species of both sundrops and evening primrose occur in the region, and they all may be difficult to distinguish. It's best to consult a technical manual for correct identification.

In general, the basic difference between sundrops and evening primrose is that sundrops opens only during sunshine, while evening primrose opens in the evening and through the night. This description may be relatively accurate, but you cannot use this as an identification factor as we've witnessed both blooming during most any time of day.

Regardless of the species or when it blooms, all are beautiful to look at and serve as food for several animals, including deer, rodents, goldfinches, and insects.

> PHOTO TIPS: Category 3
>
> *A straightforward portrait of one or two blossoms works best, but the plant often grows in a habitat suitable for a wider-angle view. Sundrops seems to photograph better than evening primrose.*

Maryland Golden Aster

Chrysopsis mariana (var. macradenia)

Sunflower Family   Asteraceae
July-October
Perennial
Common

75-300mm lens, 5T diopter, ¼ sec. at f/22   Adams

HABITAT AND RANGE

Old fields, woods, roadsides; throughout—

DESCRIPTION

A cluster of flowerheads, made up of a yellow center of disc flowers and yellow ray flowers that are narrower at each end, grow on a 1- to 2-foot stem. Young plants have fine, soft hairs on the stem. The leaves are oblong to lanceolate.

Maryland golden aster is not a true aster, but it is in the same family and has the same general characteristics. The genus name is derived from the Greek *chyrsos*, "gold," and *opsis*, "aspect," and obviously refers to the golden color of the flowers. The species name is Latin for "of Maryland." This name possibly refers to the site of the plant's discovery. It is a conspicuous plant in late summer.

PHOTO TIPS: Category   3

The flowerheads of Maryland golden aster are so densely clustered that it is difficult to separate one for a closeup. It's usually better to shoot a portrait of the entire cluster, along with part of the stem. Of course, you have to be very careful not to include a cluttered background.

Coreopsis

Tickseed

Coreopsis major (includes var. stellata)

Sunflower Family   Asteraceae
June-August
Perennial
Common

HABITAT AND RANGE
Dry, open woods, fields, and roadsides; throughout—

DESCRIPTION
The 1- to 2-inch flowerheads have approximately 8 unnotched, yellow rays, and yellow (sometimes red) disc flowers. The flowerheads grow on a 2- to 3-foot stem. The stalkless, paired leaves are each divided into 3 lance-shaped leaflets, so that there seems to be a whorl of 6 leaves. The stem and leaves are usually smooth but may be hairy. Previous treatments divided the smooth and hairy species into separate subspecies.

RELATED SPECIES
Lance-leaved coreopsis, *C. lanceolata* (var. *villosa*), blooms a little earlier than coreopsis. It has mostly basal, lance-shaped leaves with 1 or 2 lobes at the base, and flowerheads with 6 to 10 yellow rays that are lobed at the tip. *C. pubescens* var. *pubescens* is similar to lance-leaved coreopsis, but its leaves are usually located toward the top of the stem. The leaves are opposite and may be entire or have 3 (rarely more) lobes. The stem is usually pubescent, and the rays have lobes at the tip. It also blooms later in the year, usually during August. Tall coreopsis, *C. tripteris*, grows to 9 feet tall and has an anise-like odor. Its lower leaves are smooth, stalked, and divided into 3 to 5 entire leaflets. Garden coreopsis, *C. tinctoria*, has escaped from cultivation into the wild. It has a reddish brown color at the base of the rays.

A few other species occur in the region. All *Coreopsis* species are somewhat similar, and it's best to consult a technical manual for distinctions.

Coreopsis is an attractive and common wildflower, often mistaken for a sunflower. The genus name is from the Greek *coris*, "a bug," and *opsis*, "appearance," and it refers to the shape of the achene.

PHOTO TIPS: Category 5
Coreopsis is a very common roadside wildflower, so if you don't find a good opportunity at first, don't waste your film. Keep looking.

75-300mm lens, 5T diopter, 4 sec. at f/32   *Adams*

Sunflower

Helianthus spp.

Sunflower Family   Asteraceae
July-October
Perennial or annual
Frequent to rare

HABITAT AND RANGE
Open woods, roadsides, borders; throughout—

DESCRIPTION
Almost everyone recognizes the common culti-vated sunflower, but it is not so easy to identify the wild species. Generally, sunflowers have large, unlobed (but often toothed), rough leaves, a flat or slightly convex central disc, and numerous bright yellow rays (purple in a few species). While separat-ing the sunflowers from other similar genera such as *Bidens, Heliopsis, Rudbeckia, Silphium,* and *Coreopsis* is fairly easy, determining individual species may be difficult. Certain distinctions do exist that enable identification, but the beginner may have difficulty applying them, and they are beyond the scope of this book. See page 155 for a discussion of 2 sun-flower species, under black-eyed susan.

One common sunflowerlike species that is easily distinguished is large-flowered leafcup, *Smallanthus uvedalia* (*Polymnia uvedalia*), which has large, hairy, maplelike leaves that flow into small raised humps along the hollow stem.

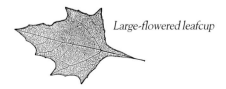
Large-flowered leafcup

75-300mm lens, 5T diopter, 1 sec. at f/16   Adams

The genus name of sunflower is from the Greek *helios,* "the sun," and *anthos,* "a flower." A popular tale is that the flowerhead of a sunflower always faces the sun, but this is not true. Nearly 2 dozen species grow throughout the southern Appalachians, as well as many sunflowerlike relatives. It may surprise you to learn the common garden sunflower does not grow naturally in the wild. It is the result of several hun-dred years of cultivation, beginning when the Plains Indians planted *H. annus,* a species native to that region. Occasionally *H. annus* has naturalized to the southern Appalachians.

PHOTO TIPS: Categories 4 and 5

Sunflowers make great subjects for the classic wide-angle closeup, as they often grow in dense patches. Even if you can't find a good patch, you can always shoot a closeup of 1 or 2 flowerheads.

Coneflower

Cutleaf coneflower, green-headed coneflower
Rudbeckia laciniata var. *humilis*

50mm lens, 5T diopter, $^1\!/_8$ sec. at f/16   *Adams*

> Sunflower Family   Asteraceae
> July-October
> Perennial
> Frequent

HABITAT AND RANGE

Moist woods, meadows, streambanks, roadside ditches, especially at higher elevations; throughout—

DESCRIPTION

The 2- to 4-inch flowerhead has 6 to 10 droopy yellow rays and a greenish yellow knob of disc flowers. The lower leaves may be divided into 1 or 2 pairs of broad, toothed lobes, while the upper leaves may be similar or mostly unlobed. The stem is smooth, branching, and grows 3 to 10 feet high.

RELATED SPECIES

R. laciniata var. *laciniata* is nearly identical except for lower leaves that are strongly divided into 3 to 7 irregularly lobed leaflets. The central cone distinguishes coneflower from most other species. See thin-leaved coneflower under black-eyed susan, page 155.

People often mistake coneflower for the well-known sunflower, or black-eyed susan. This is an easy mistake to make for those who identify wildflowers from an automobile. However, those who take the time to stop and closely examine the plant will discover a handsome wildflower, well deserving of individual recognition.

Coneflower-root tea was used by Indians for indigestion, and the young shoots were used as a spring potherb.

PHOTO TIPS: Category 5

Coneflower usually grows in such large, thick clumps that a wide-angle scenic is the only technique that effectively records it. If you want to photograph it at popular sites like Clingmans Dome parking lot in the Smokies, you better get there early in the day. By midmorning the parking lot is so full it's impossible to make a wide-angle photograph that doesn't include a vehicle. A better option is to travel north on the Blue Ridge Parkway to get away from the crowds.

Ox-eye

False sunflower
Heliopsis helianthoides

Sunflower Family   Asteraceae
May-October
Perennial
Frequent

PHOTO TIPS: Category 5

Where you find one ox-eye, there are usually many more, along with great opportunities for moderate and true wide-angle compositions. The biggest problem is dealing with the wind. The best thing to do, no matter how hard the wind is blowing, is to set up your camera and wait for a lull. It may take a few hours—as it did with the accompanying image—but that's all part of the nature-photography adventure.

HABITAT AND RANGE

Woods, meadows, streambanks; throughout—

DESCRIPTION

The 2-inch (sometimes larger) flowerheads have a cone-shaped yellow disc surrounded by 10 or more yellow ray flowers. At the base of each ray is a tiny forked pistil. The stalked, ovate leaves are toothed and arranged oppositely on the essentially smooth, 2- to 5-foot stem.

SIMILAR SPECIES

See black-eyed susan and coneflower on pages 155 and 153 respectively. True sunflowers, with which ox-eye is often mistaken, do not have the tiny forked pistils at the base of the rays.

By midsummer, the fields and roadsides are so covered with different kinds of yellow-rayed flowers that it might be tempting to lump them all into one category called "sunflowers." However, upon closer examination you will discover many unique and interesting species. Remember, you can't identify wildflowers from the car.

28mm lens, 4 sec. at f/22   *Adams*

Black-eyed Susan *

Coneflower
Rudbeckia hirta

Sunflower Family   Asteraceae
May-August
Perennial, biennial, or annual
Common

HABITAT AND RANGE
Roadsides, open fields, wasteplaces; throughout—

DESCRIPTION
The flowerhead consists of 10 to 20 yellow, daisylike, ray flowers surrounding a chocolate brown center of disc flowers—a form typical of the sunflower family. The bases of the rays are sometimes reddish purple. The stems are covered with bristles, as are the leaves, which are entire to slightly toothed. Plants grow 1 to 3 feet tall.

SIMILAR AND RELATED SPECIES
Many species are confused with black-eyed susan. The following 4 are the only similar ones that also have a dark central disc:

R. triloba var. *rupestris* (*R. triloba* var. *beadlei*), thin-leaved coneflower, is distinguished by the 3 lobes of some of its lower leaves, and flowers about half the size of black-eyed susan, with only 8 or so rays. It blooms from late July to October.

Two species of sunflower, genus *Helianthus*, may be mistaken for black-eyed susan. Narrow-leaved sunflower, *Helianthus angustifolius* (*H. angustifolius* var. *planifolius*) is hairy, but not bristly, and its leaves are very narrow and rigid. Though presently rare in the wild, it is now propagated as a major highway wildflower. *H. atrorubens* (*H. atrorubens* var. *alsodes*) is easily distinguished by its somewhat ovate leaves, much reduced upward on the stem.

See purple-headed sneezeweed, page 156.

Linnaeus, the "Prince of botany," named this wildflower for his mentor, Swedish botanist Olaf Rudbeck. The common name *black-eyed susan* refers to the dark-colored center, though it is more brown than black. If there was a Susan involved in its naming, we hope she was not as unfortunate as the name suggests. Coneflower is a name given to several wildflower species with obvious disc centers and daisylike ray flowers.

Black-eyed susan is a native North American species originating in the plains states. It was probably transferred to the East in grain shipments.

PHOTO TIPS: Category 5
Black-eyed susan tends to grow in dense clumps, making wide-angle lenses used up close a good choice. However, it also makes a good subject for isolating individual flowers, or unopened buds. As with several other "field" wildflowers, it is host to hoards of insects.

75-300mm lens, 5T diopter, 1 sec. at f/22   *Adams*

Purple-headed Sneezeweed

Helenium flexuosum (H. nudiflorum)

75-300mm lens, 5T diopter,
¼ sec. at f/22

Adams

Sunflower Family	Asteraceae
June-October	
Perennial	
Frequent	

Sneezeweed
75-300mm lens, 5T diopter,
¼ sec. at f/32

Casstevens

HABITAT AND RANGE

Wet meadows, swamps, and fields; throughout—

DESCRIPTION

The flowerhead of sneezeweed is made up of a purplish brown knob-shaped central disc surrounded by yellow, wedge-shaped drooping rays that have 2 notches at the tip. The lance-shaped or elliptic leaves have bases that run down along the stem (decurrent), causing it to look winged. Larger leaves may be toothed. The stem, which bears numerous flowerheads, is smooth, branching, and grows 1 to 3 feet tall.

RELATED SPECIES

Sneezeweed, *H. autumnale* var. *parviflorum*, has a yellow disc and grows from 2 to 6 feet high. Fine-leaved sneezeweed or bitterweed, *H. amarum* var. *amarum* (*H. tenuifolium*) is easily distinguished by its numerous needlelike leaves that are not decurrent. This plant leaves a distinct bitter taste on the hands upon handling.

Aaaachoo! God bless you! True to its name, the pollen and dried leaves of sneezeweed will make you sneeze. Indians made a snuff from the plant to clear nasal passages during head colds. The National Cancer Institute has revealed antitumor properties in its experiments with helanalin, a substance isolated from sneezeweed.

Fine-leaved sneezeweed has become a serious pest in places, especially where it may be mixed with livestock forage. When eaten by cows, the resulting milk has a bitter taste.

PHOTO TIPS: Category 3

Since purple-headed sneezeweed is a field flower, it makes a good subject for early morning insect-and-dew photography. Don't photograph the wildflower when it first emerges, though, because within a few weeks there will be many more plants to choose from, and they will have many more flowerheads than the one or two that first appear.

uttercup

Crazy weed, crowfoot
Ranunculus spp.

Crowfoot Family	Ranunculaceae
March-July	
Perennial	
Common	

HABITAT AND RANGE
Woodlands, meadows, roadsides, fields; throughout—

DESCRIPTION

Buttercup flowers usually have 5 shiny yellow petals, 3 to 5 sepals, and numerous bushy stamens. Most species have the same familiar leaf shape as shown above, though it varies in some. There are nearly 20 species in the southern Appalachians. A few of these species are easily distinguished, but most present real problems for identification. Without mastering the key system of the technical manuals, it may be best to treat this genus as a whole.

75-300mm lens, 5T diopter, $^1/15$ sec. at f/11   Adams

Buttercups are called "crazy weed" because it is said that if you hold one near your neck during a full moon you will become insane. Another old wives' tale says that if you hold the flower under your chin and your chin reflects yellow, it means you love butter.

Many species of buttercups are poisonous and may cause skin blisters. Beggars often used them to blister their feet to arouse sympathy. Grazing animals are also affected by the irritants, but the acrid flavor of the plant usually prevents them from eating too much.

Spectacular displays of some species occur in farm fields and along roadsides. In places, the ground is literally carpeted with the golden yellow flowers.

PHOTO TIPS: Categories 2 and 6

Buttercups make good subjects for artsy, soft-focus images. Compositions that isolate a few blossoms against a background of out-of-focus flowers work well. If you discover a field of the flowers and wish to use a wide-angle lens, remember that perspective changes as you change position. This means that the way the field looks from the road is not the way it will look from the edge of the field. To retain the look of yellow carpet, try backing up and using a long telephoto lens. This compresses the perspective and makes the flowers appear closer together.

75-300mm lens,
5T diopter, 2 sec. at f/22

Casstevens

Yellow Stargrass

Hypoxis hirsuta

Lily Family	Liliaceae
March-June; May-July	
Perennial	
Frequent	

HABITAT AND RANGE
Woodlands, meadows, streambanks; throughout—

DESCRIPTION
The yellow starlike flowers have 3 petals, 3 similar looking sepals, and 6 stamens. They grow in clusters of 1 to 9 on 2- to 6-inch flowerstalks. The long, hairy, grasslike leaves grow up to 10 inches long, rising above the flower clusters.

This perennial might be mistaken for a common grass until the yellow flower appears. Then, it becomes a distinctive wildflower that deserves close inspection.

PHOTO TIPS: Category 2

Yellow stargrass is just small enough to include the whole plant without creating background problems. If the background does appear cluttered, you can shoot a tight closeup of just the flower and immediate foliage.

Large Yellow Wood Sorrel

Sourgrass, sleeping beauty
Oxalis grandis

Wood Sorrel Family	Oxalidaceae
May-July	
Perennial	
Occasional	

HABITAT AND RANGE
Moist, rich woods; throughout—

DESCRIPTION
The bright yellow flowers of this species have 5 petals, 10 stamens, and are about 1 inch wide. The leaves have the typical shamrock shape of all *Oxalis* species, with 3 notched leaflets on each leaf. Each leaflet may be 1 to 2 inches wide and is edged with a narrow purple-to-maroon border. The plant grows 1 to 3 feet tall.

RELATED SPECIES
O. stricta, O. dillenii ssp. *filipes* (*O. filipes, O. florida*), and *O. dillenii* ssp. *dellenii* are smaller plants with flowers and leaves roughly half the size, and leaves that lack the purple border of *O. grandis*. A technical manual is needed to distinguish between these 3 species.

The leaves of all yellow wood sorrels are edible as salad greens, though they have a very sour, acrid flavor, accounting for the common name *sourgrass*. If you do eat them, be advised that the leaves contain oxalic acid, which is toxic in large quantities. The name *sleeping beauty* was given to the plant because the leaves and flowers close up at night.

PHOTO TIPS: Categories 1 and 6 ☼

No matter which Oxalis species you shoot, be sure to include the distinctive foliage in the photograph. The shamrock-shaped leaves complement the flowers well, and sometimes make suitable subjects by themselves.

75-300mm lens, 5T diopter, ½ sec. at f/16   *Casstevens*

Dwarf Cinquefoil

Five finger

Potentilla canadensis

Rose Family   Rosaceae
March-May; April-May
Perennial
Common

HABITAT AND RANGE
Fields, lawns, woodlands; throughout—

DESCRIPTION
This low-growing plant (2 to 6 inches) has yellow flowers with 5 petals and numerous stamens. The flowers grow in the leaf axils, on runners (up to 20 inches) close to the ground. The palmate leaves have 5 leaflets that are toothed only above the middle. The first flower of the season grows in the axil of the first fully developed leaf.

Rough-fruited cinquefoil

SIMILAR AND RELATED SPECIES
P. simplex, cinquefoil, is slightly larger, with wedge-shaped leaflets toothed over most of their length. Its first flower of the season grows in the axil of the second fully developed leaf. *P. recta*, rough-fruited cinquefoil, grows up to 3 feet on a leafy, hairy, and multibranched stem. Its leaves have 5 to 7 narrow, coarsely toothed leaflets. *P. norvegica*, rough cinquefoil, is similar to *P. recta* but has 3 leaflets. See the wild strawberries on page 222.

During the Middle Ages, cinquefoil was believed to have strong, or potent, medicinal value. Thus the name *Potentilla*. Some species contain tannin, which helps to stop bleeding and fight infection. The com-

105mm macro lens, 2 sec. at f/32   Casstevens

Rough-fruited cinquefoil 75-300mm lens, 5T diopter, ½ sec. at f/16

Adams

mon name *five finger* refers to the leaves, which have five leaflets in most species.

PHOTO TIPS: Category 1

Cinquefoil is everywhere, so don't be satisfied until you find an ideal situation—one that doesn't have a lot of ground clutter. Sometimes you'll get lucky and find it growing on a nice bed of moss.

160

Downy Yellow Violet, Smooth Yellow Violet

Viola pubescens var. *pubescens* and var. *leiocarpon*

> Violet Family   Violaceae
> April-May, sometimes later
> Perennial
> Frequent

HABITAT AND RANGE
Rich woods; throughout—

DESCRIPTION
The *Kartesz* taxonomic treatment has combined two previously separate species into the single *V. pubescens*, with 3 varieties. Variety *pubescens* (*V. pubescens*), downy yellow violet, has soft hairs that cover the stems and leaves, especially along the veins and margins. The stem leaves are broad with a cordate base and prominent veins. Occasionally there will be one basal leaf. The yellow flowers have purple veins on the lower 3 petals. Variety *leiocarpon* (*V. pensylvanica*), smooth yellow violet, is quite similar but is less hairy, has one or more basal leaves, and the leaves have fewer veins. The third variety, *peckii*, is apparently not found in our area.

Halberd-leaved violet   Round-leaved yellow violet

RELATED SPECIES
Round-leaved yellow violet, *V. rotundifolia*, is the only yellow violet in the region with flowers and leaves on separate stalks. The flower is similar, but the leaves are round, and they generally are not prominent until after flowering. In summer, long after flowering, the leaves tend to lie flat and close to the ground. Halberd-leaved violet, *V. hastata*, produces 2 or 3 arrow-shaped leaves. The backs of the yellow petals are purple tinged. Three-part-leaved violet, *V. tripartita*, an uncommon species, is the only yellow violet in our region with leaves that are deeply divided into 3 or more segments. All 3 of these species tend to bloom earlier in the year, begining in March.

The delicate violets are a favorite of almost every flower enthusiast, including Shakespeare, who frequently referred to them as a symbol of love and humility. Napoleon also favored the violets, promising to return from exile to France while they were in bloom.

Violets can be exceedingly difficult to properly identify as hybridization is frequent and the taxonomic treatment varies so much between texts.

> PHOTO TIPS: Category 6
>
> *Resist the urge to photograph the yellow violets when they first appear. Wait a few weeks and they will become more numerous, often growing in dense clumps that allow a wide-angle approach.*

75-300mm lens,
5T diopter,
1 sec. at f/22
Adams

Rugel's Indian Plantain

Rugel's ragwort
Rugelia nudicaulis

Sunflower Family	Asteraceae
July-August	
Perennial	
Rare	

75-300mm lens, 5T diopter, 2 sec. at f/22   *Adams*

HABITAT AND RANGE
Forest openings; higher elevations of the Smokies—

DESCRIPTION
Compact flowerheads of tan disc flowers (ray flowers are absent) nod on the 8-inch to 2-foot stem. The tips of the stigmas are split and curve in opposite directions. The long-stalked basal leaves are ovate and toothed; stem leaves are smaller and sessile.

Rugel's Indian plantain grows only in the higher elevations of the Smokies. There, it is quite common in openings in spruce-fir forests, especially along the Appalachian Trail and on Mount LeConte, where it forms an interesting and almost continuous ground cover beneath the spruce canopy.

PHOTO TIPS: Category 2

Most people photograph this plant because it is rare and endemic to the Smokies, not for its aesthetic virtues. If you are making such a representative image, you should try to include both flowers and foliage in the composition. Often, wide-angle landscape opportunities exist in which it can be incorporated as a foreground. If you can't find such a setting, you can always shoot a tight closeup of the flowers alone. Try to find 2 or more flowers on the same plane.

Large-flowered Bellwort
Uvularia grandiflora

> Lily Family   Liliaceae
> April-May; July-August
> Perennial
> Frequent

75-300mm lens,
5T diopter,
¼ sec. at f/16

Adams

HABITAT AND RANGE
Rich woods, especially limestone-rich soils; throughout—

DESCRIPTION
Droopy yellow flowers (usually 1 to each branching stem, rarely as many as 4) grow at the top of the stalk and are almost hidden by the leaves. The inside surface of the 1- to 2-inch petals and sepals has an orange stripe and is smooth. The underside of the oblong, veined leaves is lighter in color than the top side and is somewhat downy. The leaves appear to be pierced by the stem (perfoliate).

SIMILAR AND RELATED SPECIES
Three related species occur in the region. The inner surface of the solitary flower of *U. perfoliata*, perfoliate bellwort, is rough, with orange granules; the leaves are smooth underneath. The leaves of *U. puberula* (*U. pudica*), mountain bellwort, are shiny green on both sides; the leaves of *U. sessilifolia*, wild oats (see photo on page 24), have a dull surface, especially underneath. These two species have smaller, creamy yellow flowers that tend to flare outward, and sessile—not perfoliate—leaves.

Yellow mandarin, *Disporum lanuginosum* (see photo on page 25), also has yellow, drooping flowers, but it has elliptic to lanceolate leaves that closely resemble those of Solomon's seal, page 188. The stem

and underside of the leaves are downy, and the 2 (rarely 1 or 3) flowers are borne at the end of the branches directly opposite the last leaf. Its fruit is a bright red or orange, ellipsoid berry.

The early days of botanical study and exploration were filled with imaginative theories and unfounded statements, most of which were based upon religious beliefs rather than scientific truths. One such theory was the *Doctrine of Signatures*, which proposed that God had given a sign when part of a plant resembled part of a human body. These "signatures" designated the plant as a medicine to cure the human body part it resembled. Following this theory, bellwort was used to cure throat ailments since the flower looks like the uvula at the back of the throat. This is also how it got the genus name *Uvularia*.

> PHOTO TIPS: Category 3
>
> *Because of the way the stems and leaves are arranged, large-flowered and perfoliate bellwort do not work well when isolating a single blossom. A composition that includes a tight clump works best for these species. Mountain bellwort and wild oats, on the other hand, make great subjects for isolation images.*

Trout Lily

Dog tooth violet, yellow adder's tongue
Erythronium umbilicatum

Lily Family   Liliaceae
March-early May; April-May
Perennial
Occasional

75-300mm lens, ½ sec. at f/22   *Adams*

HABITAT AND RANGE
Rich, moist woods, streambanks, spruce-fir forests; throughout—

DESCRIPTION
Two brown-mottled or white-splotched green leaves grow at the base. The leaves are 3 to 8 inches long, elliptical in shape, and smooth on the edges. Purple or yellow stamens protrude from single yellow flowers, which nod on a 2- to 7-inch stem. The 3 petals and 3 sepals, which are strongly reflexed, usually have purple spots at their base. The flowers tend to close up at night and on cloudy days.

SIMILAR AND RELATED SPECIES
E. americanum is nearly identical, differentiated only by the presence of small, earlike appendages at the base of the petals, and the shape and orientation of the fruit. *E. albidum*, white trout lily, a rare plant of the southern Appalachians, has a white flower. See bluebead lily on page 165.

Trout lily is one of spring's first wildflowers, blooming in conjunction with the beginning of trout season—thus the common name. It has also been suggested that the mottled brown leaves resemble trout. The name *dog tooth violet* is misleading since the plant is in no way related to the violets. Perhaps the most fitting name is yellow adder's tongue. The nodding flowers do indeed resemble a viper poised to strike.

Gray's only lists *E. americanum*; *E. umbilicatum* was not considered a separate species at the time of its printing.

PHOTO TIPS: Category 6   ☼

Trout lily often grows so densely that it is difficult to isolate a single blossom without having others in the frame. You can shoot from above with a wide-angle lens and include many blossoms, but this doesn't represent the flowers well. Try a tight closeup of a single blossom isolated against a background of out-of-focus flowers.

Bluebead Lily

Clinton's lily, corn lily
Clintonia borealis

Lily Family   Liliaceae
May-June; August-September
Perennial
Occasional

HABITAT AND RANGE
High-elevation moist woods, heath balds, and especially spruce-fir forests; throughout—

DESCRIPTION
This wildflower has a small umbel of 4 to 8 greenish yellow flowers that nod on a leafless stalk. The 2 to 5 basal leaves are shiny, elliptic, and 4 to 16 inches long. The fruit is a dark blue berry.

SIMILAR AND RELATED SPECIES
See speckled wood lily on page 212 and trout lily on page 164.

Clintonia was named for DeWitt Clinton, a former governor of New York and a devoted naturalist. The species name, *borealis*, refers to the boreal forests in which it usually grows, although the southern Appalachian spruce-fir forests are not true boreal forests as are those further north. Indians used the plant for a number of ailments including infections, burns, diabetes, heart problems, and to ease the labor of childbirth. The roots do contain an anti-inflammatory agent, as well as one of the ingredients of progesterone, though it is not currently harvested from the plant. The edible leaves are said to taste like cucumbers.

Bluebead lily often grows profusely in suitable habitats, carpeting the forest floor with its shiny leaves. Sadly, though, the spruce-fir forests it prefers are among the most endangered natural communities in the Appalachians.

PHOTO TIPS: Category 2

The leaves of bluebead lily are more attractive than the flowers, and you should include as many of them as you can in the composition. With a little searching, you should be able to find several flowering stems growing close together amidst a dense tangle of leaves.

50mm lens, 4 sec. at f/22   *Adams*

Yellow Trillium

Trillium luteum

Lily Family   Liliaceae
April–May
Perennial
Frequent

75-300mm lens, 3 sec. at f/16   *Adams*
(See additional photo on page 25.)

HABITAT AND RANGE
Rich woods; southern portion of region—

DESCRIPTION
The sessile flower has 3 yellow, elliptic petals which stand erect, along with 3 greenish yellow sepals. The stamens are also greenish yellow. The 3 ovate, wide, sessile leaves grow in a whorl and are mottled with green or purple. There is a pleasant lemon fragrance to the plant, which grows 8 to 12 inches tall.

RELATED SPECIES
T. discolor also has sessile flowers but the petals are more rounded or spatulate in shape, have a cream-to-pale-yellow color, and the stamens are purple. It is restricted to the Savannah River drainage area. Yellow trillium may hybridize with sweet betsy, *T. cuneatum* (page 116), producing intermediate color forms.

Variety is something that is never lacking in trilliums. Although most species have a primary color for identification, variations occur in nearly all of them. Variations also occur in shape, reproductive parts, etc. Plus, some species hybridize with each other. This produces fodder for scientific debate as to just which species is a true species, and which is only a variety. This variety makes identification for the beginner especially difficult.

Yellow trillium is common in the lower elevations of the Smokies, particularly on the Tennessee side of the park.

PHOTO TIPS: Category 2

Yellow trillium often grows in small, dense patches that allow the use of a wide-angle lens. Also, the sessile, erect flower of this species makes a good subject for tight closeups.

Small Yellow Lady's Slipper

Cypripedium parviflorum (C. calceolus var. parviflorum)

Orchid Family	Orchidaceae
April-May	
Perennial	
Scarce	

HABITAT AND RANGE
Rich, wet woods, wooded slopes; throughout—

DESCRIPTION
The bottom yellow petal of this showy flower stretches out into a hollow, 1-inch pouch. The remaining petals are brown to purple, and spirally twisted. The leaves (3 to 5 per plant) are 2 to 4 inches wide, strongly veined, and grow alternately on the hairy stem.

RELATED SPECIES
C. pubescens (*C. calceolus* var. *pubescens*), large yellow lady's slipper, has a 1¼- to 2-inch pouch and yellow-green petals that are less twisted.

The orchid family is the largest plant family in the world, with more than 20,000 species. When one thinks of orchids, the tropics come to mind; indeed, most orchids do grow in tropical climates, but there are roughly two dozen genera that grow in the region encompassed by this book. As with most orchids, however, none of these genera grow in great abundance, and the continual loss of habitat where they do grow reduces their numbers even more. In areas where habitat is preserved, their beauty and rarity contribute to their loss, as misguided people dig them up in hopes of transplanting them. However, the specialized growing needs and mechanisms for reproduction make transplantation nearly impossible. Almost all orchids dug from the wild soon die.

75-300mm lens, 5T diopter, 1 sec. at f/22   Adams

Indian Cucumber Root

Cushat lily
Medeola virginiana

Lily Family   Liliaceae
May-June; September-October
Perennial
Frequent

75-300mm lens, 5T diopter, ½ sec. at f/16   *Adams*

HABITAT AND RANGE
Moist, rich woods; throughout—

DESCRIPTION
A whorl of 6 to 10 lance-shaped leaves surrounds the midpoint of the 1- to 3-foot stem. A second whorl of 3 (rarely more) leaves grows at the top. The greenish yellow flowers have reflexed sepals and petals, and reddish purple stamens. The flowers droop under the top whorl of leaves. Plants with only one whorl of leaves have no flowers.

SIMILAR SPECIES
Starflower, *Trientalis borealis*, has 2 star-shaped flowers just above a whorl of 5 to 9 lance-shaped leaves. It is an infrequent species found mostly in the northern end of the range.

Large whorled pogonia, *Isotria verticillata* (see photo on page viii), has somewhat similar foliage, but with only 5 whorled leaves at the summit of the purplish brown stem. This uncommon orchid of rich woods and streambanks grows throughout the range. It flowers from April into July.

See the loosestrifes on page 140.

Indian cucumber root is as beautiful in fruit as it is in flower. In autumn, the bases of the upper leaves become crimson red, and the stem straightens to support a cluster of dark purple berries. The berries are not edible, but as the common name suggests, the root is safe to eat and has a cucumberlike flavor. Interestingly, Indians also used the chewed root for fish bait.

> PHOTO TIPS: Category 3
>
> *If the background is not distracting, you might try including both whorls of leaves in the composition, or at least part of the bottom whorl. If the background is distracting, you can shoot a tight closeup of just the flower and part of the upper leaves. Be sure to return in the fall and photograph the plant in fruit.*

quawroot

Cancer root, bear corn
Conopholis americana

Broomrape Family	Orobanchaceae
March-June	
Perennial	
Frequent	

75-300mm lens, 5T diopter, 8 sec. at f/32   Adams

HABITAT AND RANGE

Dry woods, usually under oak trees; throughout—

DESCRIPTION

This unusual wildflower looks more like a pine cone than a flower. The fleshy, yellowish brown plant is 3 to 10 inches tall and covered with overlapping scales. Numerous yellow flowers grow along the spike, each with obvious protruding stamens. It usually grows in small, dense clumps.

Persons not familiar with squawroot are often surprised to learn that it is actually a wildflower, and not some type of fungi. The plant lacks the chlorophyll that gives most plants their green color and harnesses the sun's energy for food. To obtain food, squawroot grows as a parasite upon the roots of trees, mainly oaks.

Upon emergence from their winter dormancy, black bears make a tasty meal of squawroot, as it is one of the more succulent of plant species to appear early.

PHOTO TIPS: Category 2

Squawroot seems tailor-made for photography. It doesn't move, even in the strongest winds, and it makes good closeup images. It also does well in compositions that include the entire plant in a bed of oak leaves. Stop the lens down as far as it will go for maximum depth of field.

Plantain-leaved Pussy Toes

Ladies' tobacco
Antennaria plantaginifolia

Sunflower Family	Asteraceae
March-May	
Perennial	
Frequent	

HABITAT AND RANGE
Dry woods, roadbanks, fields; throughout—

DESCRIPTION
The fuzzy, white flowers of plantain-leaved pussy toes grow in small, tightly clustered flowerheads. Male (staminate) and female (pistillate) flowers grow on separate plants. Male flowers are smaller, brighter, and have brown dots of pollen on the flowerheads. Female flowers are silkier and may have a pink tint. The leaves are mostly basal, spatulate, woolly on the top surface, and have 3 to 7 (usually 3) prominent veins. A few small lanceolate leaves occur on the 3- to 18-inch stem. It often grows in large colonies.

RELATED SPECIES
Smooth pussy toes, *A. parlinii*, has mostly smooth basal leaves. Field pussy toes, *A. neglecta*, is usually smaller and has narrower basal leaves. Each basal leaf has 1 main vein, or 3 obscure veins. Smaller pussy toes, *A. howellii* ssp. *petaloidea* (*A. neodioica*), is an extremely variable species that also has basal leaves with only 1 main vein. It is best to consult the technical manuals for proper identification of it and the other species of pussy toes. Solitary pussy toes, *A. solitaria*, is the only species that produces only one flowerhead.

This herb—with flowers as soft as a kitten's paws—is intriguing. The plant produces a growth inhibitor that prevents other plants from growing nearby. This ensures that it will get its share of water and nutrients. The growth inhibitor doesn't keep away the insects though; the American painted lady butterfly lays her eggs on the underside of the leaves.

PHOTO TIPS: Category 2, sometimes 9

Pussy toes are more photogenic and interesting in fruit than in flower.

75-300mm lens, 5T diopter, ½ sec. at f/22   Casstevens

Pale Indian Plantain

Arnoglossum atriplicifolium (Cacalia atriplicifolia)

> Sunflower Family   Asteraceae
> July-September
> Perennial
> Occasional

75-300mm lens, 5T diopter, ½ sec. at f/22   Casstevens

HABITAT AND RANGE
Woods and pastures; throughout—

DESCRIPTION
This 3- to 6-foot plant has flat-topped clusters of small flowerheads. Each flowerhead contains 5 or more white or yellowish green flowers with 5 lobes and stiff bracts. The stem and underside of the leaves have a waxy, white coating. The leaves, which become larger at the base of the stem, are irregularly lobed, or toothed.

SIMILAR AND RELATED SPECIES
Great Indian plantain, *A. muehlenbergii* (*C. muhlenbergii*), grows to 9 feet high, lacks the white coating, and has rounder, toothed leaves. Its purplish brown stem is angled and grooved. Sweet-scented plantain, *Synosma suaveolens* (*C. suaveolens*), also lacks the white coating. It has sharply toothed, arrow-shaped leaves.

Pale Indian plantain is one of those herbs that mostly goes unnoticed. From a distance, the flower is unremarkable, but those who take the time for a closer look will be rewarded with an interesting sight. It is relatively common along the Blue Ridge Parkway and Skyline Drive.

> PHOTO TIPS: Category 4
>
> *Unlike most flowers that grow this tall, the best approach with pale Indian plantain is usually a closeup composition. This reveals detail in the flowers and helps to reduce background clutter problems. Try to find a low-growing plant and use a stem stake to prevent some of the wind movement.*

28mm lens,
polarizing filter,
¼ sec. at f/22
Adams

Goat's Beard

Aruncus dioicus

Rose Family   Rosaceae
May-June; June-September
Perennial
Frequent

HABITAT AND RANGE
Rich, moist woods, roadsides; throughout—

DESCRIPTION
Large clusters of branching spikes with small, densely crowded, creamy white flowers top this stately 3- to 7-foot plant. Individual flowers have 5 petals, 15 to 20 stamens, and 3 or 4 pistils. The male and female flowers are on separate plants; female flowers are slightly smaller, with shorter, sterile stamens. The leaves are compounded 2 or 3 times with ovate, pointed, toothed leaflets.

SIMILAR SPECIES
False goat's beard, *Astilbe biternata*, is nearly identical; however, its flowers have only 10 stamens and 2 pistils, and the terminal leaflet usually has 3 lobes.

Both the common and genus names of goat's beard refer to the shape of the flowers, which supposedly resemble a goat's beard. The species name indicates that the plant is dioecious, meaning the male and female flowers grow on separate plants. The Indians used a poultice made from the roots of the plant for bee stings.

PHOTO TIPS: Category 8

Bees and other insects frequent goat's beard and keep it in a constant state of motion, producing blurred images when shooting tight closeups. However, if you back up a little with a wide-angle lens the movement is not as noticeable.

172

Tall Meadow Rue

Thalictrum pubescens (T. polygamum)

Crowfoot Family   Ranunculaceae
May–July
Perennial
Frequent

75-300mm lens, 5T diopter, ¹/₈ sec. at f/16   Adams

HABITAT AND RANGE

Rich woods and meadows; throughout—

DESCRIPTION

This is a tall (3- to 10-foot) plant with branching clusters of greenish white flowers. Although the flowers have no petals, they make up for it with a showy tassel of several club-shaped stamens. The leaves are light green, divided, and subdivided into oval leaflets with 3 lobes.

SIMILAR AND RELATED SPECIES

Early meadow rue, *T. dioicum* (see photo on page 45), which has male and female flowers on separate plants, blooms from March to April. The male flowers have showy, drooping stamens and 4 to 5 greenish white or purple-tinged sepals. Female plants are less showy, with a few purple pistils. Skunk meadow rue, *T. revolutum*, is similar to early meadow rue, but beneath the dark green leaves are waxy glands that have a skunklike odor when disturbed.

Blue cohosh, *Caulophyllum thalictroides* (see photo on page 16), has very similar leaves (the species name reflects this), but its flowers are dissimilar. They are greenish yellow to purplish brown, and have 6 pointed sepals and 6 smaller petals. Young plants are covered in a white, waxy coating. It grows in rich woods and blooms in April and May.

See tassel rue, page 179.

The species name for tall meadow rue found in *Gray's* indicates that it is polygamous, meaning flowers of an individual plant can have either stamens (a male, or staminate flower) or pistils (a female, or pistillate flower), or both. Conversely, the species name of early meadow rue indicates that it is dioecious, meaning that an individual plant has either male flowers or female flowers, but not both.

> **PHOTO TIPS: Category 8**
>
> *This is a tough one. Probably the best approach is to shoot a closeup of only a small section of the flower. Otherwise, background distractions become a big problem. We have yet to see a good situation for shooting a wide-angle scene of tall or early meadow rue, but the situation probably does exist.*

Queen Anne's Lace *

Wild carrot, bird's nest
Daucus carota

> Carrot Family   Apiaceae
> May-September; June-October
> Biennial
> Common

Scientists developed our familiar garden carrot from a subspecies of Queen Anne's lace.

> PHOTO TIPS: Categories 4 and 9
>
> *Queen Anne's lace sometimes grows profusely in abandoned fields, providing good wide-angle opportunities. In almost all situations, however, you can shoot a closeup up of just the flowerhead. The best time is early morning while the flower, and any insects that spent the night on it, are still covered in dew.*

HABITAT AND RANGE
Roadsides, fields, wasteplaces; throughout—

DESCRIPTION
The lacy flowerhead is made up of numerous, small white flowers (the central flower is often purple) in a tight, round umbel that is 3 to 4 inches wide. The bracts are thin and deeply lobed, and the 2- to 3-foot stem is hairy with finely divided alternate leaves that resemble parsley.

SIMILAR SPECIES
See the listings under cow parsnip, page 175.

A popular story about the origin of the name of Queen Anne's lace is that Anne, Queen of England, held a contest with her attendants to see who could make lace as beautiful as the white flower growing in her garden. During the lace tatting, she pricked her finger, and the resulting drop of her blood is said to be the dark center floret. However, this story is not true. The name actually refers to Anne of Denmark, wife of James I, who loved fine clothes and lace. The name *bird's nest* is used because, after fruiting, the umbel becomes concave as it dries, resembling a bird's nest.

75-300mm lens, 5T diopter, $^1/_{15}$ sec. at f/11   Adams

Cow Parsnip

Masterwort

Heracleum maximum

> Carrot Family   Apiaceae
> Late May-July; July-August
> Perennial
> Frequent

HABITAT AND RANGE

Moist ground of roadsides, meadows, streambanks, mostly at high elevations; throughout—

DESCRIPTION

This plant is big! The flowerhead is an umbel, 4 to 8 inches wide, with white flowers (sometimes tinged with purple). The flowerhead grows atop a 4- to 10-foot, thick, stout, woolly stem. The petals are of unequal size. Smaller petals are notched; larger petals are deeply lobed. The leaves, up to 12 inches wide, are divided into 3 lobed leaflets and resemble maple leaves. The leaf sheath is greatly enlarged and clasps the stem. There is a pungent odor when parts of the plant are crushed.

SIMILAR SPECIES

Hairy angelica, *Angelica venenosa*, has a much smaller flowerhead (2 to 4 inches wide) that is covered with dense hairs, as is the upper stem. Like cow parsnip, it has inflated leaf sheaths, but the leaf segments are elliptic to lanceolate and the stem is much thinner. It grows 2 to 6 feet high, usually at mid-to-low elevations. Filmy angelica, *A. triquinata*, lacks the dense hairs of hairy angelica and usually grows in high-elevation openings, balds, and thickets.

Water hemlock, *Cicuta maculata* (see photo on page 22), is a smaller, thinner-stemmed plant, with flowers in a looser arrangement. It too has inflated leaf sheaths, but both stem and leaves are smooth.

The stem is purplish brown. The plant grows in swamps and on stream banks, usually at lower elevations.

Poison hemlock, *Conium maculatum*, has finely divided, fernlike leaves and a hollow, purple-spotted stem. The stem usually grows 2 to 6 feet tall, although it occasionally reaches much taller heights. It is not as common as the other species and is limited to the northern portion.

Cow parsnip's root contains psoralen, a substance that is currently being studied for treatment of psoriasis, leukemia, and AIDS. Folk remedies used the root to treat gas and indigestion. However, livestock have been poisoned from eating the root.

Water hemlock and poison hemlock are both extremely poisonous to livestock and humans, and should not be handled. The species name of hairy angelica implies that it, too, is poisonous, but that is not the case.

> PHOTO TIPS: Category 4
>
> *All the plants mentioned above are so large they require a wide-angle lens to adequately portray them. Fortunately, they often grow in settings ideally suited for these lenses, such as grassy balds and open meadows. Visit at sunrise and sunset to get the best lighting, and use the flowers as a foreground in a landscape composition.*

35-70mm lens,
½ sec. at f/32

Casstevens

Silverrod

White goldenrod
Solidago bicolor

Sunflower Family   Asteraceae
September-October
Perennial
Frequent

75-300mm lens,
5T diopter,
¼ sec. at f/22

Adams

HABITAT AND RANGE
Roadsides and woodlands; throughout—

DESCRIPTION
A slender, erect, branched or spikelike panicle of white flowerheads in tight clusters tops this 1- to 3-foot herb. Each flowerhead has tiny disc flowers surrounded by 7 to 9 rays. The elliptical leaves have soft hairs on the top and bottom sides, though the hairs are sparser on top. Lower leaves are slightly toothed, while the upper leaves are entire.

RELATED SPECIES
See the yellow goldenrods on page 134.

Of the three dozen or so species of *Solidago* (goldenrod) in the southern Appalachians, silverrod is the only white-colored species, making identification easy. A good place to see it is the high-elevation, open roadsides of the Blue Ridge Parkway.

PHOTO TIPS: Categories 3 and 5

Silverrod tends to grow in high-elevation open areas, which makes it susceptible to the seemingly constant winds. You should plan to shoot the plant early in the morning before the winds pick up. This gives the added benefit of having dew on the flower.

White Snakeroot

Ageratina altissima var. *roanensis*
(*Eupatorium rugosum* var. *roanensis*)

Sunflower Family   Asteraceae
July-October
Perennial
Common

HABITAT AND RANGE
Rich woods, especially higher elevations; throughout—

DESCRIPTION
The flowers are in flat-topped, fuzzy, white clusters atop tall (1- to 5-foot), branching stems. The paired leaves are ovate to heart shaped, dull on the top, and have stalks that are usually longer than ¾ inch.

75-300mm lens, 5T diopter, ¼ sec. at f/16   Adams

SIMILAR AND RELATED SPECIES

Smaller white snakeroot, *A. aromatica* var. *incisa* (*E. aromaticum* var. *incisum*), is a smaller version of snakeroot with tinier leaves (shiny on top) on stalks that are usually less than ¾ inch. It also has fewer flowers per flowerhead. Despite its Latin name, it is not aromatic.

The next 2 wildflowers are similar in general appearance to snakeroot. Boneset, *Eupatorium perfoliatum*, has wrinkly, paired, lanceolate leaves. The leaves are so distinctively pierced (perfoliate) by the hairy stem that they appear as a single leaf.

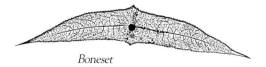

Boneset

Upland boneset, *E. sessilifolium*, has sessile, lance-shaped, finely toothed leaves on a smooth stem. They are not perfoliate.

Wild quinine, *Parthenium integrefolium* var. *integrefolium*, somewhat resembles snakeroot and boneset. It has ¼-inch-wide, white flowers that look like they aren't fully opened. The leaves have a rough, leathery appearance. Its basal leaves have long stalks and rounded teeth, while the upper stem leaves are sessile and have sharper teeth. The stem and leaves have short, appressed hairs. *P. integrefolium* var. *hispidum* (*P. hispidum*) is nearly identical but with long, spreading hairs.

Several other similar and related species occur in the region with varying frequency. Consult a technical manual for exact identification.

The white, fuzzy flowerheads of white snakeroot join the goldenrods and asters in decorating roadsides and woodland margins from midsummer to frost. It is rather abundant along sections of Skyline Drive and the Blue Ridge Parkway, particularly the high-elevation vicinities of Mount Mitchell, Richland Balsam, and Waterrock Knob.

This is another wildflower the Indians used to treat snakebites. Also, the pungent smoke released from burning the plant was used like "smelling salt" to stimulate unconscious persons.

An ailment called "milk sickness," characterized by extreme nausea, may occur in humans who drink the milk of cows who have eaten white snakeroot.

PHOTO TIPS: Category 4

If you shoot too close up, the resulting image will be indistinguishable from any of the dozen or so similar wildflowers. It's better to back up a little and show an entire flowerhead or two, along with some of the foliage. Admittedly, this means background conditions must be ideal, but with so many plants to choose from, that shouldn't be a problem.

Yarrow*

Milfoil
Achillea millefolium

Sunflower Family   Asteraceae
May-October
Perennial
Common

have been for burns, earaches, toothaches, menstrual pain, chills, fever, and upset stomach.

PHOTO TIPS: Category 3

Like most field wildflowers, yarrow is best photographed early in the morning, when it is covered in dew and any insects that have spent the night on it are too sluggish to crawl or fly away. Ladybug beetles, in particular, like yarrow.

HABITAT AND RANGE
Meadows, fields, wasteplaces; throughout—

DESCRIPTION
The dull-white flowerheads of this species form flat-topped clusters on the 1- to 3-foot branching stem. Tiny, white disc flowers are surrounded by 4 to 6 white (occasionally pink), petal-like rays. The soft, alternate leaves are finely dissected and fernlike in appearance. Stem leaves are sessile; basal leaves are on stalks. The plant is quite aromatic.

SIMILAR SPECIES
See Queen Anne's lace, page 174.

Yarrow is almost as common in fields and wasteplaces as dandelion is in lawns. Some people consider it to be just another nuisance "weed"—just like dandelion is to the gardener. However, its value over the years as a medicinal herb redeems its reputation. A common use has been as an astringent to stop blood flow from a wound. The genus name, *Achillea*, comes from the Greek hero Achilles. He is supposed to have taken the plant to the Trojan Wars for the treatment of wounded soldiers. Other uses

75-300mm lens, 5T diopter, 2 sec. at f/16   Adams

Tassel Rue

False bugbane
Trautvetteria caroliniensis

Crowfoot Family	Ranunculaceae
June-July	
Perennial	
Occasional	

75-300mm lens, 5T diopter, 1 sec. at f/22   Adams

HABITAT AND RANGE
Moist woods, streambanks, seeps; throughout—

DESCRIPTION
Flat clusters of small (¼- to ½-inch) white flowers with 3 to 5 sepals and a "tassel" of many stamens top the branching, 1- to 4-foot stem. The basal leaves grow on long stalks, are 6 to 8 inches wide, and have 5 to 11 pointed, toothed lobes. The stem leaves are similar in shape, but smaller in size.

Tassel rue

SIMILAR SPECIES
Mountain meadow rue, *Thalictrum clavatum*, has very similar flowers, grows in the same habitat, and blooms at roughly the same time. However, it is easily distinguished by its compound leaves which have the typical shape of members of the *Thalictrum* genus.

The genus name honors the distinguished nineteenth century Russian botanist Ernst Rudolph von Trautvetter. Interestingly, tassel rue also grows in Japan.

PHOTO TIPS: Categories 3 and 10

You will probably want to isolate a few of the blossoms to keep the background from being distracting. This allows you to stake off the stem, but the tassels will still blow in the wind. Only on the calmest of days can you make a sharp photo. Tassel rue sometimes grows on steep slopes that cannot be climbed without destroying the soil. Also, the slightest touch to the tassels causes them to fall off.

179

Canadian Burnet

Sanguisorba canadensis

> Rose Family   Rosaceae
> July-September; September-October
> Perennial
> Scarce

HABITAT AND RANGE

Bogs, seepage slopes, wet meadows; throughout—

DESCRIPTION

The small white flowers grow in dense spikes on branched stems. The stems are usually 3 to 8 feet tall, but some populations contain reduced species with stems that are only 6 to 12 inches tall. The flowers lack petals but have a calyx with 4 lobes and 4 long, showy stamens. The large, basal leaves are pinnately divided into 7 to 15 oblong and sharply toothed leaflets.

SIMILAR SPECIES

See black snakeroot, page 181.

Canadian burnet is primarily a northeastern species that is at the southernmost extent of its range in the southern Appalachians. Its scarcity here is reflected in the listings of the states' natural heritage programs. It is an endangered species in Tennessee and Kentucky, and a threatened species in Georgia.

The genus name is from the Latin *sanquis*, "blood," and *sorbere*, "to absorb," referring to reported styptic qualities of a Eurasian species.

> PHOTO TIPS: Category 8
>
> *Including all the spikes in the composition creates a cluttered background because the magnification is not high enough. Instead, isolate one or two spikes and shoot at more magnification. This also shows off the tiny flowers better.*

75-300mm lens, 5T diopter, ½ sec. at f/22 Adams

Black Snakeroot

Black cohosh, bugbane
Cimicifuga racemosa

Crowfoot Family Ranunculaceae	
May-August	
Perennial	
Frequent	

300mm lens, ¹/₃₀ sec. at f/8   Adams

HABITAT AND RANGE

Rich woods; throughout—

DESCRIPTION

The slender raceme of black snakeroot may be 3 feet long, with foul-smelling, white flowers opening upward from the bottom. The flowers have tiny, almost unnoticeable petals. The sepals fall soon after the flower opens, leaving it with conspicuous, bushy stamens and a single pistil with a broad stigma. The leaves are mostly basal, alternate, and divided into numerous ovate, toothed leaflets. The plant grows 3 to 8 feet tall.

SIMILAR AND RELATED SPECIES

American bugbane, *C. americana* (see photo on page 42), blooms later and does not have a foul odor. The flowers have 3 to 8 pistils with reduced stigmas. See Canadian burnet, page 180.

It is always a shock to the senses to find an at-

tractive flower like black snakeroot and discover that it has a disagreeable odor. Even insects allegedly avoid it, as the name *bugbane* and the genus name suggests. *Cimicifuga* derives from the Latin words *cimex*, "a bug," and *fugere*, "to drive away." However, we have witnessed several different kinds of insects visiting the plant. Indeed, flies, the main pollinators of black snakeroot, are attracted to the plant like, well, flies.

Black snakeroot and the related American bugbane were used by both Indians and early colonists to treat snakebites.

PHOTO TIPS: Category 8

The racemes of black snakeroot are often so large that you have to use a fairly wide-angle composition to include everything. Look for a landscape opportunity that allows you to use the plant as a foreground. Occasionally, you can back up with a longer lens and isolate the flowers, but only if the background is fairly dark and uncluttered.

 Fly Poison

Amianthium muscitoxicum (A. muscaetoxicum)

> Lily Family   Liliaceae
> June-July; July-September
> Perennial
> Occasional

80-200mm lens, 1 sec. at f/16   *Adams*

HABITAT AND RANGE

Dry woodlands, meadows, mostly at higher elevations; throughout—

DESCRIPTION

The plant grows 1 to 4 feet tall and has a tightly clustered raceme of white flowers. During fruiting, the flowers remain and become green. The basal leaves are long (15 to 20 inches) and grasslike, with a center rib and blunt tips. The flowerstalk is leafless.

SIMILAR SPECIES

Feather bells, *Stenanthium gramineum*, has similar foliage, but its flowers form a branched cluster up to 2 feet long. Each individual flower has 3 pointed petals and 3 sepals that are much longer than wide. Two species of bunchflower, *Melanthium virginicum* and *M. latifolium* (*M. hybridum*), have flowering clusters similar to feather bells, and leaves somewhat similar to fly poison. Their flowers have petals and sepals (3 each) that narrow abruptly to a short stalk. *M. virginicum*, which grows only in the northern portion, has grasslike leaves less than ¾ inch wide. *M. latifolium* has oblanceolate leaves that are between ¾ to 2¼ inches wide.

In ideal habitats, fly poison may be rather common, filling woodland meadows with its showy white flowers. As indicated by its name, the plant is poisonous. All parts, especially the bulb, contain toxic alkaloids which can cause dizziness, vomiting, heart irregularities, and even death if poisoning is severe. Settlers put out sugar water and crushed parts of the plant to kill house flies. It is advisable to wash your hands after handling it.

In Kentucky, fly poison is a threatened species.

> PHOTO TIPS: Category 3
>
> *Fly poison is such a beautiful plant that it's a shame to have to shoot a closeup of just the flowerhead. Still, that is what you'll have to do most of the time as surrounding vegetation usually clutters up the base. Don't stop looking for wide-angle opportunities, though. They do occasionally exist.*

Foamflower

False miterwort
Tiarella cordifolia

Saxifrage Family	Saxifragaceae
April-June	
Perennial	
Common	

75-300mm lens, 5T diopter, ¼ sec. at f/16   Adams

HABITAT AND RANGE

Rich woods; throughout—

DESCRIPTION

The raceme of white (sometimes tinged in pink) flowers grows on a leafless stalk, 6 to 12 inches tall. The flowers have 5 petals, and 10 long stamens (with red or orange anthers) that protrude beyond the petals. The hairy leaves resemble those of red maple and are basal, heart shaped, lobed, and toothed.

Alumroot

Foamflower

SIMILAR SPECIES

As the second common name suggests, foamflower has often been confused with miterwort (page 210), though they are not at all similar. Another plant sometimes confused with foamflower is alumroot, *Heuchera villosa*, a summer-blooming plant with very similar, though much hairier, leaves. It is distinguished by its taller stem (8 to 30 inches), its loose raceme of inconspicuous white flowers, and its preference for shaded ledges and rocky banks. Two other species of *Heuchera* are occasionally encountered. Check a technical manual for distinctions.

The name, *Tiarella*, is Greek for "little tiara." It refers to the way the long stamens of foamflower rise above the petals like the points on a royal crown.

Indians used foamflower-leaf tea as a diuretic and for sore eyes and mouth. The plant is high in tannin, which may account for these uses.

PHOTO TIPS: Category 2

Because foamflower grows in a woodland setting, you'll have problems with background distractions. Look for a small raceme, which will allow you to shoot at a higher magnification. This will help eliminate the clutter. Also, choose an angle in which there are no trees or branches directly behind the flower for several feet.

Turkeybeard

Xerophyllum asphodeloides

Lily Family   Liliaceae
Late May-June; July-August
Perennial
Scarce

75-300mm lens, 5T diopter, ¼ sec. at f/22   Adams

HABITAT AND RANGE
Dry, open woods, heath balds; throughout—

DESCRIPTION
A dense raceme (3 to 6 inches long, 2 to 3 inches wide) of white flowers grows at the top of a rigid, 2- to 5-foot stalk. The needlelike leaves grow in a dense tuft at the base of the stem. The stem is covered with short, grasslike leaves.

SIMILAR SPECIES
See fly poison on page 182.

It is unlikely you will encounter turkeybeard unless you happen to be in the few specific localities where habitat is ideal. Where it does grow, it is a bold and imposing wildflower that cannot be mistaken for any other.

Turkeybeard is listed as a threatened species in Tennessee and South Carolina. Kentucky sites no reliable observation of the plant since 1970. It is rare in Virginia and West Virginia, and is on the North Carolina plant-watch list. Deer contribute to the plant's scarcity by eating the flowerheads. Deer browsing on wildflowers is a problem in several national parks and other areas where the deer populations are expanding.

PHOTO TIPS: Categories 4 and 10

Some locations where this plant grows allow the use of a wide-angle lens, with turkeybeard as a foreground. Usually, there is no acceptable alternative to a simple, tight closeup of the flowerhead. Be careful not to overexpose the white flowers.

 Doll's Eyes

Baneberry
Actaea pachypoda

Crowfoot Family   Ranunculaceae
April-May; August-October
Perennial
Occasional

75-300mm lens, 5T diopter, 2 sec. at f/16   Adams

HABITAT AND RANGE
Rich woods; throughout—

DESCRIPTION
White flowers with 4-to-10 small, narrow petals and a tassel of many white stamens grow on a compact, 1- to 3-inch raceme. The compound leaves have pointed, toothed leaflets. The plant grows 1 to 2 feet high.

Though they may be pretty, the small white flowers of this plant are not nearly as well known as the fruit. Growing at the end of thick red stalks are round, shiny white berries with a distinctive black dot at the tip, thus the name *doll's eyes*. See photo of fruit on page 21.

All parts of this plant are poisonous; even so, Indians used small amounts of it to relieve pain in childbirth.

PHOTO TIPS: Category 3

The leaves often grow tightly together, sometimes from 2 or more plants, and present a good opportunity for an intermediate image that includes the flower along with some of the leaves. You can always shoot a tight closeup of just the flower, but since there are so many different species with similar white racemes, the photograph will not be very distinctive.

Wild Mints, Mountain Mints

Pycnanthemum spp. and others

Mint Family   Lamiaceae
July-October
Perennial
Varies with species

75-300mm lens, 5T diopter, ½ sec. at f/22   Adams

HABITAT AND RANGE
A wide range of habitats; throughout—

DESCRIPTION
These herbaceous perennials have the typical square stem of the mint family, and grow 1 to 4 feet high on single or branching stems. The flowers are usually some shade of whitish pink to lavender, and are often purple spotted. The flowers have 2 lips; the upper lip is entire or notched, and the lower lip has 3 lobes. They can be arranged in round, dense flowerheads, or singularly in the leaf axils. Four stamens usually protrude from the corolla; the upper pair is longer than the lower pair. The leaves may be toothed or entire, and vary in shape. A strong minty aroma is usually present.

While some species are quite distinctive and easy to distinguish, many are difficult to identify. During our research, we discovered numerous cases of contradictory descriptions between several respected literary sources. Compounding the problem is the fact that some species can vary substantially in leaf shape and pubescence, among other features.

First, try to identify an unknown mint with this or other guidebooks. If absolute, positive identification cannot be made, simply label the plant as a mint.

PHOTO TIPS: Category 3

The photographic approach varies greatly depending on the species, but in almost every case, it is effective to shoot a standard isolation closeup of one or two flower clusters.

False Solomon's Seal

Solomon's plume, false spikenard
Maianthemum racemosum
 ssp. *racemosum (Smilacina racemosa)*

Lily Family   Liliaceae
April-June; August-October
Perennial
Common

HABITAT AND RANGE
Moist, rich woods; throughout—

DESCRIPTION
A terminal cluster of small white flowers with enlarged stamens decorates the end of a 1- to 3-foot arching stem that zigzags from one set of leaves to another. The elliptic, pointed leaves have prominent veins and grow alternately along the stem. The berries, produced in the fall, begin as a mottled red then turn bright red all over.

SIMILAR SPECIES
See true Solomon's seal on page 188.

It's a shame that this graceful and elegant plant should have such a negative name. It is more common and showy than its counterpart, the true Solomon's seal, and deserves its own identity. Solomon's plume is a flattering and more descriptive name that we prefer.

PHOTO TIPS: Category 8

First, try to find an attractive setting that allows the use of a wide-angle lens. If you can't, you'll have to shoot a moderate closeup, but it's tough. Ideally, you'll want to include part of the leaves, but that requires shooting from overhead to align the film plane. Ordinarily, the plant doesn't grow that low to the ground, but you might get lucky. Otherwise, you'll have to shoot from the side and settle for little depth of field in the leaves. You might try experimenting with shooting from underneath, looking up.

50mm lens, 1 sec. at f/16   Adams

187

Solomon's Seal

Polygonatum biflorum

75-300mm lens, 5T diopter, ½ sec. at f/16   *Adams*

> Lily Family   Liliaceae
> April-June; August-October
> Perennial
> Frequent

HABITAT AND RANGE

Moist, rich woods; throughout—

DESCRIPTION

Two rows of smooth, broadly lance-shaped, prominently veined, alternate leaves line the 1- to 4-foot, gracefully arching stem of this plant. The flowers are small (½ to ⅔ inch), greenish yellow, and cylindrical. Each flower has 6 small lobes. They dangle from the leaf axils along the length of the stalk in clusters of 1 to 4. Dark blue berries replace the flowers in the fall.

SIMILAR AND RELATED SPECIES

Great Solomon's seal, *P. biflorum* var. *commutatum* (*P. canaliculatum*), is a larger, more robust plant with longer leaf and flower stalks, and larger flowers. It may be difficult to distinguish, but it is OK to label all plants as *P. biflorum.* Hairy Solomon's seal, *P. pubescens*, has leaves that are hairy on the underneath veins, and the slightly smaller flowers grow singly or in pairs. Rose twisted stalk or rose mandarin, *Streptopus roseus*, has similar leaves, but it is differentiated by its zigzag stem and rose-colored flowers.

See false Solomon's seal, page 187.

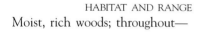

One of the most popular of all wildflowers,

Solomon's seal has a "look-at-me" disposition. Because the stem is so long, it often grows out over hiking trails, making it impossible to miss. The roots have circular scars, which are said to resemble the royal seal of King Solomon. Besides his wisdom in settling child-custody disputes, Solomon also was wise in the use of medicinal herbs. It is believed that this plant, which is named for him, was one of those herbs.

The root scars are an indicator of the plant's age—each year produces a new circle. Some plants have been determined to be at least 50 years old.

> PHOTO TIPS: Category 4
>
> *Unless you find a perfect setting, you'll be most likely shooting a closeup of the plant, possibly including 4 or 5 sets of flowers and a few leaves. Since the stem grows horizontally, you can stake it off on each side, stabilizing the plant even when the wind is blowing. You will still have to wait for a lull, however, since the flowers will dangle in the wind regardless.*

Umbrella Leaf

Diphylleia cymosa

Barberry Family   Berberidaceae
May-June; July-August
Perennial
Scarce

75-300mm lens, 5T diopter, 8 sec. at f/11   Adams

HABITAT AND RANGE
Wet wooded coves, rich seepage slopes; throughout—

DESCRIPTION
The 2 huge leaves are 1 to 2 feet wide and are located on a 2- to 4-foot-long stem. They are deeply cleft in the middle, and each half has 5-to-7 toothed lobes. The white flowers have 6 petals, 6 sepals, and 6 stamens. The flowers bloom in a cluster above the leaves. Nonflowering plants have only one leaf.

While attractive in flower, it is most appealing in fruit, when the deep blue berries contrast sharply with the bright red stalks.

Umbrella leaf is restricted to the southern Appalachians, where it is encountered infrequently except along a few stretches of the Blue Ridge Parkway and in the Smokies. It may have medicinal value as an anticancer treatment (a closely related Chinese species is used as such), although one resource suggests its scarcity may limit interest in further study.

PHOTO TIPS: Categories 3 and 10

Isn't it frustrating when you find the perfect setting for a wildflower after it has finished blooming? This happened to us with umbrella leaf. The best shooting approach in this case was a closeup of just the flower and part of the leaf, but good wide-angle opportunities do exist.

Umbrella leaf grows in wet, shallow soil, and often on steep slopes. Please watch your footing; one careless slip could take several plants down the hill with you.

 Rabbit Tobacco

Cudweed, everlasting
Gnaphalium obtusifolium var. *praecox*

> Sunflower Family   Asteraceae
> August-October
> Annual
> Common

75-300mm lens, 5T diopter, ¹/₃₀ sec. at f/16   *Casstevens*

HABITAT AND RANGE
Roadsides, fields, wasteplaces; throughout—

DESCRIPTION
Branching clusters of white, tubular flowerheads top the 1- to 2-foot stem. The stem, undersides of the leaves, and the base of the bracts are covered with dense, white, woolly hairs. The narrow, elliptical leaves are aromatic when crushed or bruised.

SIMILAR SPECIES
Cudweed, *Gamochaeta purpurea* (*Gnaphalium purpureum*), is similar in general form, but it has spatulate to lance-shaped leaves and brown, green, or purple bracts.

This aromatic herb was a favorite of young boys who used the leaves as a substitute for tobacco—thus the common name.

PHOTO TIPS: Category 3

To reveal the intricate beauty of the flowerheads, shoot a tight closeup into the plant. One feature of this type of shot is that you only have to move the camera position slightly for a totally new composition.

ℐndian Physic

Bowman's root, false ipecac
Porteranthus trifoliatus (*Gillenia trifoliata*)

50mm lens, 1 sec. at f/16   *Adams*

> Rose Family   Rosaceae
> Late April–early July; July–August
> Perennial
> Common

HABITAT AND RANGE
Rich woods, roadsides; throughout—

DESCRIPTION
The flowers have 5 long, white or pinkish white petals. The petals are unequal in length and somewhat twisted, giving the flowers a scraggly appearance. The leaves are divided into 3 pointed, slightly toothed leaflets. The 2- to 4-foot, reddish brown stem is branching, contributing to the plant's ragged appearance.

RELATED SPECIES
The rare American ipecac, *P. stipulatus* (*Gillenia stipulata*), has a similar flower; however, the leaves are divided into 5 segments. Each segment consists of 3 leaflets and 2 stipules that look like smaller leaflets.

Tea made from both potentially toxic species of this genus has been used as a laxative and to induce vomiting. It is a common plant along the Blue Ridge Parkway, often growing so large and dense that it looks more like a shrub than an herbaceous wildflower.

> PHOTO TIPS: Category 5
>
> *A 50mm, or similar, lens positioned close to the plant works well to include several flowers along with foliage. Try to find a setting that has most of the flowers parallel to the film plane— and be careful not to overexpose the white petals.*

Michaux's Saxifrage

Saxifraga michauxii

Brook saxifrage

Lettuce saxifrage

Michaux's saxifrage

Saxifrage Family	Saxifragaceae
June-August	
Perennial	
Frequent	

HABITAT AND RANGE

Moist, rocky areas, seepage slopes; primarily the southern portion of the region—

DESCRIPTION

The basal rosette of hairy, strongly toothed, lance-shaped leaves is the strongest identifying characteristic of this species. When mature, the leaves are a deep maroon underneath. The small white flowers grow on a hairy, slender, branching stem, 6 to 20 inches high. Each flower has 5 petals; 3 larger petals with 2 yellow spots at the base, and 2 smaller petals without spots. The flowers are not radially symmetrical.

50mm lens, ¼ sec. at f/16   Adams

SIMILAR AND RELATED SPECIES

Lettuce saxifrage, *S. micranthidifolia*, has less branching in the stem, much larger leaves (up to 12 inches), and the flowers are radially symmetrical. It blooms from April to June and is always rooted in water or very wet soil. Early saxifrage, *S. virginiensis*, is a plant of very dry habitats. It blooms from March to May, has egg-shaped basal leaves (1 to 3 inches), and radially symmetrical flowers.

Brook saxifrage, *Boykinia aconitifolia*, has similar flowers, but the leaves strongly resemble those of monkshood, page 67.

Michaux's saxifrage is a rather common plant in wet, rocky areas, sometimes seeming to grow from the rock itself. In fact, the genus name may have derived from this trait. The name comes from the Latin *saxum*, "a stone," and *frangere*, "to break." Another possible derivation of the name comes from the stone-like granules on the roots of a European species. The *Doctrine of Signatures* (page 163) implied that the plant had the ability to dissolve kidney and gallbladder stones because of the presence of these stonelike granules. The species and common names honor the plant's discoverer, the famous French botanist André Michaux.

> PHOTO TIPS: Category 6
>
> *This plant is not very tall, but because of its preference for rocky slopes, it is difficult to use plastic wind barriers or diffusers. Try to shoot on an overcast, calm day.*

75-300mm lens,
5T diopter, ¼ sec. at f/16
Adams

White Wood Aster

Mountain wood aster
Aster chlorolepis (A. divaricatus)

HABITAT AND RANGE

High-elevation woodlands and open areas; only in the southern segment—

DESCRIPTION

The lower leaves of this aster are mostly ovate; upper leaves are elliptic to lanceolate. It usually has more than 10 white rays per head.

RELATED SPECIES

A. divaricatus, a plant of mid-to-low elevations throughout the range, is nearly identical to white wood aster, but with less than 10 rays per head. *Gray's* lists only *A. divaricatus*, with *A. chlorolepis* listed as a synonym. There is no easy method for the beginner to distinguish between the many *Aster* species, including those listed here. If in doubt, simply label it as *Aster* sp.

While you may not always know exactly which species you're examining, you should have no trouble recognizing this plant as an aster. It looks just like the typical bluish purple varieties except for the color. White wood aster is a very showy wildflower, often growing in uninterrupted patches along the high-elevation roadways of the southern mountains. Two particularly good places to see it are on the Blue Ridge Parkway spur heading to Balsam Mountain and along the road to Clingmans Dome in the Smokies.

PHOTO TIPS: Category 6

You should have no trouble locating a good situation for shooting white wood aster. It grows in dense patches, often among other wildflowers, creating great closeup and wide-angle opportunities. An especially fine photogenic aspect of the plant is that it often grows at the base of tall, late-summer wildflowers like Joe-Pye weed.

Great Chickweed

Star chickweed, giant chickweed
Stellaria pubera

Pink Family Caryophyllaceae
April-June
Perennial
Common

75-300mm lens, 5T diopter, ⅛ sec. at f/16   Adams

HABITAT AND RANGE

Rich to dry woods; throughout—

DESCRIPTION

The starlike, white flowers have conspicuous dark anthers. The flowers are in small terminal clusters on a 6- to 16-inch stem, and they often grow in dense, reclining mats. The 5 petals, which are longer than the sepals, are so deeply cleft that they appear to be 10 petals. The paired leaves are broadly elliptic and mostly sessile.

SIMILAR AND RELATED SPECIES

S. corei, Core's chickweed, is almost identical except that its petals are equal to, or shorter than, the sepals. It is an infrequent species found mostly in the Smokies, Great Balsams, Roan Mountain, and westward. The petals of common chickweed, *S. media*, are also shorter than the sepals, and the lower leaves are stalked. Its petals are half the length of *S. pubera*. Lesser stitchwort, *S. graminea*, a plant found in fields and open areas, has petals that are longer than the sepals, and small, narrow, sessile leaves. It has delicate stems and tends to grow in tangled masses. Mouse-ear chickweed, *Cerastium fontanum* ssp. *vulgare* (*C. vulgatum*), has petals and sepals of about equal length, a hairy stem, and hairy, sessile, ovate leaves. Other *Cerastium* species may be encountered. Consult a technical manual for exact identification of these species and the *Stellaria* species.

Chickweed provides more than just delicate beauty. The leaves are high in vitamins A and C, and make a tasty addition to salads. Medicinally, it has been used to treat scurvy, skin infections, congestion, coughs, and constipation. It even predicts the weather; according to folklore, if the blossoms begin to close up, rain is approaching.

In late April and early May, great chickweed is one of the most conspicuous wildflowers you'll see on a drive along the Blue Ridge Parkway.

PHOTO TIPS: Category 6

If you keep looking, you should be able to find a large clump that has a flat plane you can align with the film plane. This is necessary to achieve maximum depth of field. Remember to calculate the exposure to maintain detail in the white petals.

ℱringed Phacelia

Phacelia fimbriata

Waterleaf Family   Hydrophyllaceae
April-May
Annual
Occasional

105mm macro lens, ¹/8 sec. at f/16   Casstevens
(See additional photo on page 46.)

HABITAT AND RANGE

Rich woods and streambanks; primarily in the southern portion—

DESCRIPTION

This is a 3- to 5-inch-high, weak-stemmed plant, growing in large colonies. The white, bell-shaped corolla is small (¹/3 to ¹/2 inch) with strongly fringed lobes. Plants produce an inflorescence of 5 to 15 flowers. The leaves have 5 to 9 unequal lobes and clasp the stem.

RELATED SPECIES

Miami mist, *P. purshii*, which looks very similar, produces an inflorescence of 10 to 30 fringed flowers that are pale blue with a cream-colored center. Small-flowered phacelia, *P. dubia*, is similar to Miami mist, but with smaller, fringeless flowers. It is more common in the northern portion. See purple phacelia, page 58.

If you pass by a colony of fringed phacelia too quickly, you may think you are seeing the remains of a late-spring snow fall. The plant often grows in extensive colonies, sometimes covering everything on the ground. Stop for a few minutes and look closely at the delicate beauty of an individual blossom.

The best place to see the plant is in the Smokies, particularly around the Chimneys picnic area, and a little later in the year along the road to Clingmans Dome.

The species name comes from the biological term fimbriate, meaning delicately fringed.

PHOTO TIPS: Categories 6 and 9
When you find fringed phacelia at its prime, you'll no doubt reach for a wide-angle lens. It is one of the few native plants in the southern Appalachians that can completely cover a large section of the forest floor.

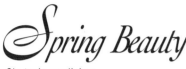

Spring Beauty

Claytonia caroliniana

| Purslane Family   Portulacaceae |
| March-May |
| Perennial |
| Common |

HABITAT AND RANGE

Rich woods; throughout—

DESCRIPTION

Delicately beautiful flowers grow in a loose raceme. The 5 petals are white or pink with dark pink veins. A single pair of lanceolate to oblanceolate, 1-inch-wide (or less) leaves with distinct petioles occurs midway up the stem. A few basal leaves may be present. The plant is 6 to 8 inches tall.

SIMILAR AND RELATED SPECIES

C. virginica, is almost identical, except its leaves are grasslike and have indistinct petioles. See common wood sorrel on page 224.

———

Spring beauty is one of our favorite harbingers of spring. Apparently we aren't the only ones to enjoy it—research indicates that over 70 different species of insects have been known to pollinate the flowers. But these insects have to visit on sunny days; the blossoms do not open on dark, cloudy days.

Geneticists are interested in spring beauty because each plant may have any one of 50 different combinations of chromosomes. This variable chromosome number makes it a good candidate for genetic study since most living organisms have the same number of chromosomes for each individual in a species.

Spring beauty is common almost everywhere, but truly spectacular displays occur in certain localities. The accompanying photographs were made in the high elevations of the Smokies, along the road to Clingmans Dome.

PHOTO TIPS: Categories 1 and 9 ☼

In ideal growing conditions, spring beauty carpets the forest floor, making a wide-angle composition an effective approach. A tighter composition—one that includes a few blossoms along with foliage—is also a good choice.

196

20mm lens, ½ sec. at f/22
(See additional photo on page 16.)

Adams

Wood Anemone

Windflower

Anemone quinquefolia

75-300mm lens, 5T diopter, 1 sec. at f/16   *Adams*

Crowfoot Family	Ranunculaceae
Mid-March–early June	
Perennial	
Occasional	

HABITAT AND RANGE

Rich, moist woods, woodland edges; throughout—

DESCRIPTION

A solitary flower with 4 to 9 (usually 5) white sepals grows on a slender, 6- to 8-inch stem. There is a single whorl of 2 to 3 leaves halfway up the stem, with 3 to 5 sharply toothed leaflets on each leaf. The lateral leaflets are often so deeply lobed that they appear as 2 separate leaflets.

SIMILAR AND RELATED SPECIES

The leaflets of *A. lancifolia*, mountain anemone, are not as deeply lobed and have even more toothing on the edges. The leaves are divided into only 3 leaflets. It grows up to 16 inches high. Thimbleweed, *A. virginiana*, grows 2 to 3 feet and has greenish white sepals. It blooms later than the other species, from early June through July.

See rue anemone on page 200.

Wood anemone is one of the first flowers to bloom in spring. The delicate white blossom is made up of sepals only and has no petals. The flowers stay open for several weeks, awaiting pollination. After pollination the sepals fall off, the fruit develops, and the leaves die back, leaving no visible evidence of the plant until the following spring.

Thimbleweed
75-300mm lens,
5T diopter,
1/30 sec. at f11
Adams

PHOTO TIPS: Category 6

The white petals display attractive detail if you are careful not to overexpose them.

Canada Violet
Viola canadensis

Violet Family   Violaceae
April-early July
Perennial
Frequent

HABITAT AND RANGE
Rich-to-mesic woods; throughout—

DESCRIPTION
The 5 petals of this violet are white with a yellow base and turn purple as they age. The 3 lower petals have dark purple stripes, and the backs of all the petals are tinged with purple. The leaves are heart shaped and toothed on the edges. One of our tallest violets, it grows 8 to 18 inches high.

RELATED SPECIES
There are 3 varieties of *V. canadensis* in the region: var. *corymbosa*, var. *rugulosa* (*V. rugulosa*), and var. *canadensis*. The distinctions between them are unclear, except that the first 2 have stolons, while var. *canadensis* does not. You are safe in labeling all plants as simply *V. canadensis*. The flower of sweet white violet, *V. blanda*, is similar; however, the upper two petals are bent backwards in a half-twist, and the shorter stem and flowerstalk are red. Pale violet, *V. striata*, has large, deeply lobed stipules, and the flowers lack the yellow base on the petals and the purple tinge on the back of the petals. The northern white violet, *V. macloskeyi* ssp. *pallens* (*V. pallens*), is short (only 1 to 5 inches) with small rounded leaves. The ½-inch flowers have purple veins and are fragrant. The common wild or field pansy, *V. bicolor* (*V. kitaibeliana* var. *rafinesquii*), has white or pale blue flowers, spoon-shaped leaves, and small, deeply lobed stipules.

Most species of violets are edible. The flowers are often coated with sugar and eaten as candies. The leaves are rich in vitamins A and C, and they complement any salad as additional greens. They also have medicinal value; tea from the dried leaves will supposedly relieve headaches, and poultices from violets have been used to heal skin abrasions.

PHOTO TIPS: Category 6

Canada violet becomes more and more prominent as the growing season progresses. Wait a while and you will find thick, bushy clumps that present good photo opportunities. This is much better than shooting the few individual flowers that first appear.

75-300mm lens, 5T diopter, ½ sec. at f/22   Adams

ue Anemone

Windflower

Thalictrum thalictroides (*Anemonella thalictroides*)

Crowfoot Family   Ranunculaceae
Late March–May
Perennial
Common

75-300mm lens, 5T diopter, ¼ sec. at f/16   *Casstevens*

HABITAT AND RANGE
Rich woods; throughout—

DESCRIPTION
This delicate herb, which has no petals, has 5 to 10 white or pink petal-like sepals and numerous stamens. There is a whorl of tri-lobed leaves just below the cluster of 2 to 3 flowers. The basal leaves are also tri-lobed and grow on long leaf stalks in 2 or 3 groups of 3. The plant grows 4 to 8 inches high.

SIMILAR SPECIES
The rare twinleaf, *Jeffersonia diphylla*, has a similar flower; however, its single leaf is almost completely divided at the middle. See wood anemone and hepatica on pages 198 and 57.

Indians used the roots of rue anemone to treat

intestinal disorders. Presently, it is occasionally used to treat foot problems.

PHOTO TIPS: Category 2 ✵

Try to photograph this delicate herb on a windy day and you'll soon realize the appropriateness of the name windflower. It moves in the slightest breeze, making wind barriers a necessity. Be careful not to overexpose the white sepals.

105mm macro lens, ½ sec. at f/16   *Adams*

$\mathcal{W}$ild Lily of the Valley

False lily of the valley, Canada mayflower
Maianthemum canadense

HABITAT AND RANGE
Rich woods, spruce-fir forests: throughout—

DESCRIPTION
Fragrant white flowers grow in a small raceme. Individual flowers have 2 petals, 2 sepals, and 4 stamens. The 1 to 3 (usually 2) leaves are veined, 1 to 3 inches long, shiny, and heart shaped at the base, where they clasp the stem. This small plant (2 to 6 inches) often grows in dense colonies.

Remember that old cliché that bid you to "take time to smell the flowers"? Well, this is one time when you'll want to do just that. What this little wildflower lacks in size, it makes up for in fragrance. We don't know if animals also like the fragrance, but we do know that grouse, mice, and chipmunks enjoy eating the dark red berries that are produced in the fall.

Wild lily of the valley is a threatened species in Kentucky.

PHOTO TIPS: Category   1

An overhead vantage point makes a good image and demonstrates the colonial nature of the plant. It does not, however, depict the individual flowers very well. That requires a ground-level closeup. Try both angles.

Trailing Arbutus

Mayflower
Epigaea repens

Heath Family   Ericaceae
Mid-February–mid-May; April–June
Perennial
Frequent

75-300mm lens, 5T diopter, 4 sec. at f/32   Adams

HABITAT AND RANGE

Sunny, dry, acid woods, roadbanks; throughout—

DESCRIPTION

This is a very low-growing evergreen shrub with alternate, leathery, oval leaves that are 1 to 3 inches long. The clusters of fragrant, white or pink flowers have 5 lobes that flare out from a short, hairy tube. The stems are trailing and hairy. This plant often grows in dense patches.

Supposedly, this early-blooming little wildflower was the first bloom spotted by the Pilgrims after a harsh winter in the new world, so they named it after their ship, the *Mayflower*. Shakers sold the plant as the "gravel plant," an aid for kidney stones. Although it does contain an effective urinary antiseptic, caution is warranted because it can convert to a toxic compound.

PHOTO TIPS: Category 1

A vantage point from directly overhead works well, both compositionally and to maximize depth of field. You may need to do a little rearranging of the blooms to make them noticeable as they are primarily hidden below the leaves.

Stonecrop

Sedum
Sedum ternatum

Orpine Family   Crassulaceae
April-June; May-July
Perennial
Frequent

75-300mm lens, 5T diopter, 4 sec. at f/32   *Adams*

HABITAT AND RANGE

Moist or dry rocks, logs, streambanks; throughout—

DESCRIPTION

The stems of this plant creep along the ground or over rocks, forming dense mats. The flowerstalks rise up from the stem and usually branch into 3 clusters of white flowers. The flowers have 4 or 5 petals which are sharply pointed, and 5 green sepals. Numerous bracts are located beneath the flower. Dark brown anthers stand out against the white flowers. The lower leaves are spatulate, smooth, thick, fleshy, and occur in whorls of 3.

RELATED SPECIES

The only other white-flowered *Sedum* you are likely to encounter is the rare *S. glaucophyllum,* which is similar but has alternate leaves.

The genus name *Sedum* is from *sedere*, which means "to sit." The name refers to the manner in which the plant clings to rocks and logs. The species name *ternatum* means "in threes" and refers to the whorl of 3 leaves.

PHOTO TIPS: Category 1

Stonecrop is one of the easiest wildflowers to photograph because it does what photographers wish all plants would do: it stays put in the wind. Keep that in mind when planning a shooting schedule and save stonecrop for the times when nothing else seems to work.

Wintergreen

Teaberry
Gaultheria procumbens

Heath Family   Ericaceae
June-August; September-November
Perennial
Common

HABITAT AND RANGE
Dry, acid woods; throughout—

DESCRIPTION
This evergreen shrub is short (2 to 6 inches) with dark green, shiny, oval, slightly toothed leaves that have a strong taste and odor of wintergreen. The urn-shaped flowers have small teeth at the tip and hang beneath the leaves. They are waxy white or pink. A bright red berry is produced in the fruiting season.

SIMILAR SPECIES
See the listings under spotted wintergreen, page 206.

75-300mm lens, 5T diopter, 4 sec. at f/22   *Adams*

Wintergreen is technically a shrub, but it looks more like an herb so its inclusion seems appropriate. The highly aromatic plant was the source of wintergreen oil until the oil began to be synthetically produced. However, the essential oil of wintergreen, methyl salicylate, is still experimentally important as an analgesic and antiseptic. It may also play a role in slowing the beginning of tumor growth. Tea from the leaves has been used to relieve headaches and sore muscle pain. This sounds reasonable, since methyl salicylate is related to aspirin.

Wintergreen is a threatened species in South Carolina.

> PHOTO TIPS: Category 1
>
> *Wintergreen has the same photographic attributes as partridge berry, page 205, but with one major difference. Instead of shooting straight down, you must shoot more or less at an angle to the flowers because of the way they hang beneath the leaves. To lessen back strain, try to find a plant growing on a steep bank.*

Partridge Berry

Twin flower
Mitchella repens

Madder Family	Rubiaceae
May-June; June-July	
Perennial	
Frequent	

105mm macro lens, 20 sec. at f/32   *Adams*

HABITAT AND RANGE

Deciduous woods, hemlock forests, streambanks; throughout—

DESCRIPTION

The fragrant, small, white flowers on this low, creeping plant occur in pairs at the ends of slender stems. They are trumpet shaped and have 4 lobes covered with dense hairs. The evergreen leaves are rounded and opposite. In fruiting season, the 2 flowers fuse to form a single red berry.

The berries of this plant are edible, if you can get to them before the quail and wild turkeys do. The fruit is formed from both flowers, which are united at their base. The two flowers in each pair differ from one another: one has a long pistil and short stamens; the other has long stamens and a short pistil. This helps to ensure cross-pollination and healthier plants.

An interesting feature of partridge berry is that it often displays both flowers and fruits at the same time, the fruits being from flowers of the previous season.

PHOTO TIPS: Category 1

If there is such a thing as a perfect photo subject, partridge berry is it. It has beautiful flowers, complementary foliage, and contrasting red berries. Plus, everything is on roughly the same plane, and it stays put in the wind. The hardest part is finding the right plant to shoot. Search for one that lets you include flower, berry, and foliage in the composition. And, of course, it helps to visit after a rain shower.

Spotted Wintergreen

Pipsissewa

Chimaphila maculata

> Heath Family   Ericaceae
> May-June; July-October
> Perennial
> Common

75-300mm lens, 5T diopter, 6 sec. at f/22   Adams

HABITAT AND RANGE
Coniferous and hardwood forests; throughout—

DESCRIPTION
The fragrant, nodding flowers have 5 waxy white (sometimes pink) petals and grow in a cluster on a 4- to 10-inch stem. The leaves usually grow in whorls, but may also be scattered on the stem. The leaves are 1 to 3 inches long, leathery, dark green with white stripes along the veins and midrib, and have widely spaced toothing on the edges.

RELATED SPECIES
Prince's pine, *C. umbellata* ssp. *cisatlantica* (*C. umbellata* var. *cisatlantica*), is similar but has solid, dark green leaves that are slightly larger and rounded at the tips, and the flowers have red anthers. Round-leaved wintergreen, *Pyrola americana* (*P. rotundifolia* var. *americana*), has similar waxy white flowers, but they are more numerous and have a prominent, protruding style.

It may surprise you to learn that spotted wintergreen is closely related to Catawba and rosebay rhododendron. Although spotted wintergreen and the rhododendrons are very different in appearance, they all have evergreen leaves which allow them to be instantly recognized during the winter.

Pipsissewa is a Creek Indian name that refers to the Indians' belief that juice from the plant could reduce bladder and kidney stones. Studies confirm that the juice has properties that increase urine flow, as well as antibiotic elements.

> ### PHOTO TIPS: Category 2
>
> *To help the flowers stand out—they tend to blend with the forest floor—try to find a plant that has a dark, neutral background. Old, wet oak leaves are a good choice, and moss is better still. Pine needles tend to be distracting, but you may not have a choice since the flower often grows beneath evergreens.*

Indian Pipe

Corpse plant, ghost flower, ice plant
Monotropa uniflora

> Wintergreen Family   Monotropaceae (Pyrolaceae)
> June-October; August-November
> Perennial
> Occasional

HABITAT AND RANGE

Rich, moist, shady woods, particularly pine forests; throughout—

DESCRIPTION

The entire plant is translucent white, occasionally pink, with a single, nodding, pipe-shaped flower (the flower turns upright during fruiting). The scale-like leaves grow alternately on the 3- to 12-inch stem. The plant often grows in small clusters.

SIMILAR AND RELATED SPECIES

Pinesap, *M. hypopithys* (see photo on page 23), is yellow or reddish yellow and has several flowers per stem. Sweet pinesap, *Monotropsis odorata*, is a purplish brown species, similar to Indian pipe, but it is often hidden beneath leaf litter. It is easily distinguished, and sometimes discovered, by its delightful fragrance.

Indian pipe does not fit in with the normal idea of a wildflower. It resembles fungi more than the leafy, green plants usually thought of as wildflowers. Chlorophyll, the substance which gives plants their green color and changes the sun's energy to food, is absent from Indian pipe. To get food, Indian pipe forms a symbiotic relationship with a fungus growing on its roots. As the fungus breaks down organic matter for its own food, nutrients are absorbed through Indian pipe's roots.

The white, ghostly appearance and the plant's tendency to turn black and "melt," or decompose when touched, is the source of Indian pipe's other common names. The stem also turns black after pollination.

Indians used the plant's juices to make an eye wash, and at one time, doctors made a sedative from the roots.

> PHOTO TIPS: Category 2
>
> *Save this one for a windy day when you can't shoot anything else—it stays put in all but hurricane weather. However, don't make the mistake of locating a promising plant and returning more than a few days later. If you do, you'll likely find it already turning black. You must photograph it soon after it pushes through the soil.*

75-300mm lens, 5T diopter, 8 sec. at f/32   Adams

Pennywort

Obolaria virginica

Gentian Family   Gentianaceae
March-April; May-June
Perennial
Occasional

75-300mm lens, 5T diopter, 4 sec. at f/22   *Adams*

HABITAT AND RANGE
Rich woods; throughout—

DESCRIPTION
The small white or purplish white, tubular flowers grow singly, or in groups of 3, in the upper leaf axils of this low-growing, 3- to 6-inch plant. Lower leaves are scalelike and arranged oppositely on the stem. The upper leaves are ovate and very small, ½ inch or less.

The genus name of pennywort is from the Greek *obolos*, which is the word for a small coin, and refers to the small rounded leaves. The coinlike leaves also inspired the common name. Although the plant is not uncommon, it is seldom seen as it blends with the forest litter.

PHOTO TIPS: Category 2

A good time to photograph pennywort is when the wind is high and light is low. It only moves in the strongest of winds, allowing you to stop down to f/16 or f/22. This provides enough depth of field to keep it, and much of the surroundings, in focus. Save the calm days for flowers that blow in the wind.

One-flowered Cancer Root

Squawroot
Orobanche uniflora

> Broomrape Family   Orobanchaceae
> April-May
> Perennial
> Occasional

105mm macro lens, 5T diopter, 6 sec. at f/22   Adams

HABITAT AND RANGE
Rich, moist woods; throughout—

DESCRIPTION
The solitary flower consists of a white-to-pale-lavender tube that flares out into 5 lobes. Soft hairs cover the outside of the flower. The pale, sticky stalk is 3 to 8 inches high and leafless. Densely overlapping leaf scales grow at the base of the stem. No parts of the plant are green. It sometimes grows in small clusters.

Like all members of the broomrape family, one-flowered cancer root lacks chlorophyll, living as a parasite on the roots of other plants. It is fairly common in some areas of the southern Appalachians, but it is inconspicuous and often overlooked.

> PHOTO TIPS: Category 2
>
> *The hardest part about photographing this wildflower is finding it. Once you do, you'll want to shoot a tight closeup to keep it from being lost in the image. This may create problems with background clutter, but you can probably do a little "gardening" to simplify the scene.*

75-300mm lens,
6T diopter,
2 sec. at f/22

Casstevens

Miterwort

Bishop's cap
Mitella diphylla

Saxifrage Family   Saxifragaceae
April-June
Perennial
Occasional

HABITAT AND RANGE

Moist, rich woods, streambanks; throughout—

DESCRIPTION

The tiny white flowers are cup shaped, with 5 fringed petals that give the flower a starlike appearance. The flowers are arranged singly on the upper portion of the 8- to 18-inch stem. A pair of stalkless, opposite, maple-shaped leaves grow halfway up the stem, while the basal leaves grow on long stalks.

Most people walk by miterwort without a second glance, but the tiny flowers are fascinating when viewed through a magnifying lens. The common and genus names are inspired by the fruit, which is shaped like a miter, the official headdress of a bishop.

PHOTO TIPS: Categories 3 and 7

To record the intricate beauty of the flower requires an extreme closeup, which is quite a problem if the wind is blowing. Try isolating a blossom and staking off the stem at both the top and bottom of the blossom. Since individual flowers face in different directions, you probably won't have enough depth of field to cover more than one.

Ramp

Wild leek, ramps
Allium tricoccum

Lily Family Liliaceae
Mid-June–July; August-September
Perennial
Frequent

HABITAT AND RANGE
Rich woods; throughout—

DESCRIPTION
An umbel of 25 to 55 white-to-pale-yellow, bell-shaped flowers sits atop the naked, 6- to 15-inch stem. The basal leaves are elliptical, 8 to 10 inches long, and have the scent of onion. They grow early in the spring and disappear before the flowers bloom.

RELATED SPECIES
A. burdickii is a recently recognized species characterized by narrower leaves with white bases (the leaves of *A. tricoccum* have pink bases), and an umbel containing only 10 to 20 flowers. Nodding wild onion, *A. cernuum* (see photo on page x), has a smaller, more open umbel of pink or white flowers that nod from a downcurved stem. Its leaves are grasslike, and it is found primarily in open woods and rocky slopes. Field garlic, *A. vineale* (see photo on page 17), has tiny bulbs mixed with the pink or white flowers, and a single spathe below the umbel. It has grasslike leaves and grows in fields and disturbed sites. Wild garlic, *A. canadense*, is similar to field garlic, but it has fewer flowers (or no flowers) and a three-part spathe at the base of the flower umbel.

The sweet-tasting bulbs of ramps are so popular in the southern portion of the region that an annual "Ramp Festival" is held near the Smokies to celebrate their arrival. They are gathered in such quantities that one wonders whether the plant can continually withstand the pressure. Although the other species of wild onions and garlic are also edible, the ramp seems to be the favorite. It is served as a cooked vegetable, in salads, pickled, or added as seasoning to other dishes. It was also popular among Indians as a spring tonic, and for relief of cold symptoms. One superstition says that wearing wild onions around your neck keeps illness away. While this may not be true, eating them will surely keep your friends away, as the foul odor has a habit of leaching through the skin for days. This led to the ramp's reputation as the "sweetest tasting, foulest smelling plant that grows."

> PHOTO TIPS: Category 3
>
> With all species of wild onion, the best approach is to shoot a closeup of the flowerhead. This is easy for the field species since the background is open and uncluttered, but ramps grow in the forest and present problems. Unless you can find a plant well separated from background foliage, you may have to resort to using an artificial background.
>
> Consider shooting the distinctive foliage of ramps in early spring and returning later to shoot the flower.

75-300mm lens,
5T diopter,
6 sec. at f/16

Adams

75-300mm lens,
5T diopter,
1 sec. at f/22
Adams

Speckled Wood Lily

White clintonia
Clintonia umbellulata

Lily Family   Liliaceae
May-June; August-October
Perennial
Occasional

HABITAT AND RANGE
Rich, moist woods; throughout—

DESCRIPTION
The leafless (it may have very small leaves) stalk stands 8 to 18 inches high and holds an umbel of 5 to 30 white flowers. The flowers are often speckled with purple. The 2 to 5 basal leaves are elliptical and have hairs along the margins and midrib. The fruit is a very dark-blue-or-black berry.

Speckled wood lily may be overlooked when in flower (though it is quite lovely), but in fruit the plant is more conspicuous, with the umbel of shiny, dark blue berries contrasting sharply with the withering leaves. The genus *Clintonia* was named in honor of DeWitt Clinton, former governor of New York and devoted naturalist.

PHOTO TIPS: Category 2

The approach here is straightforward: shoot at an angle to include both leaves and flower. Shooting at an angle results in the greatest depth of field and reduces background coverage, cutting down on distractions. Be sure to return when the plant is in fruit.

Goldenseal

Orangeroot
Hydrastis canadensis

Crowfoot Family	Ranunculaceae
April; May-July	
Perennial	
Rare	

HABITAT AND RANGE
Rich woods; mostly throughout—

DESCRIPTION
The distinctive solitary flower has no petals and sepals that fall off early, leaving a tassel of greenish white stamens. The 8- to 24-inch stem bears 1 basal leaf and 2 stem leaves, all of which are thick, broad, heart shaped, and deeply lobed. The leaves are not fully developed at the time of flowering. The fruit is dark red (see photo on page 10).

Goldenseal has a rich medicinal history. For centuries it has been used as a general health tonic, to heal skin wounds, to treat watery eyes, heal inflamed mucous tissues, relieve liver and stomach problems, and to treat malaria. Nonmedical uses included insect repellent and clothing dyes. Experimental use has shown the plant has antibacterial, anticonvulsant, and sedative properties, as well as the ability to lower blood pressure. For a while, drug users consumed goldenseal to mask the presence of morphine and heroin in urine, but improved testing procedures have rendered this use of the plant ineffective.

Unfortunately, this history of medicinal use has been the demise of goldenseal. For the past several years, it has been a top seller in the health food market. Years of overcollecting and commercial exploitation have seriously reduced its numbers in the wild. If you are lucky enough to discover the plant in the wild, please do not contribute to its demise by harming it or reporting the location to others. It is possible to propagate the plant outside of its natural habitat. This is encouraged to establish stock for possible reintroduction to the wild.

PHOTO TIPS: Categories 2 and 10

You should be extremely careful while photographing this plant. Besides the usual concerns about inadvertently stepping on the plant, the stamens of goldenseal fall off at the slightest touch, which is devastating to its survival.

75-300mm lens, 5T diopter, 4 sec. at f/22   Adams

213

Daisy Fleabane

Erigeron annus

> Sunflower Family   Asteraceae
> May–October
> Annual
> Common

However, this belief, like so many other folk tales, is unfounded.

> PHOTO TIPS: Category 3
>
> *The fleabanes are field flowers, which means they are host to a number of insects. Try visiting early in the morning when the dew and low temperatures makes the insects sluggish and you can include them in the image.*

HABITAT AND RANGE
Fields, roadsides, and wasteplaces; throughout—

DESCRIPTION
Numerous small, aster-like, white or pink flowers grow on a branched, hairy stem. The hairs spread out from the stem, as opposed to lying flat against it. The mostly sessile leaves are usually more than $3/8$ inch wide, hairy, and obviously toothed. The leaves are elliptic to oblanceolate.

RELATED SPECIES
Lesser daisy fleabane, *E. strigosus* var. *beyrichii*, is similar except its leaves are usually less than $3/8$ inch wide and usually entire. The hairs on its stem are short and appressed. Common fleabane, *E. philadelphicus*, has more rays (100 to 150), and clasping stem leaves. Despite its name, it is the least common of the 3 species.

See robin's plantain on page 81.

The fleabanes are common and beautiful sights along the roadways and fields of the region, and they are wholly undeserving of the "weed" status attributed by some. The suffix *bane,* applied to numerous wildflowers, means "harmful" or "poisonous." The name *fleabane* suggests this plant might repel fleas.

75-300mm lens, 5T diopter, $1/15$ sec. at f/16   Adams
(See additional photo on page 32.)

*Daisy**

Ox-eye daisy
Leucanthemum vulgare (*Chrysanthemum leucanthemum*)

Sunflower Family   Asteraceae
April-August
Perennial
Common

HABITAT AND RANGE
Roadsides and fields; throughout—

DESCRIPTION
The solitary flowerhead has a compact, central yellow disc, which is depressed in the center and surrounded by 15 to 30 white rays. The 1- to 3-foot stem bears alternate, irregularly lobed leaves.

SIMILAR SPECIES
Feverfew, *Tanacetum parthenium* (*C. parthenium*), is a rare roadside flower that looks almost identical to the daisy, except it has numerous flowerheads on a bushy, branching stem.

The daisy is probably the only wildflower recognized as often as the dandelion. Most children, and probably a few adults, have pulled the petals off one by one to see what was happening in their love life.

Of course, those who know that daisies usually have an odd number of petals know whether to start with "loves me" or "loves me not."

The daisy is typical of the Sunflower family, with each ray being a separate female flower containing a pistil, while the tiny disc flowers contain both pistils and stamens.

The common name is a merging of the phrase "day's eye."

PHOTO TIPS: Categories 3 and 9

Numerous species of insects frequent daisies and provide the opportunity for a unique image of this ordinary flower. Visit early in the morning, while the dew and cool air keep the critters from crawling or flying away. In places, entire roadsides and fields are carpeted in daisies, permitting the use of wide-angle lenses.

75-300mm lens, 5T diopter, 1/15 sec. at f/11   *Adams*

Bloodroot

Puccoon root, red Indian paint
Sanguinaria canadensis

Poppy Family   Papaveraceae
Mid-March–April; April–May
Perennial
Common

75-300mm lens, 5T diopter, 1 sec. at f/22   Adams

HABITAT AND RANGE
Moist, rich woods; throughout—

DESCRIPTION
A solitary white flower with 8 to 12 showy petals and numerous yellow stamens grows on a 6- to 12-inch stem. The single leaf, born on a separate stalk, is deeply lobed and wraps around the stem.

SIMILAR SPECIES
The rare twinleaf, *Jeffersonia diphylla*, has a similar 8-petaled flower; however, its single leaf is almost completely divided at the middle. The delicate flowers are vulnerable to the elements and usually last only a few days.

Bloodroot is one of the first flowers to bloom in spring, subjecting it to the dangers of late frost. The leaf provides some protection as it remains wrapped around the stem at night, and the flower closes up at night until pollination occurs, further protecting the reproductive parts. The light green seedpod appears 2 to 3 weeks after pollination. At maturity the pod splits open, releasing the seeds that are often carried away by ants.

The genus name *Sanguinaria* (Latin for "blood") and all the common names refer to the bright orange- red juice in the stems and the roots. The juice, an effective stain, was used by Indians for war paint and to dye cloth.

Bloodroot contains sanguinarine, an alkaloid that has antiseptic, anesthetic, and anticancer properties. Indians used the plant as a cough medicine, appetite stimulant, emetic, insect repellent, snakebite antidote, and for rheumatism. These were dangerous practices since the plant is slightly toxic.

PHOTO TIPS: Category 2 ☼

Be careful not to overexpose the pure-white petals. To illustrate the plant's unique adaptation for surviving the cold, photograph it in the morning when the flower is closed and the leaf is tightly wrapped around the stem.

Mayapple

Mandrake
Podophyllum peltatum

Barberry Family	Berberidaceae
Mid-March–mid-May; May–June	
Perennial	
Common	

HABITAT AND RANGE
Rich woods, meadows; throughout—

DESCRIPTION
The 2 large (6 to 12 inches long), umbrellalike leaves of mayapple are deeply lobed into 5 to 9 segments. The leaves hide the solitary, 1- to 2-inch flower. The flower has waxy white petals and yellow stamens, and grows in the notch where the two leaf stems meet (the axil). Plants with a single leaf do not flower. The plant grows up to 18 inches tall and is often found in large colonies.

Mayapple is a popular wildflower and one of the harbingers of spring. After flowering, an egg-shaped, yellow fruit develops that is about 2 inches long. When ripe, the fruit is edible and is sometimes used to make jelly. Caution is advised, though, as the un-ripened fruit and the rest of the plant are poisonous and will cause severe diarrhea if eaten. However, many of nature's poisons can be beneficial when used properly. Two modern drugs are derived from mayapple: podophyllin and etoposide.

Unless you want to become a mother-to-be, you are advised against picking this wildflower. According to superstition, those who do so become pregnant.

PHOTO TIPS: Category 3

It's hard to include all the leaves and still make a clean, uncluttered image, so usually you'll want to isolate the blossom along with only part of the leaves. Because the flower is usually nodding, you'll have to shoot from underneath. Shooting from such a position may cause strain on the back, so look around for a flower that doesn't nod as much. However, a nodding flower presents a unique perspective when shot from underneath. Occasionally, you will find a single plant or patch of plants that warrant the use of a wide-angle lens.

50mm lens, extension tube, 4 sec. at f/16   Adams

Southern Nodding Trillium

Trillium rugelii (T. cernuum)

> Lily Family   Liliaceae
> April-May; June-July
> Perennial
> Scarce

75-300mm lens, 5T diopter, ½ sec. at f/22 Adams

HABITAT AND RANGE

Cove hardwoods, basic to neutral soil; only in the southern portion—

DESCRIPTION

The flower nods on a short flowerstalk beneath a whorl of 3 wide, ovate leaves. The 3 white-to-pale-pink (rarely dark purple or brown) petals curve backward at the tip. Purple anthers are displayed in the center. The plant grows 6 to 20 inches high.

RELATED SPECIES

Nodding trillium, *T. cernuum*, is a rare plant in the northern range that prefers damp woods with black ash and American elm. The only recognizable difference between it and *T. rugelii* is the length of its anthers, but this is not a good indicator for the layperson. In fact, *T. rugelii* has been only recently listed as a separate species. Sweet white trillium, *T. simile*, is an interesting species that looks like a cross between the white form of *T. erectum* and *T. rugelii*. It has wide white petals that are usually located above the leaves, and it has the fragrance of green apples. It grows only in the southern portion of the region.

Southern nodding trillium is one of the rarer species of trillium found in the southern Appalachian mountains, and it is also one of the most beautiful. *T. cernuum* is on the endangered species list for Virginia and West Virginia.

> PHOTO TIPS: Categories 3 and 10
>
> *You'll need to shoot from underneath looking up to adequately portray this wildflower. In most cases, this requires a 50mm or similar lens because you are so close. It also requires dirty knees and a commitment to a sore back. To lessen the muscle strain, and to allow the use of a longer lens—reducing background clutter—try to locate a specimen growing on a steep hillside. This allows shooting at a less-acute angle. Some photographers attach a right-angle view finder to their cameras for such a shot, but it can be troublesome to use.*

Painted Trillium

Trillium undulatum

> Lily Family   Liliaceae
> Mid-April–May; July–August
> Perennial
> Occasional

75-300mm lens, 5T diopter, 3 sec. at f/22   *Adams*

HABITAT AND RANGE
Acid soil of bogs, hemlock, and spruce-fir forests, usually beneath heaths; throughout—

DESCRIPTION
The 3 petals are white with a rosy red inverted "V" at the base and thin pink veins throughout the rest. A single whorl of ovate, pointed, stalked leaves grows beneath the flower on an 8- to 20-inch stem. The leaves are not fully mature during flowering, and they are often purplish brown.

This attractive little woodland herb is one of our favorite trillium species. Ants, too, enjoy the painted trillium, and most other trilliums, though probably not for their beauty as we do. They like to gather and take the seeds to their nest, where they eat the outside crest and discard the seed, which later germinates. This is the primary means for trillium seed dispersal.

Painted trillium is a threatened species in Kentucky.

> PHOTO TIPS: Category 2
>
> *Compositions that include the whole plant as well as closeups of the blossom work well. Be careful not to overexpose the white petals.*

Large-flowered Trillium

White trillium
Trillium grandiflorum

Lily Family   Liliaceae
April-June; July-August
Perennial
Common

HABITAT AND RANGE

Rich woods, shady coves, slopes, basic-to-neutral soil; throughout—

DESCRIPTION

Three is the magic number for identifying all trilliums. The 2- to 4-inch flower has 3 green sepals and 3 bright white, lance-shaped petals. The petals are tightly rolled in the center of the flower, forming a funnel-like opening decorated with yellow anthers. The petals flare out from this funnel above a single whorl of 3 broadly ovate, sessile leaves. Most white-flowered species of trillium, especially large-flowered trillium, have petals that change to pink with age; although some flowers may be pink upon emergence. The plant is 8 to 18 inches tall and often grows in large colonies.

RELATED SPECIES

Catesby's trillium, *T. catesbaei* (see photo on page 35), has a 1½-inch white flower that is often nodding below its elliptic leaves. Some of its distinguishing features are sickle-shaped sepals, yellow anthers that are irregularly twisted outward, and white petals that change to a rich pink with age. It is a relatively uncommon inhabitant of dry oak and oak-pine woods (and extending into rich woods) in the southern portion of the region. Wake robin or red trillium, *T. erectum* (page 116), has an occasional white form. It has smaller petals that spread outward from the base without forming the funnel as in large-flow-ered trillium. This white form of wake robin (see photo on page 242) is found primarily in the southern portion of the region, where it is common in some areas, especially in the Smokies.

See southern nodding trillium on page 218.

There is nothing quite so dazzling as a forest floor carpeted with the blooms of hundreds or thousands of large-flowered trilliums. It is one of the most common of the dozen or so species found in the southern Appalachians. Yet its population decreases when it is harvested for sale through garden nurseries. Once harvested from an area, trillium takes many years to repropagate—it takes 6 years for large-flowered trillium to go from seed to flower. In the first year, only underground rhizomes grow. A small leaf appears the second year, followed by several years of various leaf stages, until a flower is finally produced. Because of this long process, some nurseries sell plants that have been dug from the wild rather than propagating their own stock. Buyers should ask for proof that the plants are nursery grown.

Large-flowered trillium is particularly common in the rich woods of the Smokies and the southern portion of the Blue Ridge Parkway; but perhaps the largest colony in the country occurs near the northern end of Shenandoah National Park in the G. Richard Thompson Wildlife Management Area. It is estimated that the colony contains over 18 million plants. For more information about the site, contact the Virginia Native Plant Society (see the appendix).

PHOTO TIPS: Categories 2 and 9

The photo tips under the other trilliums usually apply to large-flowered trillium as well. One difference here is that the plant's tendency to grow in large patches enables the use of a wide-angle lens, letting the photographer create the quintessential southern Appalachian image. Be careful not to overexpose the white petals.

50mm lens, 2 sec. at f/22
(See additional photo on page 17.)

Adams

Wild Strawberry
Fragaria virginiana

Rose Family Rosaceae
March-June
Perennial
Common

75-300mm lens, 5T diopter, 1 sec. at f/16   *Adams*

HABITAT AND RANGE
Roadsides, fields, and woodland borders; throughout—

DESCRIPTION
Often found in large colonies, this low-growing plant (3 to 10 inches) has small white flowers with 5 petals. The leaves are divided into 3 ovate, toothed leaflets, 1 to 3 inches long. Flavorful red, ½-inch berries are produced in the fruiting season.

Three-toothed cinquefoil

SIMILAR SPECIES
Indian strawberry, *Duchesnea indica*, has a similar leaf structure and fruit; however, its flowers are yellow. Three-toothed cinquefoil, *Sibbaldiopsis tridentata* (*Potentilla tridentata*), is a similar flower of rock outcrops and balds. It has narrow, shiny, three-part evergreen leaves with 3 (rarely 5) teeth on the tips of each leaflet. It is uncommon, though where it does occur, it is often in large colonies.

The fruits of wild strawberry may not be as large as the cultivated variety, but they are often sweeter and more flavorful, and the dried leaves can be used to make a refreshing tea. A common belief is that the fruits of Indian strawberry are poisonous, but this is not true. Still, you probably won't want to eat them—they are rather bland and tasteless compared to those of wild strawberry.

PHOTO TIPS: Category 1
Shoot early in the morning or just after a rain when the dew or rain droplets cling to each tooth of the leaflets.

Grass of Parnassus

Parnassia asarifolia

Saxifrage Family   Saxifragaceae
August-October
Perennial
Scarce

105mm macro lens, ¼ sec. at f/16   Adams

HABITAT AND RANGE
Bogs, seepage slopes, streambanks; throughout—

DESCRIPTION
The white flowers have 5 clawed petals with prominent green veins and 5 stamens that grow alternately with the petals. The plant grows 8 to 10 inches high and has a rosette of kidney-shaped, long-stalked basal leaves. There is a single clasping leaf on the stem.

RELATED SPECIES
P. grandifolia is a very rare species that has ovate to oblong leaves, and petals that are not clawed.

P. asarifolia

P. grandifolia

Nothing about this plant resembles grass, and it is uncertain just how it got that name. "Parnassus" is a mountain in central Greece that was considered sacred to Apollo. The first-century naturalist Dioscorides observed a similar plant on Parnassus, possibly growing in meadows in a manner that resembled grass. It is believed that the plant Dioscorides named was *P. palustris*, a species also found in the northern United States and Canada, and one which has thinner leaves. The common name has since been attributed to all the species in the genus.

PHOTO TIPS: Category 2
A good possibility with grass of Parnassus is to find a couple of flowers that are roughly on the same plane and shoot a tight closeup. This reveals the delicate beauty of the blossoms.

Common Wood Sorrel

Wood shamrock, sourgrass
Oxalis montana

Wood Sorrel Family	Oxalidaceae
May-July; June-September	
Perennial	
Frequent	

105mm macro lens, 6 sec. at f/32   Adams

HABITAT AND RANGE

Rich, moist woods and hemlock forests, usually at high elevations and especially in spruce-fir forests; from the Smokies northward—

DESCRIPTION

This plant is easily recognized by the shamrock-shaped leaves consisting of 3 inverted heart-shaped leaflets. The single flower has 5 white (rarely pink) petals with obvious deep pink veins. It often grows in colonies.

SIMILAR AND RELATED SPECIES

Violet wood sorrel, *O. violacea*, has a small cluster of rose-purple flowers without the pink veining. See spring beauty, page 196.

A welcome sight on a hike through the cool, high-elevation forests of the region, this "St. Patrick's Day" flower is as well known by its leaves as it is by its flower. Legend says that St. Patrick used the leaf to explain the Doctrine of the Trinity to a tribal chief during one of his missionary journeys. Its history in Ireland goes back even further to the time when it served as a symbol for the Druids.

> **PHOTO TIPS: Category 1** ☼
>
> *Common wood sorrel often grows out of moss, which makes a perfect background. Try to find a plant that grows close to the moss and not a few inches above it. This will allow enough depth of field to keep everything in sharp focus. You might try to press the flower and leaves gently into the moss, but be careful not to damage them.*

Dutchman's Breeches

Dicentra cucullaria

75-300mm lens, 5T diopter, ½ sec. at f/16   Adams

HABITAT AND RANGE

Rich woods, northern slopes; scattered localities throughout—

DESCRIPTION

An arching stem holds 4 to 10 white "breeches" above fernlike, segmented leaves. Two inflated petals form spurs (the "pant's" legs), while two smaller petals and a little yellow color form the "waistline." The plant grows 6 to 12 inches tall.

RELATED SPECIES

See squirrel corn, page 226.

It's easy to see where Dutchman's breeches gets its name after watching the little "pants" blowing in a breeze on the "washline" (stem). Though it is quite pretty, it is also poisonous, containing alkaloids that act as a depressant to the central nervous system. In the past, it was used by veterinarians to preanesthetize large animals. Some animals, such as cattle, have died from eating the flowers in the wild.

In South Carolina, Dutchman's breeches is a threatened species.

PHOTO TIPS: Category 6

Ideally, you'll want to include some of the foliage in the image. However, since the flowers grow above the leaves and not in the same plane, depth of field becomes a problem. Look for a situation where the flowers grow a little closer to the leaves, allowing you to keep more of the scene in focus.

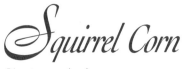

Squirrel Corn

Dicentra canadensis

HABITAT AND RANGE

Rich woods; throughout, but mostly in the southern portion—

DESCRIPTION

The sweet-scented white flowers (sometimes with a tinge of purple) have 2 outer petals that form rounded basal spurs. The flowers grow in a raceme at or just above the segmented, fernlike leaves.

SIMILAR AND RELATED SPECIES

Wild bleeding heart, *D. eximia* (see photo on page 30), is a plant of rich, rocky woods and bluffs. It closely resembles squirrel corn, but wild bleeding heart has pink flowers. Pale corydalis, *Corydalis sempervirens*, is a closely related and similar species with single-spurred, pink flowers with yellow tips. Yellow corydalis, *C. flavula*, is similar to pale corydalis except for its all-yellow flowers. See Dutchman's breeches, *D. cucullaria*, on page 225.

All three species of *Dicentra* mentioned here contain poisonous alkaloids in the leaves and roots of the plant. Cattle have been known to die from eating the new spring leaves. The belief that squirrels favor the tubers, which are shaped like kernels of corn, prompted the common name, but one wonders how the squirrels survive the poison if they eat the roots.

The genus name *Dicentra* is from Greek, meaning "two-spurred."

PHOTO TIPS: Category 6

See the photo tips under Dutchman's breeches, page 225.

75-300mm lens, 5T diopter, 4 sec. at f/11   Adams

Oconee Bells

Shortia, coltsfoot
Shortia galacifolia var. *galacifolia*

> Diapensia Family   Diapensiaceae
> Early March–mid-April; July–August
> Perennial
> Rare

HABITAT AND RANGE
Rich woods, especially along stream banks, usually associated with rhododendron and mountain laurel; a few isolated localities in western and southwestern North Carolina, northwestern South Carolina, and northeastern Georgia—

DESCRIPTION
The solitary flowers resemble nodding bells, and have 5 white or pinkish white petals with notched and wavy edges. Five conspicuous, fertile, yellow stamens curve inward, while 5 sterile stamens are hidden at the base of the petals. The rounded, evergreen leaves are shiny and leathery, and have sharp teeth. The plant grows in dense patches.

SIMILAR AND RELATED SPECIES
Plants with styles that are mostly $^3/_{16}$ to $^3/_8$ inch long are referred to as variety *brevistyla*, while plants with styles mostly $^9/_{16}$ inch or longer are variety *galacifolia*. The beginner may wish to label all plants as simply *Shortia galacifolia*.

Oconee bells is unmistakable in flower, but at other times its leaves may be confused with galax, page 235. However, galax leaves are larger, with finer, more numerous teeth. Also, galax has an earthy, unpleasant (to some) odor.

For a discussion on the interesting history of Oconee bells see page 31. This history, combined with the attractive evergreen leaves and the delightful flowers, has made Oconee bells one of the most popular wildflowers with gardeners and photographers alike. Unfortunately, this popularity may contribute to its rarity, as irresponsible persons remove the plant from the wild. It is now so well established in public and private gardens that anyone wishing to propogate their own supply, or photograph it, should not consider using wild plants.

Oconee bells is an official symbol of the Carolinas' Nature Photographers Association.

> PHOTO TIPS: Categories 2 and 10
>
> *Two good possibilities are a closeup of the flower alone and an overall shot that includes the flower and some of the distinctive foliage. During late fall and persisting into winter, the leaves become varying shades of orange, red, and green.*

75-300mm lens,
5T diopter,
3 sec. at f/22
Adams

Lily of the Valley

Convallaria majuscula (C. montana)

> Lily Family   Liliaceae
> Mid-April–early June
> Perennial
> Scarce

75-300mm lens, 5T diopter, 2 sec. at f/22   Adams

HABITAT AND RANGE

Rich woods, wooded slopes and coves; throughout—

DESCRIPTION

The fragrant white flowers are bell shaped and hang on one side of the 4- to 10-inch stem. The plant has 2 or 3 elliptical, veined leaves that are 5 to 12 inches long. It normally grows in scattered patches, though it is not really colonial.

SIMILAR AND RELATED SPECIES

C. majalis is an introduced species that occasionally escapes cultivation. It is quite similar but smaller in size, with leaves less than 6 inches long. See wild lily of the valley on page 201.

Perfume makers have often attempted to imitate the delicate fragrance of lily of the valley. While their perfumes may have a pleasing aroma, there is no substitute for the flower's scent as it blends with the woodsy, earthy smell of outdoors.

The flowers and roots have been used as a substitute for *Digitalis purpurea*, a plant used in the treatment of heart disease. Lily of the valley is listed as a threatened species in South Carolina and an endangered species in Kentucky.

> PHOTO TIPS: Categories 2 and 10
>
> *Photographers should pay special attention to the flowers that are not in the image to make sure they don't step or sit on them. See if you can photograph a plant at the edge of the patch to lessen the chance of damage.*

Cut-leaved Toothwort

Pepper root

Cardamine concatenata (Dentaria laciniata)

Mustard Family   Brassicaceae (Cruciferae)
Late March-May; April-May
Perennial
Common

HABITAT AND RANGE
Rich woods; throughout—

DESCRIPTION
The white or pink flowers have 4 petals and grow in a terminal cluster on an 8- to 15-inch stem. The stem has soft hairs on the upper half. A whorl of 3 leaves attaches at the middle of the stem. The leaves are divided into 2 to 5 (usually 3) toothed segments. Basal leaves develop after flowering.

SIMILAR AND RELATED SPECIES
Toothwort, *C. diphylla* (*D. diphylla*), has a pair of stem leaves, each divided into 3 broadly lanceolate, toothed leaflets. The basal leaves are similar but egg shaped. Toothwort grows in wetter environments, often along streambanks. The scarce slender toothwort, *C. angustata* (*D. heterophylla*), also has only 2 stem leaves, but the leaves are divided into 3 narrow, lance-shaped leaflets. The basal leaves of *C. angustata* are much broader than the stem leaves. Several other species of *Cardamine*, collectively

called bitter cress, have similar flowers. They are distinguished from the toothworts by the lack of a whorl of deeply divided stem leaves. Garlic mustard, *Alliaria petiolata* (*A. officinalis*), a common spring plant in Shenandoah National Park and the surrounding region, has similar flowers, but it is much taller (1 to 3 feet) and has heart-shaped, coarsely toothed leaves.

Because the rootstock of some *Dentaria* species resembles teeth, the name toothwort was applied. Additionally, according to the *Doctrine of Signatures* (see page 163) it was once believed that the plant would relieve toothaches. This is not true, but the peppery-tasting roots are often used as a spice.

Cut-leaved
toothwort

Toothwort

Garlic
mustard

PHOTO TIPS: Category 2 ☼

Be careful not to overexpose the white petals.

75-300mm lens, 5T diopter, ¼ sec. at f/16 Adams

White Campion *

Evening lychnis
Silene latifolia ssp. *alba* (*Lychnis alba*)

75-300mm lens, 5T diopter, ½ sec. at f/16   *Adams*

> Pink Family   Caryophyllaceae
> April–July
> Annual or Perennial
> Occasional

HABITAT AND RANGE
Roadsides, fields, wasteplaces; throughout—

DESCRIPTION
This plant can be identified by the inflated, hairy, and veined calyx, and the 5 white, cleft petals. Another identifying characteristic is the generally sticky nature of the plant. The flowers grow in loose, branching clusters on a 6- to 20-inch stem. Female flowers have 4 or 5 (rarely 6) obvious curved styles, while male flowers have 10 stamens. The sessile leaves are ovate to elliptic.

SIMILAR AND RELATED SPECIES
Bladder campion, *S. vulgaris* (*S. cucubalus*), has a distinctively veined, smooth calyx. Forking catchfly, *S. dichotoma*, is a hairy species with sessile flowers, deeply cleft petals, and very slender, paired leaves. Its calyx has 10 ribs and is only slightly inflated, and the flowers seem to all grow on one side of the stem. The night-flowering catchfly, *S. noctiflora*, an uncommon species that opens in the evenings, is quite similar to white campion, but has only 3 styles. Sleepy catchfly, *S. antirrhina*, has very small white or pink flowers that open for a short time in sunshine. Its stem is covered with black, sticky secretions. Starry campion, *S. stellata*, is eas-ily distinguished by its fringed petals. Also, its leaves are arranged in pairs at the top and bottom of the stem, while the middle leaves are in whorls of 4. *S. ovata* is similar to starry campion, but its petals are more deeply fringed, and it does not have whorled leaves.

The name of the genus *Silene* is said to have come from Silenus, foster-father of Bacchus in Greek mythology. Silenus was often intoxicated, with his face covered in frothy beer, which reminded the authors of the sticky secretions of many members of the *Silene* genus.

> PHOTO TIPS: Category 3
>
> *Most of the time you will want to shoot a tight closeup of 1 or 2 blossoms, possibly including a little foliage. The most distinguishing feature of the campions is the inflated calyx, so be sure to shoot at an angle that adequately portrays it. This may mean settling for incomplete focus on the petals.*

Bladder campion
75-300mm lens, 5T diopter, $^1/_8$ sec. at f/11   Casstevens

Starry campion
75-300mm lens, 5T diopter, 2 sec. at f/16   Adams

75-300mm lens,
5T diopter,
4 sec. at f/32

Adams

Downy Rattlesnake Plantain

Goodyera pubescens

> Orchid Family   Orchidaceae
> June-August
> Perennial
> Frequent

75-300mm lens, 5T diopter, 1 sec. at f/11

Casstevens

HABITAT AND RANGE

Woodlands; throughout—

DESCRIPTION

A distinctive feature of this orchid is the basal rosette of oval, blue-green leaves, with a network of white veins and a wide, white center vein. The cluster of small (¼-inch) flowers forms a 1- to 5-inch conical spike at the top of the 6- to 20-inch, hairy stem. It often grows in colonies.

RELATED SPECIES

Lesser rattlesnake plantain, *G. repens* (var. *ophioides*), has a shorter spike of flowers that only grows on one side of the stem, and smaller leaves with variable white markings. It only grows to 12 inches tall.

The beautiful, variegated leaves of the rattlesnake plantains are evergreen, adding welcome green color to the forest floor during the winter. The leaf patterns are said to resemble the markings of a rattlesnake, and in fruit the spike actually rattles when thumped—thus the common name. The plant was used by Indians with great faith as a remedy for snake bites.

> PHOTO TIPS: Category 3
>
> *You can shoot an isolation image of the spike, but this does not represent the flower well and does not show the beautiful leaves. Try to find a situation that lets you include both, although this may create background problems.*

Nodding Ladies' Tresses

Fragrant ladies' tresses
Spiranthes cernua

Orchid Family   Orchidaceae
Late July-October
Perennial
Occasional

75-300mm lens,
5T diopter,
½ sec. at f/22

Adams

HABITAT AND RANGE

Swamps, meadows, wet roadsides, often at high elevations; throughout—

DESCRIPTION

Small (¼- to ½-inch), white, slightly downcurved, double-lipped flowers grow in 2 to 4 spiraling rows on the 8- to 18-inch stem. The flowers are often fragrant. Three or 4 slender leaves, up to 12 inches long, grow from the base of the stem and may be withered before the flowering period.

SIMILAR AND RELATED SPECIES

Spring ladies' tresses, *S. vernalis*, is the tallest species of this genus, sometimes reaching 4 feet. The flowers are white to pale yellow, with downy hairs, and a lower lip that curves down and under. Its grass-like leaves are usually present at flowering.

The following 3 *Spiranthes* species all have flowers that are arranged on a single spiral, and flower lips less than ³/16 inch long: Little ladies' tresses, *S. tuberosa* (var. *grayi*), is the smallest species in the genus and is easily overlooked. Its 2 or 3 egg-shaped basal leaves usually fade before the flowers appear. The flower lip of slender ladies' tresses, *S. lacera* var. *gracilis* (*S. gracilis*), has a green stripe on the inner surface, and the smooth flowers are tightly spiraled. Its 3 to 5 basal leaves are oval and may be absent at flowering. This

species is more common in the southern section. *S. lacera* var. *lacera* (*S. lacera*) is similar to the previous species except its leaves are present at flowering, and the flowers are minutely hairy. This species is more common in the northern section.

Colicroot, *Aletris farinosa* (see photo on page 25), is a woodland species very similar to *Spiranthes*, but its flowers do not grow in a spiral.

One look at any of the ladies' tresses orchids and you will instantly see how they got their genus name. *Spiranthes* is from the Greek *speira*, meaning a "coil" or "spiral," and from *anthos*, a "flower." As with many species that have small blooms, these tiny, spiral flowers deserve a close look. *S. cernua* is relatively common along the high-elevation roadsides of the Blue Ridge Parkway.

PHOTO TIPS: Category 2

Ladies' tresses are easy to photograph since they are low growing and don't blow around much. Also, the magnification required to shoot a revealing closeup causes the background to blur into a pleasing posterlike effect. If possible, include all of the flowering portion of the spike instead of cropping off the bottom.

Devil's Bit

Blazing star, fairy-wand
Chamaelirium luteum

> Lily Family   Liliaceae
> Early April-May; September-November
> Perennial
> Frequent

ground," and from *leirion*, for "lily." An immature specimen was used as the foundation of the genus, and it was incorrectly assumed that this lily normally grows on the ground.

HABITAT AND RANGE

Rich woods; throughout—

DESCRIPTION

Small white flowers are tightly clustered on a spike or raceme that may be 4 to 8 inches long. The raceme is located on the end of an 8- to 18-inch stem. Staminate (male) and pistillate (female) flowers are on separate plants. The male plant has a longer raceme (rarely a spike) that often curves downward. The female plant grows in racemes or spikes and tends to be leafier. The evergreen basal leaves are oblanceolate, smooth, and form a rosette; stem leaves are narrower. The flowers turn yellow with age.

SIMILAR SPECIES

Lizard's tail, *Saururus cernuus*, has a similar drooping raceme of white flowers, but its leaves are heart shaped. It grows in swamps and shallow-water areas where it forms large colonies; however, it is scarce in our region.

The scientific name of devil's bit provides a good lesson in the necessity of observing mature plants to achieve accurate identification. The genus name is from the Greek *chamai*, which means "on the

50mm lens, 81A warming filter, 4 sec. at f/22   Adams

Galax

Beetleweed

Galax urceolata (G. aphylla)

> Diapensia Family   Diapensiaceae
> May-July; August-October
> Perennial
> Common

HABITAT AND RANGE
Heath woodlands, rocky slopes; throughout—

DESCRIPTION
The shiny evergreen basal leaves identify this plant at any time of year. They are rounded, slightly toothed, and 3 to 4 inches wide. A dense raceme of small white flowers, with stamens growing together to form a tube, graces the 8- to 24-inch, bare stem.

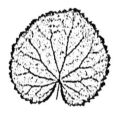

SIMILAR SPECIES
See Oconee bells, page 227.

Galax plants are harvested by the thousands in the national forests and private lands of the southern Appalachians—the only place it grows. The evergreen leaves make a long-lasting addition to floral arrangements. Although the plant is presently common in many areas, often occurring in large patches,

75-300mm lens, 5T diopter, 4 sec. at f/16   Adams

it is distressing to see so many plants taken from the wild. Persons who wish to use it for decoration are encouraged to propagate their own supply.

> PHOTO TIPS: Category 3
>
> *The distinctive leaves of galax are more attractive and photogenic than the flower, and you should include them in your photos. Unless the plant is growing on a steep bank—it often does—there are usually problems with background clutter. Maybe you can locate a suitable situation for a forest landscape, using galax as a foreground.*

Ragged Green Fringed Orchid

Platanthera lacera var. *lacera* (*Habenaria lacera*)

Orchid Family   Orchidaceae
June-August
Perennial
Scarce

HABITAT AND RANGE
Wet woods and meadows, bogs; throughout—

DESCRIPTION
The 10- to 30-inch stem holds a raceme of greenish yellow flowers and erect, linear-to-lanceolate leaves. The uppermost leaves are small and bractlike. The flowers have a distinctive three-part lip, each part of which is divided into threadlike fringes. A slender spur curves downward beneath the lip.

SIMILAR AND RELATED SPECIES
The following species are all members of the orchid family.

Large round-leaved orchid, *P. orbiculata* var. *orbiculata* (*H. orbiculata*) (see photo on page 9), a plant found in rich woods, has somewhat similar flowers that aren't fringed. However, the most distinctive part of the plant is the pair of large, round basal leaves that rest flat upon the ground.

Southern rein orchid, *P. flava* var. *herbiola* (*H. flava* var. *herbiola*), has a slender raceme of greenish yellow flowers with a small lip curved underneath.

There is a tiny lobe on each side of the base of the lip and in the center of the upper surface. It is a leafy plant, with leaflike bracts beneath each flower, which usually extend beyond the flower.

Green adder's mouth, *Malaxis unifolia*, a small plant of moist woods and streamsides, has a short raceme of green flowers and a single, clasping, oval leaf about midway on the stem.

Small green wood orchid, *P. clavellata* (*H. clavellata*), is a small plant found in bogs and wet woods. It ranges from a few inches to a little over a foot tall and has 1 (rarely 2) oblong-to-oblanceolate leaf located near the middle of the stem. The leaf is much larger than that of green adder's mouth, ranging from 2 to 7 inches long. The few flowers on this plant are greenish yellow with 3 rounded teeth on the rectangular lip. The flowers have a spur that curves downward, just beneath or to the side of the flower.

Viewing any of these orchids requires a keen eye and knowledge about their habitat, as they are quite inconspicuous and blend with their surroundings. The previous genus name, *Habenaria*, is from the Latin *habena*, which means "rein." This name refers to the spur that is present in all members of the genus *Platanthera*. The species name of ragged green fringed orchid, *lacera*, means "torn or lacerated," and refers to the obviously fringed flowers.

PHOTO TIPS: Categories 2, 3, and 10

Locating these orchids is the hardest part about photographing them. Once you do, the best approach in most circumstances is relatively straightforward: a closeup of the raceme. However, large round-leaved orchid, which is unique with its distinctive leaves, is much better represented with a composition that includes the whole plant.

75-300mm lens, 5T diopter, ½ sec. at f/22   *Adams*

False Hellebore

White hellebore
Veratrum viride

Lily Family   Liliaceae
June-August; July-September
Perennial
Occasional

HABITAT AND RANGE
High-elevation openings in bogs, meadows, and wet woods; throughout—

DESCRIPTION
This stout, leafy plant has a hairy stem, grows 2 to 8 feet tall, and bears large clusters of star-shaped, yellow-green flowers. The sepals and petals are covered in soft hairs. The numerous large leaves clasp the stem. The leaves are elliptic, tapered at both ends, and strongly pleated.

SIMILAR SPECIES
Melanthium parviflorum, a plant found in rich woods, has leaves that are mostly basal and stalked, and sepals and petals that are smooth.

False hellebore is an unusual plant in that it is most attractive long before it blooms. During early May—early spring in the highlands—the plant begins to unfurl its leafy shoots, creating a beautiful green display in the otherwise wintry landscape (see photo on page 43). By the time it flowers, it is hard to distinguish among the ferns and other foliage of its environment, and its leaves have usually been heavily ripped and torn.

False hellebore is highly poisonous if ingested (especially the roots), causing heart rate and respiration to slow. At one time, it was added to heart medications, but overdoses and cases of accidental poisonings ended its use. There is a story that some Indians were selected as chiefs only if they survived eating the plant.

This wildflower is very similar to the California corn lily, *V. californicum*, that is common in western states.

PHOTO TIPS: Category 8

This plant is rather ugly at the flowering stage, but that's OK. When the young leaves are just beginning to appear, they make outstanding photo subjects. Sometimes, you can even photograph them popping through a late spring snow. This is especially likely at the high-elevation Mount Mitchell State Park, one of the best places to photograph the plant.

50mm lens, ¹/₆₀ sec. at f/11   Harry Ellis

Jack-in-the-Pulpit

Indian turnip, lords and ladies
Arisaema triphyllum

> Arum Family   Araceae
> April-June; July-September
> Perennial
> Frequent

HABITAT AND RANGE
Moist, rich woods; throughout—

DESCRIPTION
The tubular spathe (pulpit) enclosing the spadix (jack), along with the 1 or 2, three-part leaves, make this plant easy to recognize. The "pulpit" may be all green or include varying shades of purple stripes.

RELATED SPECIES
A. dracontium, green dragon, is an uncommon plant with a narrower spathe and a spadix extending several inches beyond the tube. The leaf is usually divided into several leaflets. *Gray's* lists 2 additional species of jack-in-the-pulpit based on slight variations. In the current treatment, these species are listed only as subspecies of *A. triphyllum*. The differences between these subspecies are difficult to discern by the beginner. Don't worry, you will be safe in labeling all the "jacks" you find as simply *A. triphyllum*.

Anyone who has found this popular wildflower and lifted its little hood to see "jack," the preacher, in his "pulpit," understands its common name. The actual flowers are at the base of the spadix. Plants with tiny, round green flowers are female, while plants with threadlike, pollen-covered flowers are male. After pollination, the fruits form. When autumn approaches, the spathe withers away, exposing the cluster of bright red berries (see photo on page 21).

An intriguing adaptation of jack-in-the-pulpit is its ability to change sex from year to year. In a year of good growing conditions, the underground corm will store an abundance of food and produce a female plant, which requires extra energy to fruit. In less adequate years, a male plant will appear in spring.

The roots of jack-in-the-pulpit are edible after extensive cooking and drying to rid the plant of calcium oxalate crystals. These crystals occur throughout the plant and cause severe burning if eaten raw. Some have suggested that the roots may serve as a natural insecticide, as the calcium oxalate seems to keep insects from eating the plant's leaves.

> PHOTO TIPS: Category 3
>
> *This is a tough one. Closeups featuring only the flower tube tend to be stale and dull, but we have yet to find a good situation for including all the leaves and the tube. Intermediate compositions that show the tube between the two bare leafstalks do not seem to work well at all. The best photographs we've seen show several whole plants growing close together.*

75-300mm lens,
5T diopter,
½ sec. at f/16
Adams

Ginseng

Panax quinquefolius

> Ginseng Family   Araliaceae
> June; August-October
> Perennial
> Rare

HABITAT AND RANGE

Rich woods; throughout—

DESCRIPTION

The single, small, and fragrant umbel of inconspicuous greenish white or greenish yellow flowers grows in the leaf axils of the plant. A whorl of 3 to 4 leaves on long stalks dominates the plant, with each leaf divided into 3 to 5 (usually 5) toothed segments. Red berries are produced in the fall. The plant grows 8 to 20 inches tall.

SIMILAR AND RELATED SPECIES

The very rare dwarf ginseng, *P. trifolius*, has a white flower, 3 sessile leaflets per leaf, and is only 4 to 8 inches tall. See photo on page 35. The closely related wild sarsaparilla, *Aralia nudicaulis*, produces 2 to 5 (usually 3) umbels of flowers per stalk and purple-black berries in the fall. Its flowering stalk is separate from the leaf stalk.

While the future of many wildflower species is uncertain, it is clear that ginseng is headed toward eradication unless collecting is halted. Traditionally, ginseng has been one of the most heavily harvested wildflowers in the Appalachian region. Chinese have valued the plant's root for centuries, using its "power" as an aphrodisiac as well as to rejuvenate the body. Export of ginseng root has been a profitable business in eastern North America since the early 1800s. In 1980, a staggering 375,000 pounds were exported, 30 percent of which was taken from the wild. Yearly exports are currently in the range of 100,000 pounds, but this is still a tremendous amount and doesn't account for the roots that remain for sale in health-food and herbal outlets in this country.

Ginseng is easily propagated outside of its natural habitat, but supposedly the propogated roots don't have the same "powers," making them less acceptable to ginseng brokers. Although some laws are in place to monitor the harvest and sale of ginseng, regulations to completely halt the operations are difficult to enact because the business is so profitable. Some states, such as Tennessee and South Carolina, list it as a threatened species. In other states it is protected as a renewable resource. Certainly, more needs to be done if this species is to remain a viable member of our flora.

PHOTO TIPS: Categories 3 and 10

Although ginseng is not necessarily fragile, it is recommended that you do not photograph it in the wild. Most people, especially other photographers, pay close attention to anyone who carries a camera bag and tripod, and ginseng does not need the publicity. Several private and public botanical gardens have fine opportunities for photography, and some even have conditions that permit the use of a wide-angle lens. The accompanying photograph was made in such a facility.

28mm lens, 81A warming filter, 8 sec. at f/22   *Adams*

Wake robin (white form), see page 220
75-300mm lens, 5T diopter, 1 sec. at f/16   *Adams*

PHOTOGRAPHY SOURCES

Applied CD Technologies, Inc.
5600 Seventy-seven Center Drive, Suite 360
Charlotte, NC 28217
704-527-6800

Bogen Photo Corporation
565 East Crescent Avenue
P.O. Box 506
Ramsey, NJ 07446
201-818-9500
In addition to their own line, Bogen also
distributes Gitzo products.

Carolinas' Nature Photographers Association
P.O. Box 1131
Mt. Pleasant, SC 29465

Keys Printing
P.O. Box 8
Greenville, SC 29602
803-288-6560

Kirk Enterprises
4670 East U.S. Highway 20
Angola, IN 46703
219-665-3670

Nature Photographer
P.O. Box 2037
West Palm Beach, FL 33402
407-586-7332

North American Nature Photography Association
10200 West 44th Avenue, Suite 304
Wheat Ridge, CO 80033
303-422-8527

Outdoor Photographer
12121 Wilshire Boulevard, Suite 1220
Los Angeles, CA 92005
310-820-1500

Really Right Stuff
P.O. Box 6531
Los Osos, CA 93412
805-528-6321

Slik Corporation
300 Webro Road
Dept. OP
Parsippany, NJ 07054

WILDFLOWER EVENTS

Spring Wildflower Symposium
Wintergreen Resort
P.O. Box 468
Wintergreen, VA 22958
804-325-8172
Held annually in May.

Spring Wildflower Pilgrimage
Great Smoky Mountains National Park
107 Park Headquarters Road
Gatlinburg, Tennessee 37738
615-436-1256
Held annually on the last weekend in April.

STATE AGENCIES

Georgia Department of Natural Resources
Georgia Natural Heritage Program
2117 US Hwy. 278, SE
Social Circle, GA 30279
706-557-3032

Kentucky Heritage Counsel
Kentucky Nature Preserves Commission
801 Schenkel Lane
Frankfurt, KY 40601
502-573-2886

North Carolina Natural Heritage Program
Department of Environment,
Health and Natural Resources
Division of State Parks and Recreation
P.O. Box 27687
Raleigh, NC 27611
919-733-7701

South Carolina Department of Natural Resources
Heritage Trust Program
P.O. Box 167
Columbia, SC 29202
803-734-3893

Tennessee Department of
Environment and Conservation
Division of Natural Heritage
401 Church Street
Life and Casualty Tower, 8th Floor
Nashville, TN 37243
615-532-0431

Virginia Department of
Conservation and Recreation
Natural Heritage Program
1500 E. Main Street, Suite 312
Richmond, VA 23219
804-786-7951

West Virginia Natural Heritage Program
Department of Natural Resources
Operations Center
Ward Road, P.O. Box 67
Elkins, WV 26241
304-637-0245

BOTANICAL GARDENS

Highlands Nature Center Botanical Garden
Highlands Biological Station
P.O. Drawer 580
Highlands, NC 28741
704-526-2602

North Carolina Botanical Garden
CB# 3375, Totten Center
University of North Carolina
Chapel Hill, NC 27599
919-962-0522

WILDFLOWER AND CONSERVATION ORGANIZATIONS

National Wildflower Research Center
2600 FM 973 North
Austin, TX 78725-4201
512-929-3600

The North Carolina Arboretum Society
P.O. Box 6617
Asheville, NC 28816
704-665-2492

North Carolina Wildflower Preservation Society, Inc.
1933 Gaston Street
Winston-Salem, NC 27103

Southern Appalachian Highlands Conservancy
34 Wall Street, Suite 802
Asheville, NC 28801
704-253-0095

Tennessee Native Plant Society
Department of Botany, University of Tennessee
Knoxville, TN 37996

Virginia Native Plant Society
P.O. Box 844
Annandale, VA 22003
703-368-9803

NATIONAL PARKS

Blue Ridge Parkway
Park Headquarters
400 BB&T Building
Asheville, NC 28801
704-298-0398
    For emergencies or to report poachers,
    call 1-800-PARKWATCH.

Great Smoky Mountains National Park
Headquarters Office
107 Park Headquarters Road
Gatlinburg, TN 37738
615-448-6222
    For emergencies or to report poachers,
    call 616-436-1200.

Shenandoah National Park
Superintendent
Rt. 4, Box 348
Luray, VA 22835
703-999-3500
    For emergencies or to report poachers,
    call 1-800-732-0911 or call collect
    at 0-703-999-2227.

ℬibliography

Blacklock, Craig, and Nadine Blacklock. *Photographing Wildflowers*. Minneapolis, Minn.: Voyageur Press, Inc., 1987.

Brown, Tom, Jr. *Tom Brown's Guide to Wild Edible and Medicinal Plants*. New York: Berkley Books, 1985.

Coffey, Timothy. *The History and Folklore of North American Wildflowers*. Boston: Houghton Mifflin Company, 1993.

Fernald, Merrit Lyndon. *Gray's Manual of Botany*. 8th ed. Portland, Ore.: Dioscorides Press, 1950.

Foster, Steven, and Roger A. Caras. *A Field Guide to Venomous Animals and Poisonous Plants: North America North of Mexico*. Boston: Houghton Mifflin Company, 1994.

Foster, Steven, and James A. Duke. *A Field Guide to Medicinal Plants: Eastern and Central North America*. Boston: Houghton Mifflin Company, 1990.

Gledhill, D. *The Names of Plants*. 2nd ed. New York: Cambridge University Press, 1989.

Gupton, Oscar W., and Fred C. Swope. *Fall Wildflowers of the Blue Ridge and Great Smoky Mountains*. Charlottesville: University Press of Virginia, 1987.

———. *Wildflowers of the Shenandoah Valley and Blue Ridge Mountains*. Charlottesville: University Press of Virginia, 1979.

———. *Wild Orchids of the Middle Atlantic States*. Knoxville: The University of Tennessee Press, 1986.

Holt, Perry C., and Robert A. Paterson. *The Distributional History of the Biota of the Southern Appalachians, Part II: Flora*. A symposium sponsored by Virginia Polytechnic Institute and State University and the Association of Southeastern Biologists, Blacksburg, Va., November 1970.

Imes, Rick. *Wildflowers: How to Identify Flowers in the Wild and How to Grow Them in Your Garden*. Emmaus, Pa.: Rodale Press, 1992.

Justice, William S., and C. Ritchie Bell. *Wild Flowers of North Carolina*. Chapel Hill: The University of North Carolina Press, 1968.

Kartesz, John T. *A Synonymized Checklist of the Vascular Flora of the United States, Canada, and Greenland*. 2 vols. Portland, Ore.: Timber Press, 1994.

Krochmal, Arnold, and Connie Krochmal. *A Field Guide to Medicinal Plants*. New York: Times Books, 1984.

Laun, Charles. *Handbook of Nature and Scientific Photography*. Columbia, Mo.: Alsace Books and Films, 1988.

Martin, Laura C. *Wildflower Folklore*. Old Saybrook, Conn.: The Globe Pequot Press, 1993.

Newcomb, Lawrence. *Newcomb's Wildflower Guide*. Boston: Little, Brown and Company, Inc., 1977.

Niering, William A., and Nancy C. Olmstead. *The Audubon Society Field Guide to North American Wildflowers: Eastern Region*. New York: Alfred A. Knopf Inc., 1979.

Peterson, Lee Allen. *A Field Guide to Edible Wild Plants: Eastern and Central North America*. Boston: Houghton Mifflin Company, 1977.

Peterson, Roger Tory, and Margaret McKenny. *A Field Guide to Wildflowers: Northeastern and Northcentral North America*. Boston: Houghton Mifflin Co., 1968.

Phillips, Harry R. *Growing and Propagating Wildflowers*. Chapel Hill: The University of North Carolina Press, 1985.

Radford, Albert E., Harry E. Ahles, and C. Ritchie Bell. *Manual of the Vascular Flora of the Carolinas*. Chapel Hill: The University of North Carolina Press, 1968.

Reilly, Ann. *American Wildflowers*. New York: Portland House, 1991.

Reveal, James A. *Gentle Conquest: The Botanical Discovery of North America with Illustrations from the Library of Congress*. Washington, D.C.: Starwood Publishing, Inc., 1992.

Roe, Charles E. *A Directory to North Carolina's Natural Areas*. Raleigh, N.C.: North Carolina Natural Heritage Foundation, 1987.

Shaw, John. *Closeups in Nature*. New York: Amphoto, 1987.

Stokes, Donald W., and Lillian Q. Stokes. *A Guide to Enjoying Wildflowers*. Boston: Little, Brown and Company, 1985.

———. *The Wildflower Book*. Boston: Little, Brown and Company, 1992.

Stupka, Arthur. *Wildflowers in Color*. New York: HarperCollins Publishers, 1965.

West, Larry, and Julie Ridl. *How to Photograph Insects and Spiders*. Mechanicsburg, Pa.: Stackpole Books, 1994.

White, Peter S. *The Flora of Great Smoky Mountains National Park: An Annotated Checklist of the Vascular Plants and a Review of Previous Floristic Work*. Gatlinburg, Tenn.: Uplands Field Research Laboratory, Great Smoky Mountains National Park, 1982. (out of print)

Wofford, B. Eugene. *Guide to the Vascular Plants of the Blue Ridge*. Athens: The University of Georgia Press, 1989.

Index

scabrum, 144
venosum, 144
Houstonia
  caerulea, 53
  longifolia, 53
  purpurea, 53
  serpyllifolia, 53
  (*tenuifolia*), 53
Hydrastis canadensis, 213
Hydrophyllum
  canadense, 83
  macrophyllum, 83
  virginianum, 83
Hypericum spp., 148
Hypochaeris radicata, 146
(*Hypochoeris radicata*), 146
Hypoxis hirsuta, 158

Ice plant, 207
Impatiens
  capensis, 128
  pallida, 128
Indian cucumber root, 168
Indian paint brush, 129
Indian physic, 191
Indian pipe, 207
Indian plantain
  great, 171
  pale, 171
  Rugel's, 162
  sweet-scented, 171
Indian tobacco, 70
Indian turnip, 239
Ipecac
  false, 191
  American, 191
Ironweed, New York, 106
Iris
  cristata, 55
  verna, 55
  virginica, 55

Iris
  crested dwarf, 55
  dwarf, 55
Isatis tinctoria, 133
Isotria verticillata, 168

Jack-in-the-pulpit, 239
Jeffersonia diphylla, 200, 216
Jewelweed, 128
Joe-Pye weed, 103

King devil, 144
Knapweed, spotted, 102
Krigia
  biflora, 146
  dandelion, 146
  montana, 146
  virginica, 146

Ladies' tobacco, 170
Ladies' tresses
  fragrant, 233
  little, 233
  nodding, 233
  slender, 233
  spring, 233
Lady's slipper
  large yellow, 167
  pink, 92
  showy, 92
  small yellow, 167
Lamium
  amplexicaule, 110
  purpureum, 110
Larkspur
  dwarf, 59
  tall, 59
Leek, wild, 211
Leucanthemum vulgare, 215

Liatris spp., 75
Lightning plant, 100
Lilium
  canadense, 124
  grayi, 124
  michauxii, 126
  philadelphicum, 124
  superbum, 126
Lily
  bell, 124
  bluebead, 165
  California corn, 238
  Canada, 124
  Clinton's, 165
  corn, 165
  cushat, 168
  Gray's, 124
  Michaux's, 126
  speckled wood, 212
  trout, 164
  Turk's-cap, 126
  white trout, 164
  wood, 124
Lily of the valley, 228
  false, 201
  wild, 201
Linaria vulgaris, 139
Lion's foot, 136
Lion's tooth, 146
Liparis
  (*lilifolia*), 112
  liliifolia, 112
  loeselii, 112
Listera
  australis, 112
  smallii, 112
Little brown jugs, 113
Live-forever, wild, 107
Liverleaf, 57
Liverwort, 57
Lizard's tail, 234
Lobelia